D1601625

Morality and Utility

MORALITY AND UTILITY

by
Jan Narveson

The Johns Hopkins Press
Baltimore, Maryland

This work has been published with the help of a grant from the Humanities Research Council of Canada using funds provided by the Canada Council.

Preface

This is an essay on the subject of the criterion of morality, a subject which was, for some time and in some of the most influential quarters of the English-speaking philosophical world, virtually in abeyance, even among those philosophers who concerned themselves with ethical questions. That period and those theorists are not to be belittled, though it is popular to do so in some other quarters today. Concern with the meanings or functions of ethical terminology, in the narrowest senses of the words 'meaning' and 'function,' is entirely proper and even logically prior to the kind of task undertaken here; my debt to these theorists will be evident to the reader. The view advanced in this book is by no means new, give or take a few details of formulation (important though these may be to the theorist); neither, I think, are the broad outlines of the manner in which it is to be defended. The purpose of this essay is merely to bring things up-to-date.

The history of utilitarianism subsequent to the mighty labors of Mill and Sidgwick is an unfortunate one. Objections—which to the minds of the philosophically untutored, seem as trivial as to the philosophers influenced by them, they seem unanswerable —have diverted and often suppressed the otherwise wholehearted acceptance of this point of view. That an act's moral rightness is proportional to its utility, its tendency to promote the general happiness, strikes many minds with all the force of self-evidence, upon its first pronouncement. Further reflection on matters of detail, however, especially when induced by some sharp-witted student of philosophy, tends to perplex the would-be adherent, and in the end to put him to rout. An aura of suspicion has always hung over these philosophical objections. So far as I'm concerned, this book is the outcome of my efforts to hunt down its sources. In general, my assessment is that the objections are due to inattention to principles of application which are not themselves normative in nature, such inattention resulting in the "deduction" of what does not actually follow, and in failure to deduce what does, from the utilitarian hypothesis. Whether I am right in this, of course, the reader must judge for himself.

One's debts in a work of this kind are bound to be many and diverse. To my former teachers at Harvard University, especially Roderick Firth and Henry Aiken, and also to J. O. Urmson of Oxford, I owe thanks for stimulation on virtually all of the matters discussed in this book, though I daresay none would agree very extensively with its results. An enormous debt is of course due to the labors of my various predecessors and contemporaries in ethical philosophy; it was both encouraging and chastening to discover, after beginning on this project, to what extent my views have been anticipated or independently arrived at by others. Finally, my gratitude is extended to the secretarial force of the University of Waterloo, Department of Philosophy (Mrs. Una Vincent and Miss Margaret Ann Cole) for their considerable labors on the text, to the University in general for its generous allotment of time for such pursuits as this to its ordinary staff members, and to the editors and readers of the Johns Hopkins Press for helpful criticism and suggestions, and for continual encouragement.

Contents

CONTENTS

CHAPTER I

Utilitarianism and Philosophical Ethics

Normative Ethics

Until the twentieth century, there seems to have been no serious doubt that at least one of the functions of moral philosophers was to tell us, in a general way, what we ought to do. They were, of course, supposed to back up these views with reasons, often of a kind which geared ethical theories to metaphysical or other philosophical views in a system; but in any case, people expected to derive a general program for *living* (at least that portion of life with which ethics was presumed to be concerned), from the philosophers who dealt with ethical questions. People would not have believed that so far as the actual conduct of life was concerned, the implications of the ethical theories of Plato, Aquinas, Hume, and Nietzsche, among others, were identical. They surely supposed that there were *some* activities which would be deplored by some of these philosophies and simultaneously recommended by others. This does not seem to be an unreasonable supposition.

But during the twentieth century, the feeling grew that philosophers cannot, or perhaps ought not to try to tell us what to do, even in the most general way. This feeling has declined since the heyday of positivism, but it is still strong. If it is correct, then presumably the task of this book is impossible and should be abandoned. It may be useful to explain, therefore, why I feel justified in attempting it; more especially, what it is that a philosopher working with this subject is presuming to attempt.

This view that philosophers cannot, or ought not, attempt to underwrite moral principles stems, I think, from two main

1

sources. The first is the general belief that philosophy consists exclusively in the analysis of concepts, meanings, or the uses of language. Such an activity presumably would discover only whether statements are, or are not, logically true ("analytic"). If a particular statement should be "synthetic," then it is not the business of philosophy to determine whether it is true at all. There is reason to claim that ethical statements that say what we ought to do are not logically true; hence, if they can be said to be true at all, it is held that it must be someone else's business to determine whether or not they are. This is a position explicitly set forth in Ayer's *Language, Truth, and Logic,* where it is said:

As for the expressions of ethical judgments, we have not yet determined how they should be classified. But inasmuch as they are certainly neither definitions nor comments upon definitions, nor quotations, we may say decisively that they do not belong to ethical philosophy.[1]

Subtler views than this are now current with regard to the nature of philosophical analysis; by and large, these later improvements continue to support the belief that ethical judgments are not, as such, capable of being supported by purely philosophical investigation. To put it broadly, philosophy is out to establish truth-by-meaning rather than truth per se. Moreover, I agree with this general understanding of the tasks of philosophy. I do not propose (if I can avoid it) to cross the borderline into psychology, nor to appeal to such spurious sources as "synthetic" metaphysics, "intuition," or the like in support of ethical statements. But I deny the inference that philosophers cannot advance substantive ethical theories, for reasons to be explained in the course of this work.

The second source of this rejection is a set of currently popular views about the meanings or logical functions of ethical language, viz., those called "emotive" and "performative." According to these views, ethical statements are not literally propositions at all—they do not state facts of any kind, but perform certain

---

[1] Alfred J. Ayer, *Language, Truth, and Logic* (New York: Dover Publications, Inc., 1947), p. 103.

other functions, such as expressing emotions or attitudes, stimulating action, advising, ordering, and so forth. It is easy to proceed from this position to say that:

Another man may disagree with me about the wrongness of stealing,
in the sense that he may not have the same feelings about stealing as
I have. . . . But he cannot, strictly speaking, contradict me. For in
saying that a certain type of action is right or wrong, I am not
making any factual statement, not even a statement about my own
state of mind. I am merely expressing certain moral sentiments.
And the man who is ostensibly contradicting me is merely expressing his moral sentiments. So that there is plainly no sense in asking
which of us is in the right. For neither of us is asserting a genuine
proposition.[2]

If we accept this particular view of Ayer's, which has had considerable following, there is good reason why philosophers should
not try to demonstrate moral principles: it is because they are
undemonstrable—by anyone—not only by philosophers. Thus
Ayer's position is not aimed especially at philosophers, as the
first one is. The first view, which concerns the nature of philosophical analysis, leaves open the possibility that someone might
be able to "verify" ethical statements, only not in the role of a
philosopher; whereas the second leaves ethical statements without the possibility of verification by anyone, regardless of profession.

The view that ethical statements are not essentially propositions, that they are imperative or performative in their logical
function is, by now, almost a truism in ethical philosophy. I do
not propose to challenge it. And if by "true" one means "corresponds to the facts," then no doubt ethical statements are
neither true nor false. But why should we say this? And what
would we mean if we did say it? Recent work on the concept
of truth should be sufficient to warn us against supposing that
expressions like "corresponds to the facts" really explain the
notion of truth. For example, Strawson has argued forcibly that

[2] *Ibid.*, pp. 107–08. Later writers continue to show this tendency. Cf.,
e.g., Patrick Nowell-Smith, *Ethics* (Harmondsworth, Eng.: Penguin Books,
Inc., 1954), pp. 192–94; Paul Edwards, *Logic of Moral Discourse* (New
York: Free Press of Glencoe, Inc., 1955), pp. 162–65, especially.

"is true" is not a predicate, any more than "is good" or "exists."[3] And if "is true" is itself essentially a performative, as Strawson argues, then there is no obvious reason for not applying it to ethical statements. On the contrary, there are numerous reasons —some of them, I think, quite obvious—for applying it to these statements. (I shall try to indicate some examples in the last chapter.) Even if we forego using "true" of ethical utterances, we can do as well with "justified," "well-grounded," or similar locutions, as Aiken and others have argued.[4]

In my opinion, neither of these two general views seems to show that philosophers ought not to do substantive ethical work. The first view would only imply this, I think, in company with a wholly unsatisfactory supposition of a parallel between non-analytic ethical statements and non-analytic "factual" statements. It would indeed be absurd to suggest that a philosopher, who is essentially an armchair theorist, might be able to decide between two statements of a factual kind when they are incompatible but both equally conceivable. What one must do in order to verify factual statements varies, of course; in all cases, except those which assert something about what is going on in the vicinity of our armchairs, it is necessary to get out and look (or otherwise investigate the world) to see whether they are true, test them. This, then, is a perfectly intelligible explanation of why a philosopher cannot set up shop to discover new facts; although he can, and should, keep track of the ones he already knows! Surely, the whole trend of twentieth-century analysis in ethics—a trend exemplified by the second of the two views—demonstrates that this could not be the case with substantive ethical statements. If these major trends are correct, any empirical investigating you can do with such statements is bound to serve to verify only the so-called "factual components" of ethical statements. Since the "specifically ethical" components of such statements are precisely the "non-factual" ones, what would be the character of an ethical investigation? If anything, these trends in analysis imply that

[3] P. F. Strawson, "Truth," *Analysis*, Vol. 9 (1948–49), pp. 83–97.

[4] Henry D. Aiken, "The Concept of Moral Objectivity," in *Morality and the Language of Conduct*, ed. Hector-Neri Castañeda and George Nakhnikian (Detroit: Wayne State University Press, 1963), pp. 101–103. See also Richard Robinson, *An Atheist's Values* (New York: Oxford University Press, Inc., 1964), pp. 28, 29.

any "investigating" that can be done has to be of the "armchair" variety.

In order to reinforce this suggestion (and to qualify it some what), consider the way we must proceed with propositions thought to be "synthetic." The philosopher who is wondering whether or not some statement is synthetic must attempt to conceptualize, imagine, or describe what it would be like for the statement to be false. If he can produce a clear description or picture of a situation in which it would be false, and another in which it would be true, then he concludes that the statement is not a conceptual truth (or falsehood). On this basis, he also concludes that its verification is not the task of the philosopher. Let us take the statement, "Killing is wrong," for example. We might test the truth of this statement by considering circumstances in which killing would be right; only our question is not whether the statement is true but whether it is synthetic. On the model for testing syntheticity of descriptive statements, this would require that we try to imagine what it would be like for killing to be right. For this purpose, it does no good to conjure up special circumstances or borderline cases such as self-defense or unintentional manslaughter; for it is the central cases of descriptive statements which can be conceived false. There is a tree in the quad—but it is perfectly conceivable that there should not be. In order to establish that the statement, "Killing is wrong" is "synthetic," we must imagine what it would be for straightforward homicide (with no excuses), to be right. But how are we supposed to go about supposing, imagining, or conceiving that homicide is *right?* If we attempt this, we must draw a blank, since this only shows that ethical statements do not express matters of fact. This strongly suggests that when ethical principles are said to be non-analytic (which is true enough, I shall argue later), this must not be taken as proof that only an empirical investigation can support them, for we have seen reason to suppose that only a conceptual investigation could support them. If we are quite convinced that there is something wrong with killing people, and observe that this is not due to any special information of the sort required for supporting scientific statements, we have no option but to conclude that if our convictions have *any* kind of support, that support must be provided by some kind of abstract argument. We may or may not want to conclude that the fundamental principles of ethics are "synthetic a priori," a phrase both obscure and misleading. That they are "a priori" seems the inescapable conclusion if, of course, there are any such principles at all.

This argument must be understood to concern only the "specifically ethical" components of ethical statements. We are all aware that a particular act is right or wrong only if it does, or does not, have certain characteristics. Then the statement that it is "right" or "wrong" will in part require observational support, to establish that the type of act in question actually does or does not have those characteristics. Here the psychologist, the sociologist, the economist, or other investigators can and must be brought into the picture. The question is not whether some facts are relevant to ethical questions, but whether we can show that they *must* be. Moreover, we must be able to do this without resorting to peculiar "specifically ethical facts" to which only certain people have access. Such a move would be tantamount to giving up the search for good arguments.

In short, it is only the contention that ethical statements cannot be rationally supported at all that would seriously imply the inability of philosophers to support them, and this view, as we have seen, would also make nonsense of the suggestion that they should be supported by anyone else. Added to this is the fact that whenever people try to say who, other than philosophers, can help us with our substantive ethical thinking, the results are unsatisfactory. Psychologists, teachers, and preachers come in for mention. But can we seriously argue that these professions prepare one for the role of general moralist better than moral philosophy? This seems doubtful.

In summary: the supposition that ethical statements are intrinsically undemonstrable is not compatible with the assertion that certain non-philosophers are better qualified to make them than philosophers. We should all be equally unqualified if that view were correct. Secondly, it is difficult to produce a plausible list of other persons who would be qualified to formulate ethical principles, if they can be rationally formulated at all.

In the final section of this book, I shall consider whether and how it is theoretically possible to demonstrate, support, or rationally advocate any substantive ethical positions by means of a general, abstract philosophical argument. For the present, it is sufficient to point out that the proposition that ethical statements are intrinsically indemonstrable is unsatisfactory. The view that we are prevented, logically and therefore forever, from really solving ethical problems seems incomprehensible, especially since people sometimes do solve them. The view that they cannot be said to be true or false is at least obscure, especially since people talk as if they were true or false. And the view that people cannot literally contradict each other on ethical questions is simply incredible. Even if there were no currently available theories to suggest a plausible way of combining the undoubted truth that ethical statements are not essentially factual with the doubted truth that they are nevertheless subject to rational investigation, we could not remain satisfied with the curious view that they are not open to such investigation, which would mean that there is no point in thinking about ethical questions at all. We should, I think, be quite justified in going ahead and trying to produce some sensible views on these questions.

In addition to casting doubt on the supposition that philosophers are not qualified to formulate ethical principles, we can produce some plausible reasons for thinking that they should be better qualified to do this than other people. It is agreed that it is precisely the philosopher's business to consider the meaning or logic of ethical sentences. This is in itself one good reason for handing to the philosopher the job of attempting to expose the fundamental principles of the subject as well. We have noted that formulating these principles is not like formulating fundamental principles in science. In the case of science, a background of experimentation and observation is logically essential before there can be theorizing to any purpose. But no special experience is necessary to formulate ethical principles. If they can be formulated at all, this must be, in some sense, a conceptual task rather than a task requiring some special types of extra-armchair investigations. Philosophers themselves are only too quick to point out that people who begin to think about ethical principles very often confuse the philosophical task of analysis with that of framing principles. But if the philosopher is able to point out the danger, why should he not be peculiarly fitted to surmount it?

He would, presumably, be ahead of the philosophically un-tutored in this respect.

In short, I have argued that the activity of formulating and supporting general principles in ethics must be conceptual if anything, and that the "analytical" task of ethics is important to anyone undertaking to engage in that activity. If this is cor-rect, it follows that philosophers ought to do this job. That it has traditionally been considered the philosopher's job can be respectfully suggested as a supporting reason under the circum-stances. They may or may not have done the job well, but it was theirs to attempt.

Method in Normative Ethics

In the introduction to a recent book on ethics, this statement occurs:

One of the points I shall hope to establish—for the beginner rather than for the advanced student to whom it will already be obvious—is this: no moral philosopher is able to legislate moral standards in the way that some earlier writers thought he could.[5]

Passages expressing a similar sentiment are easily found in many recent works on moral philosophy, and they are doubtless justified. It is indeed impossible for philosophers to legislate moral standards, or to create them, or to be in any other way the originators of them. Again, this is merely because they can-not be legislated, created, or originated at all.[6] But why should it be expressed with particular reference to philosophers when it could be addressed equally well to anyone? Suppose that in the same statement we substitute the word 'discover' for 'legis-late.' It would then be a good deal less plausible, I think. Now suppose we substitute the words 'support' or 'advance' for 'legis-

---

[5] John Hartland-Swann, *An Analysis of Morals* (London: George Allen & Unwin, 1960), p. 15.

[6] See the clear and convincing argument of Kurt E. M. Baier in *The Moral Point of View: A Rational Basis of Ethics* (Ithaca, N. Y.: Cornell University Press, 1958), pp. 177–180.

late.' In that case, it appears that we could fairly doubt it. Why should not a philosopher be able to support, or advance, or even to discover a moral "standard," just as a scientist might support, advance, or discover a proposition in chemistry? The fact that moral principles are not on the same subject as chemical ones, and even the fact that they are of a logically different type, is hardly sufficient to make this impossible. In any case, previous philosophers have not attempted to "legislate" moral standards, although they have attempted to support, defend, and sometimes discover them. Philosophers do admit that philosophy can help to make our thinking on moral subjects more coherent and more rational. If this is true, why can they not actually hope to improve or correct it?

The suggestion that philosophers cannot "legislate" morality serves to remind us of the method which the philosopher must adopt as he attempts to formulate general ethical principles. The point is (as in all cases of rational inquiry), that we will not be able to progress unless our proposals are subject to some kind of control imposed by the sense that our theorizing is testable by reference to some sort of "data." As in the case of other theories, a philosophical theory is an effort to account for something, not an exercise performed in intellectual vacuo. We must now attempt to specify just what these "data" are.

Most of the classical moral philosophers, as well as recent writers on ethics, are in agreement that broadly speaking, data for the moral philosopher consist in the "deliverances of our ordinary moral consciousness," or words to that effect. They are correct, but we need a more precise characterization, in the first place. Secondly, we deserve an argument to show that that is the way it must be.

All of us who study ethics have some more or less well-defined ethical beliefs. If we did not, we should be quite unable to proceed. This is commonplace, and the only question is how much to make of it. Too much certainly can be made of it. Any number of ethical writers have made this observation into a theory: the theory, for instance, that we all come equipped with a ready-made source of authoritative ethical deliverances known as "conscience," "practical reason," or perhaps "the moral sense," the deliverances being referred to as "intuitions." That this is unsatisfactory is, I trust, sufficiently well-established by now to obviate further argument. But the need to present an alternative and more neutral characterization is evident if we are to continue to maintain that our pre-existing ethical beliefs play an important role in ethical analysis.

We employ the words 'good,' 'right,' and 'just,' very often, applying them to some things and withholding them from others. These tendencies to apply ethical words may be referred to neutrally as "ethical beliefs" but there are also ethical hunches, doubts, hesitations, and downright quandaries, as well as times when we feel confident or certain. In addition to variation in degree of confidence of application, there are variations in precision of formulation. Some of our ethical beliefs are reasonably well-defined, and others extremely vague. The fact that there are variations is sufficient reason in itself to deny that they can be accounted for as authoritative intuitions. Often we change our minds and even have inconsistent beliefs without being aware of it. The question concerning all these beliefs is: can we say that the object of ethical theory is to "account" for them? Many writers have talked as if it were so. Around the turn of the century, in particular, they tended to refer to ethics as a "science," the "science of moral phenomena," or some such thing.[7] This is not a satisfactory way of looking at the matter.

One obvious objection to characterizing ethical theory as a "science" is that there are sciences properly so-called which do concern themselves with the same subject matter. Cultural anthropology and sociology are cases in point. But if one presents ethical philosophy merely as a systematic description of a certain set of ethical beliefs, one will miss the point; for no normative conclusions will appear to follow. It would therefore be misleading to classify moral philosophy as a "science."

Perhaps a more serious reason for not considering ethical philosophy as closely parallel to science is that the parallelism in structure is not as great as it might appear. The assumption is

[7] Thus Henry Sidgwick: "It [his book] claims to be an examination, at once expository and critical, of the different methods of obtaining reasoned convictions as to what ought to be done which are to be found— either explicit or implicit—in the moral consciousness of mankind generally." *The Methods of Ethics* (Preface to 1st ed.; London: Macmillan Co., 1907), p. v.

that there is a structural resemblance between ethics and empirical science, in that there is a field of data consisting of observations. These observations are to be accounted for in terms of a comprehensive theory which will also suggest new experiments and observations by which they can be tested. It cannot be denied that there is some similarity here. But there is an essential difference which suggests that the comparison is inappropriate on the whole. The observations behind an empirical science are not, generally speaking, open to much doubt. We do not ordinarily suffer from illusions, hallucinations, or other mistakes in perception when we observe phenomena. Moreover, our observations cannot be construed as vague hunches of which the final theory is a more precise formulation. But in the case of ethical beliefs this is just the status we do have to ascribe to them. When we judge that some particular act was right or wrong, we are making a judgment, not an "observation." It is entirely possible for the judgment to be wrong; in fact, most people would probably claim no more than a modest success in their ethical judgings. In science, we can distinguish reasonably well between facts and the theories which are designed to account for them; but in ethics, the very status of the "facts" is continually in question. Moreover, disagreement in judgments is quite common in ethics: as much so as disagreements among ethical theories of different philosophers. Therefore, it is not very satisfactory to view these theories as attempts to account for essentially undoubted facts.

Indeed, the role of theorizing is rather pervasive in ethics. People do not ordinarily have hunches about matters of high-level scientific theorizing; but they very often theorize about ethics. Take a random groups of students into a classroom, introduce them to some of the problems of ethics, and nearly all of them will in short order be found advocating some theory or other. Take the same group into a classroom, expound to them some tolerably comprehensible scientific theories, and most of them will sit back and say, "How interesting!" It seems that a need is felt to theorize in ethics, which is not felt in the sciences. It seems unlikely that this is just a happenstance psychological fact about people.

Nevertheless, we are obliged to think of ethical theories as having an "inductive" aspect in the sense that they must be capable of implying many of the ethical beliefs we already hold. How are we to describe this, in view of the foregoing difficulties? I suggest that the situation is as follows. We noted at the outset of this discussion that we have tendencies to apply ethical words to some things and to withhold them from others. Now, if we try to formulate what ethics is about, we shall begin by listing some of these ethical words and envisaging cases in which we should apply them. If we are presented with a theory which implies that certain acoustically similar words apply to a totally different and unrelated set of things (acts, events or objects), then what reason could we have for supposing that it is a theory about the same concepts as those we have been employing? This is not exactly a "paradigm case" argument, although it is similar. A better parallel, however, is with the philosophical question of the existence of the external world. We make mistakes in perception now and again—things are not always as they seem. From this observation, a philosopher concludes that we always *might* be wrong in our statements about the world; from this he concludes that we might *always* be wrong. But the last inference is logically unsupportable. No sense can be made of the supposition that we are always wrong, despite the fact that we might be wrong in any particular case.[8] Similarly, no clear sense could be made of the theory that nothing is ever right or wrong. The set of activities which *define* the problems of morals do not make sense without the supposition that something is right or wrong. So what can we do but choose standard examples and ask for a theory which will, at least, make sense of those?

It is for this reason, then, that we must test ethical theories by reference to what we already believe on the subject. No theory that will do justice to ethics can fail to do justice to at least a fair share of them. If it does not, it will be judged either false or not an ethical theory at all. And to apply these considerations to our present case, we must therefore begin our appraisal of the utilitarian theory by seeing whether or not it will account for what is already recognized to be right or wrong.

Theorizing activity also has some force of its own, as philos-

[8] This point is delightfully made in O. K. Bouwsma's paper, "Descartes' Evil Genius," *Philosophical Review* (1949), p. 2.

ophers recently have urged with regard to science.[9] An ethical theory, to be adequate, must account for many of our previous ethical beliefs. But suppose it does so extremely well for most of them and yet that there remain a few aberrant cases which cannot be reconciled with it. There may well come a time, under these circumstances, when the supposed "data" will themselves be rejected. It is important to recognize that there is more room for this in ethics than in science. For we do make sense of the notion of ethical reform, and we do not, if we are sensible, repose too thoroughgoing a confidence in our ethical judgments. Exactly how the process of ethical reform occurs is not easy to discover, but the possibility of it cannot be denied, although the possibility of a complete, wholesale, top-to-bottom alteration can. It seems likely that the force of a simplifying ethical insight plays a major role in this process of reform.

Moreover, it must be borne in mind that although this "inductive" method, as it might be called, of testing the adequacy of ethical theories is perhaps the basic one, there is also another way of arguing for such a theory. This might be called the "a priori" method, by which a comparatively short argument purports to establish the whole theory all at once. For instance, if we could show that the Principle of Utility is true by arguing that it is necessary, demonstrable, undeniable, or self-evident, that would be a conclusive proof. People have doubted that there can be such arguments for ethical theories, and certainly some that have been used are open to criticism. It would be dangerous to argue that the principle of utility is "analytic," for reasons which will be adduced in the next chapter; the category of the "synthetic a priori" is more than open to suspicion. Nevertheless, I am inclined to think that such an "all-at-once" argument is possible, and I shall formulate one in the last chapter. What I am suggesting here is merely that if a plausible argument of that kind can be produced, and if the theory it supports is also plausible by the "inductive" tests of accounting for our presently firm ethical beliefs, then that fact must be taken as very powerful support for the theory.

[9] Cf. Willard V. O. Quine, *Word and Object* (Cambridge, Mass.: The M.I.T. Press, 1960).

Utilitarianism and Its Problems

Let us now turn our attention to utilitarianism in particular. If we look at the standard "text book" pictures of the utilitarian theory, we find that it reads approximately as follows. Utilitarianism is a species of hedonism, which is a philosophy of life. According to this philosophy, the goal of man's life is pleasure. An "egoistic" hedonist would hold that each man ought to "pursue" his own pleasure and nothing else; utilitarianism, on the other hand, says that we are to "pursue" the general pleasure, that is, to endeavor to produce as much pleasure as possible, no matter where it is found, nor whose it is. He is, correlatively, to shun pain (others' as well as his own). Since in most situations what we do is likely to produce both some pleasure and some pain, we have to settle for the maximum "balance" of pleasure over pain. Pleasure is, by definition, good, or perhaps "*the* good"; pain is, by definition, bad, or perhaps "*the* bad." Our duty at each moment, under any circumstances, is (by definition) to produce the maximum balance of pleasure over pain in as many people as possible.

The standard interpretation of this picture is open to numerous well-known objections. G. E. Moore showed that it is fallacious to define the word "good" as meaning "pleasurable"; in fact, that it is incoherent to maintain that "good" means pleasurable" and also that "*the* good" is pleasure.[10] Ross argued that even the apparently innocuous premise, "It is our duty to produce the most good," cannot be held to be true by definition.[11] He claimed that it is false. He alleged that on the utilitarian view, it would follow that if someone made a promise to someone else to do something, and then discovered that more good could be brought into the world by ignoring it, it would be his duty to ignore it. By this reasoning, it is easily shown that there is no point in making promises at all; since our duty is to act in the same way in any case, whether we make them or not. (If more

[10] George E. Moore, *Principia Ethica* (London: Cambridge University Press, 1903), Chs. 1 and 3.
[11] William D. Ross, *Right and the Good* (London: Oxford University Press, 1930), Chs. 1 and 2.

INTRODUCTION

good would be brought into the world by doing what was promised, it would be one's duty anyhow; whereas, if more good
would not be accomplished, then it would be one's duty to break
a promise if made.) Numerous authors have objected that the
"calculus" which would be needed to put the Principle of Utility
into practice cannot be carried out, certainly not in practice and
perhaps not even in principle.[12] Again, they hold that utilitarianism cannot be squared with the demands of justice. It is held,
for example, that we have a duty to distribute good things equitably as well as felicifically, and that this is incompatible with
utilitarianism.[13] As to criminal justice, they argue that if, for
example, it were discovered that everyone would be made happier if an innocent man were imprisoned, then he should be
imprisoned, if utilitarianism holds true.[14] Alternatively, if a certain criminal could no longer harm anyone, then he ought not
to be imprisoned.[15] And it also has been fashionable to hold up
utilitarianism as a "pig philosophy."[16] Some have denied that
pleasure is a good at all; many have held that there are, in any
case, other good things besides pleasure. Is not a life of pleasure-
seeking, even if combined with an effort to secure that life for
others as well as oneself, ignoble, befitting only the low-browed?
Critics have pointed to Mill's celebrated defense of liberty and
have claimed that a concern for freedom, as such, is incompatible
with the view that ultimately pleasure is the only good.[17] Theorists also point out that at least Bentham and Mill appear to have
been "psychological hedonists," holding that man is incapable,

[12] Cf., for example, William Lillie, *An Introduction to Ethics* (New
York: Barnes and Noble, Inc., 1961), pp. 171–77. Lillie's characterization of
utilitarianism approximates this picture rather closely. Also, for example,
D. M. MacKinnon, *A Study in Ethical Theory* (Riverside, N.J.: Collier
Books, 1962), p. 38.
[13] Cf., for example, William Frankena, *Ethics* (Englewood Cliffs, N.J.:
Prentice-Hall, Inc., 1963), pp. 38–42.
[14] See, for instance, G. E. M. Anscombe, "Modern Moral Philosophy," in
Philosophy (1957), pp. 16, 17.
[15] E. F. Carritt, *Ethical and Political Thinking* (London: Oxford University Press, 1947), Ch. 5.
[16] Friedrich Nietszche, *Beyond Good and Evil* (New York: Macmillan
Co., 1907), par. 225; Francis H. Bradley, "Pleasure for Pleasure's Sake" in
Ethical Studies (New York: Liberal Arts Press, Bobbs-Merrill Co., Inc.,
1951).
[17] Henry D. Aiken, "Utilitarianism and Liberty: John Stuart Mill's Defense of Freedom" in *Reason and Conduct* (New York: Alfred A. Knopf,
Inc., 1962), Essay XIV, pp. 293–314.

"by nature," of seeking anything except pleasure. They have striven to show that this premise is false,[18] and that it is incompatible with ethical hedonism, of which utilitarianism is supposed to be a species.[19]

Since the time of Bentham and Mill, there have been many improvements in ethical theory, and not a few of the preceding objections are due to these improvements. There have also been developments within the utilitarian tradition itself. Of the improvements in question I shall make considerable use in the remainder of this book, but two of the developments are worth mentioning here. The first, historically, is what Hastings Rashdall called "ideal utilitarianism," though Moore, who also held this view, called it simply "utilitarianism."[20] In this theory, the identification of "good" with "pleasure" is abandoned. "Good" is chosen as a primitive term (indefinable, as well as undefined, in Moore's view), and various things besides pleasure are held to be good in themselves. The Principle of Utility is amended simply to read that our duty is to produce the most good, rather than the most pleasure or happiness. This, indeed, is the theory which Ross was particularly concerned with in his refutations of "utilitarianism." It is still regarded as a generalization, or perhaps idealization, of the original view.

The other, more recent, development is known as "rule" utilitarianism. Its chief modification, or as some claim, interpretation,[21] of the original utilitarian view is the idea that instead of evaluating particular acts by the principle of utility, we must think of this principle as applying only to general rules. Acts are right if they conform to the rules, which in turn are justified on the ground that they in general produce more good than any alternative.[22] As this formulation suggests, they also tend to

[18] Hastings Rashdall, *The Theory of Good and Evil* (London: Oxford University Press, 1907), Vol. I, Ch. 1.

[19] John Hospers, *Human Conduct* (New York: Harcourt, Brace, and World, Inc., 1961), pp. 141, 142.

[20] George E. Moore, *Ethics* (Oxford: Home University Library, 1912; reset by Oxford University Press, Inc., 1947), Chs. 1 and 2.

[21] J. O. Urmson, "The Interpretation of the Philosophy of John Stuart Mill," in *Philosophical Quarterly* (January, 1953), Vol. 3, No. 10, pp. 33–39.

[22] *Ibid.;* see also, Richard B. Brandt, *Ethical Theory, The Problems of Normative and Critical Ethics* (Englewood Cliffs, N.J.: Prentice-Hall, Inc., 1959), Ch. 15, sec. 3.

adopt "ideal utilitarianism" as their version of the principle of utility.

The "textbook picture" of utilitarianism sketched at the outset is, I shall argue, unsatisfactory. Moreover, I regard both of the developments of utilitarian theory briefly outlined above as misguided. In succeeding chapters, I propose to show what is wrong with the picture in question, and what is wrong with the developments. I shall argue that the numerous standard objections, many of which were briefly mentioned above, are based either on the travesty in question, or on erroneous reasoning as to what utilitarianism does imply. The "developments" are plausible, if at all, only because they appear to meet these objections. Since the objections are incorrect, the developments are unnecessary; they are open to serious objections themselves; and to the extent that they are helpful, they are not incompatible with utilitarianism.

I shall present an alternative picture of the Principle of Utility which, in my opinion, does more justice to the apparent intentions of the theory's founders. But I shall not devote very much effort to arguing this. Historical questions concerning the intentions of philosophers are fraught with difficulty. I am not primarily concerned with such questions. Whether or not my picture of utilitarianism is in accord with the original intentions of Bentham and Mill, I believe that it is a considerable improvement over what we have come to accept as the standard picture. It is an improvement in the sense that it seems to me to be true, and its truth is what I propose to argue for, in the main.

Since utilitarianism is a view of the whole of normative ethics, its defense is a complicated business. In order to meet a certain objection, one has to explain other implications of the theory. Soon, one discovers that nothing less than a complete exposition is enough to convince the critic, or to make one's view clear. This poses severe problems of organization, which, I fear, are not very well-solved in this work. I therefore beg the reader's indulgence on two scores: first, that he read the work in its entirety before he leans too heavily on a particular criticism of any one part; and secondly, that he forgive the nonconsecutiveness of exposition.

As an aid to the reader, I shall begin by painting in very broad

strokes the alternative picture of utilitarianism I propose. I shall
then fill in individual chapters with the different elements of the
picture and present them completely, with the necessary arguments to support them. The general picture is as follows:

To begin with, utilitarianism is a *moral* theory. It is not a
"metaethical" theory, that is, one which purports to define, ex-
plicate, or analyze the language of morals. It is not a "theory of
value," that is, one which attempts to lay bare the fundamental
features of anything, in any context whatsoever, that make it
good, bad, or indifferent. It is not a theory of "intrinsic value,"
in the sense of G. E. Moore. It is not a "philosophy of life." It
is not, therefore, a species of "hedonism" in any straightforward
sense. It is a theory of what makes any act good or bad, right or
wrong, from the moral point of view, in short, a theory of moral
value. It is, to put it another way, a theory of the moral criterion,
as Mill said.[23] The criterion in question, stated briefly, is that the
moral value of an act is proportional to its productiveness in all
those whom it affects, of what they hold to be *non*-morally good;
and inversely proportional to its productiveness of what they
hold to be (non-morally) bad. I take this to be a more accurate
way of saying that moral value is determined by the general
interest, welfare, or happiness. We could say that utilitarianism
is the view that the whole of morals can be summed up as the
taking of everyone's point of view, and not just our own, when
we act. The theory of utilitarianism is the theory that we can
deduce from this principle, together with relevant statements of
fact plus suitable definitions of the more specialized ethical terminology, any true statement of a moral kind. It is the business
of an exponent of utilitarianism to bring this theory to bear
on all of the different kinds of judgments properly called moral
judgments. If there are differences of this kind however (and
there are), the theorist must have some view of the differences
in meaning of the different moral terms in which these judgments
are stated. This activity is a metaethical one. Therefore it is not
a task which can be solved by making deductions from the Principle of Utility. To be specific: I believe that it is a different

[23] John Stuart Mill, in *Utilitarianism, Liberty, and Representative Government* (New York: Everyman's Library, E. P. Dutton and Co., 1926),
p. 1. (All further references to these works will be taken from this edition.)

thing to say that an act is a morally good one, a morally right one, a just one, or an obligatory one. The utilitarian must show us which acts are good, which are right, which are just, and which are obligatory. In order to make it possible to deduce general statements such as "All and only acts of type F are good," "All and only acts of type G are right," etc., from the Principle, we must evidently have a view as to what we are saying when we say of an act that it is good, right, or just, etc. Views on these subjects belong to metaethics, and there is nothing especially utilitarian about them. Thus, we can go wrong in either of two ways when applying the utilitarian principle. We may have gotten the distinction wrong, i.e., have failed to have an adequate view of just what we are saying when we say that an act is 'just' as opposed to 'good,' for instance; in which case, it will not be surprising if we also come out with a wrong theory as to which acts are just, however correct our deductions. On the other hand, the resulting deductions can be wrong. Only if we are successful on both counts can we hope to appraise the utilitarian theory itself. As we have seen, such an appraisal must proceed by seeing whether the resulting view of what is good (right, just, etc.) is adequate; that is, accord with what really is right, just, etc. so far as we can see by our pre-analytical lights.

To sum up: it is absurd to suppose that promises have no moral force; that inequitable distribution is just as good as equitable; that innocent men sometimes ought to be punished; that we should live like pigs. It is also absurd to maintain that if I like jam, then it is my duty to eat jam, that a theory of the moral criterion should be incompatible with analytic propositions, and that twice as many people being half as happy is as good as half as many people being twice as happy. These are all results which any theorist, and hence the utilitarian, must avoid. I have, in previous paragraphs, made a number of general assertions about this theory which, if carefully understood, will I think be seen to go a great way toward avoiding all of these various absurdities which people have claimed to deduce from the Principle of Utility. We shall now proceed to their explicit statement and defense.

CHAPTER II

The Logical Status of Moral Principles

Logical Status of the Principle of Utility

At the beginning of the nineteenth century, when Bentham and his followers embarked on a defense of the utilitarian viewpoint in ethics, it was possible to announce the principle and then plunge right in, deducing consequences, warding off attacks, and so forth. Since the time of G. E. Moore, it is necessary to proceed more cautiously. In the previous chapter, utilitarianism was classified as a "substantive" moral theory as opposed to a "meta-ethical" one. This classification calls for explanation, especially since there has been, and still is, a tendency among the critics of the utilitarian theory to question it, or to ignore it even as a possibility. We need, then, some tolerably clear account of the status which the Principle of Utility is supposed to have. I shall follow up my discussion of this matter with some brief historical remarks to indicate that my interpretation is not out of line with the apparent intentions of Mill and Sidgwick, and probably Bentham.

We can easily produce examples of discourse which seem unproblematically of an ethical kind: "A man ought to be willing to die for his country if necessary"; "Jimmy, you ought to be nicer to Mrs. Smith"; "It is wrong to tell lies." These are pretty obvious examples, of different varieties. On the other hand, we can produce examples of explicitly metaethical statements: " 'Good' connotes a unique, non-natural property"; "To say 'You ought not to have stolen that money' is equivalent to saying 'You stole that money!' in a peculiar tone of horror." The difference between these two classes of statements can perhaps be described best in terms of the distinction of use and mention. In the former class, ethical expressions are being *used*; in the latter, they are being *mentioned*; and the fact that they are is clearly indicated by the inverted commas surrounding their apparent occurrence. Indeed, we can say that the ethical expressions in question do not occur at all in statements of the second class.[1]

It would be reasonable to say that statements of the first kind are ethical statements, as they stand, and to say that they give (or normally, would be used to give) advice, instruction, or criticism of a moral kind. We could speak sensibly of a person's obeying or living up to, or failing to live up to, what is said in statements of the first kind; but there is no evident sense in speaking of living in accordance with the statement, " 'Good' denotes a nonnatural property." In a rather quixotic sense, we might say that philosophers could model their behavior on such a statement; but all we mean is that they could consider it, believe it, defend it, and so on.

Metaethical statements, we would like to say, are those which purport to describe the meaning, the use, or the logic (if these are distinguishable) of ethical expressions; that is, they purport to tell us *what* we are saying when we say that something is good, right, wrong, a duty, or whatever evaluative word is in question. As Moore pointed out, it is not sensible to construe such statements as of the kind which support particular evaluations: " 'You must do this, because many people use a certain word to denote actions of this nature.' "[2] Recent questionings of the distinction between fact and value or of the analytic and the synthetic are out of place against this obvious observation. It is hard to see how a philosophical investigation could proceed at all without "countenancing" such a distinction.

Unfortunately, there are many statements which seem to lie betwixt and between these two pretty clear categories. Philosophers rightly puzzle over such sentences as "We ought to do what is right," "What is right is what produces the most good

[1] Cf., Benson Mates, *Elementary Logic* (New York: Oxford University Press, Inc., 1966), pp. 18–20.
[2] Moore, *Principia Ethica*, p. 12.

22

on the whole," or "It is one's duty to do evil," all of which have, one might say, a logically peculiar ring to them. Recently, such sentences as "We ought to keep our promises" and "Cheating is wrong" have been argued to have a rather special status, too. Some of these examples might plausibly be classified as analytic, or as self-contradictory, although doing so would no doubt upset the digestions of some philosophical readers, the notions of analyticity, etc., having been subjected to skeptical doubts of late. An analysis of such sentences is needed, since they are neither explicitly about language nor obviously and straightforwardly ethical as they stand. The question naturally arises whether the Principle of Utility, however formulated, is not also in limbo. In particular, the question arises as to whether we are to think of it as a disguised metaethical sentence.

To begin with, a sentence cannot wear a disguise by itself. If a sentence appears to be of one sort but is in reality of another sort, this must be the fault of the persons using it. The question is, how are we to understand this Principle? If it has not been clear in the hands of other writers, at least we can assign it a definite logical status here, if it us useful to do so. The reason we are interested in the question, of course, is to find out what sort of arguments it would be relevant to advance in order to persuade people to adopt it. We want to avoid being influenced by arguments of the following type, about which Moore was rightly concerned: (1) "By 'right' I *mean* 'in accordance with the wishes of the Master Race' "; *therefore* (2) "To do what is in accordance with the wishes of the Master Race is right." Such arguments are worthless, since they do nothing to show what is right in our sense of the term. It is arguable that no mere definition, even a correct one, can supply any help of this kind. Moore went on to criticize the utilitarians in particular for committing the same sin, and numerous critics have followed him in this. It will be worthwhile to devote a bit of attention to setting the historical record right on this matter. The three most important utilitarians are Bentham, Mill, and Sidgwick, whom we shall consider in reverse order. Sidgwick, the latest and perhaps the clearest of the three, recognized a clear distinction between questions of analysis and questions of substance, and produced explicit analyses of both 'right' and 'good.' On the question of the meaning of 'right' and the other "deontological words," he says:

What definition can we give of 'ought', right', and other terms expressing the same fundamental notion? To this I should answer that the notion which these terms have in common is too elementary to admit of any formal definition.[3]

This view would certainly avoid the danger of trivializing the Principle of Utility, which Sidgwick formulates as follows:

By Utilitarianism is here meant the ethical theory, that the conduct which, under any given circumstances, is objectively right, is that which will produce the greatest amount of happiness on the whole; that is, taking into account all whose happiness is affected by the conduct.[4]

Mill's statement is similar:

The creed which accepts as the foundation of morals, Utility, or the Greatest Happiness Principle, holds that actions are right in proportion as they tend to promote happiness, wrong as they tend to produce the reverse of happiness.[5]

What of Mill's view of the meanings of ethical expressions? He rarely discussed this subject explicitly, but there are two places in which he does: the fifth chapter of *Utilitarianism*, and the final book of his *System of Logic*. In the latter, it appears that he is a forerunner of Stevenson, Ayer, and Hare, for he says that moral and other evaluative judgments do "not express themselves in the indicative, but more properly in the imperative mode, or in paraphrases equivalent to it."[6] Clearly, this analysis would also avoid the danger of trivialization. (He has a narrower and more special analysis of 'just,' which we will be considering in detail in Chapter VI.)

[3] Sidgwick, *Methods of Ethics*, p. 32.
[4] *Ibid.*, p. 411.
[5] Mill, *Utilitarianism*, p. 6.
[6] John Stuart Mill, *A System of Logic* (London: Longmans, Green and Co., 1959), Book VI, Ch. xii, p. 616.

What, finally, about Bentham, the earliest of the three? Certainly he is the most plausible one to choose as having committed some sort of Naturalistic Fallacy. He tends, for instance, to say of 'benefit, advantage, pleasure, good, or happiness' that 'all this in the present case comes to the same thing.'[7] But how much can we make of this? I submit that the evidence available from Bentham's work does not support any particular assessment of his meta-ethical views. Much of the evidence suggests that he would not want to say, explicitly, that 'right' (for instance) *means* 'conducive to the general happiness.' For example, Bentham discusses a principle he calls the "principle of asceticism," which asserts just the opposite of the Principle of Utility. He certainly regards this "principle" as wildly irrational and incredible, saying that it "never was, nor ever can be, consistently pursued by any living creature. Let but one-tenth part of the inhabitants of this earth pursue it consistently, and in a day's time they will have turned it into a hell."[8]

Nevertheless, this does not square with the supposition that he thought it was self-contradictory. It is impossible to "follow" a self-contradictory "principle" at all; thus, no concern about the "consequences" of doing so would be relevant.

Finally, turning to recent times, we can point to the example of Smart who, in his recent defense of utilitarian ethics, explicitly adopts an emotivist position.[9] Therefore, there is no excuse left for criticizing the utilitarian position in general, or in particular for trying to pull the wool over our eyes by defining itself into acceptance. This general assessment is supported by recent work on Mill, e.g., that of Urmson[10] and Aiken.[11]

What, then, is the status of this principle? Is it supposed to be analytic or synthetic, for example? I suggest that for the time

---

[7] Jeremy Bentham, *An Introduction to the Principles of Morals and Legislation* (Garden City, N.Y.: Dolphin Books, Doubleday and Co., Inc., 1961), Ch. I, par. III, p. 18.

[8] *Ibid.*, Ch. II, par. X, pp. 27, 28.

[9] See J. J. C. Smart, *An Outline of a System of Utilitarian Ethics* (Cambridge: Melbourne University Press, 1961), p. 2. ". . . will assume for the purposes of this study the truth of some such meta-ethical analysis as that of Hare's *Language of Morals*."

[10] Urmson, *Philosophical Quarterly* (January, 1953), pp. 33–39.

[11] Aiken, "Definitions, Factual Premises, and Moral Conclusions," in *Reason and Conduct*, Essay III.

being we regard it as "synthetic," if we must make our choice; although, as it was pointed out earlier, in Chapter I, 'synthetic' does not function in quite the same way for ethical statements as for the obvious examples of factual statements. My reasons for suggesting this are as follows:

It would generally be said that utilitarianism consists in the assertion that the Principle of Utility is the *fundamental* principle of morality. It is this word, "fundamental," which causes the trouble here. For there is a tendency to suppose that if a statement is fundamental relative to another group of statements, then it must be of different epistemological status.[12] This calls for a brief look into this matter.

To begin with, let us consider a scientific generalization. We observe a number of animals, and we notice that each of them has a heart; in fact, we never discover one which does not have a heart. We conclude that all animals have hearts. Now, "All animals have hearts" is a more general statement than "Fido is an animal, and Fido has a heart"; but it is no more *necessary* than the latter. In fact, no general statement can be more necessary than any statement it implies. To put it in general terms, if a statement, S_1, implies another statement, S_2, and S_2 is not necessary, then S_1 cannot be necessary. The situation is analogous to that of "validity" in logic.[13] If the function of a statement is to sum up several particular statements, then it is a waste of time to argue that the (general) statement in question is necessary, unless you are willing to argue that the particular statements in question are also necessary.

The Principle of Utility, then, is to have whatever status typ-

---

[12] Exemplified in Whewell's philosophy of science, for example: Cf. Robert Butts, "Necessary Truth in Whewell's Philosophy of Science," *American Philosophical Quarterly* (1965).

A similar view seems to be suggested in Stephen Toulmin's *Philosophy of Science* (New York: Hutchinson University Library, Hillary House Publishers, Ltd., 1960). One might, for that matter, consider the "Principle of Causality" itself as an example. Numerous philosophers, most notoriously Kant, have supposed that the proposition that every event has a cause is necessarily true; even though the proposition about any particular event that it has any particular cause is contingent. This juxtaposition is, in my opinion, flatly inconsistent.

[13] Cf., e.g., Willard V. O. Quine, *Methods of Logic* (New York: Holt, Rinehart, and Winston, Inc., 1959), Ch. 26, p. 150, rule iii.

ical "low-level" moral principles have, the difference being merely one of generality. If we want to call these typical moral statements "synthetic," then we must regard the Principle of Utility as synthetic. This reflects, especially, the contrast with metaethical or implicitly metaethical statements, which is the main thing here. If arguments turn up eventually (e.g., Chapter IX), which suggest that the Principle is in some sense "necessary," then this will show that all of the particular, low-level statements that follow it are also necessary. In no case will there be a contrast of logical status between the "supreme" principle and the "lesser" ones.

There are two qualifications to this, neither of which alters the question of the analyticity of the Principle of Utility. First, the Principle is intended to be supremely general, in the sense that the "other things being equal" clause need not be attached to it; whereas, typical moral principles such as "Stealing is wrong," or "You ought to keep your promises" have to be understood as having an 'unless' . . . clause. More will be said on this point in the sections below. Secondly, all "particular" moral statements and many general ones have a factual element. Thus, if Bill stole an apple, then what Bill did was wrong; but that Bill stole an apple is just a matter of fact. Similarly, 'Adultery is wrong' is, according to the utilitarian account, only true to the extent that adultery causes such things as psychological pain and inconvenience. This, if it is true, is only contingently true. In the cases of these ethical statements, then, we can analyze them into a "factual" and an "ethical" element. Then we can say that if the Principle of Utility is a priori, then the "ethical element" of every ethical statement is also a priori.

In summary, if the Principle of Utility is true, we must be able to set it down as an axiom. Then, from a non-moral description of any act, together with definitions of specific moral terms, we can deduce from it the moral status of that particular act. The same holds true for classes of acts. If the Principle of Utility is adequate, we ought to be able to deduce all of the general moral truths as well as all of the particular ones from it, given the facts. The project undertaken in this book is to make it plausible that this can be done. Of course, I do not propose to deduce all of the particular moral truths from it, being neither in possession of them nor in a position to be so. I do propose to show how a number of very important moral principles, generally regarded as true, follow from it, and especially how certain principles which have been thought not to follow from it, in reality do.

Now, what is the point of this? It is, in part, a question of theoretical interest. The theoretician is always interested in elegance and simplicity. It can hardly be denied that utilitarianism has these attributes; indeed, people tend to criticize it because it has them in too high a degree. However, this is not a question of theoretical economy for its own sake. As I see it, there are two serious reasons for wanting to be able to sum up morality in a simple system. First, and most importantly, it allows one to raise the question of proof more efficiently. Instead of having to ask, "Why should I resist my impulses to do violence to others?" "Why should I pay my debts?" "Why should I . . . ?" thus raising a new question for each particular duty or other moral practice, we shall, so to speak, be in a position to ask all of them at once. If we can find some predicate 'F' such that every right act has it and every wrong act has its opposite, say 'F₁'; then, if we can advance an argument for doing acts of type F and refraining from acts of type F_1, we shall have answered all of these questions at once. To those who do not believe that there can be a serious question why a particular right act is right, this apparent advantage will seem fraudulent. But most people, I think, as well as most philosophers, have felt uncomfortable from time to time about doing what morality requires, and have felt the need of some solid reason for continuing to do it. This feeling might be dispelled by insisting that ethical principles are self-evident, or that they are commands of God; this isn't very likely, and it is no more likely that it will be allayed by philosophers who insist that such questioning is out of place.[14] In any case, recent philosophers have enabled us to put together a really strong argument for utilitarianism, which I shall discuss in the last chapter. I shall wait until then because, as argued earlier in Chapter I, it serves no useful purpose if it doesn't prove what needs to be proved; and what needs to be proved is that the basic body of our moral beliefs is correct.

[14] Cf. Baier's statement in *The Moral Point of View*, p. 1.

The other serious advantage is that once we have found a plausible fundamental principle, we need no longer rely heavily on the strength of a patchwork fabric of independent principles to bear the weight of moral thinking. Instead, we can reason things out by making deductions from the basic principle. Thus, there is less reliance on memory and more on reasoning. This has an additional advantage in making sense of moral *change*. Moral beliefs can easily become ossified, rigidified, and thus distorted, if one has no sense of a general purpose, common to them all. One of the main troubles with intuitionism of any kind is that it tends to lead to this kind of rigidity, as such writers as Dewey (and recently, Smart and Warnock) have emphasized. Who is more intolerable than a misguided but fanatical moralist?

The seriousness of these advantages will be weighted differently by different readers. But it seems to me that each of them singly, and surely all of them jointly, justify a serious effort to explore the possibility of reducing ultimate ethical principles to a single one. It may be asked what the criteria of individuation for "principles" is, and to this I have no answer. I think it is natural to view the Principle of Utility as "unified," or "single" in some sense. I shall have to rely on this tendency, although I do not think there is any serious danger of its simplicity being exposed as fraudulent. We just have to realize that this simplicity is not incompatible with extreme complexity and multiplicity of secondary principles; and to those to whom simplicity of underlying assumptions is intrinsically suspicious, I can only add, "Wait and see."

Utilitarianism is a Moral Theory

If we are to have any hope of plausibly explaining and defending the utilitarian theory, we must have a precise idea of the work to be done by it. This question has not been very clearly faced, and sometimes barely faced at all, either by defenders or opponents of utilitarianism in the past. In the previous section, I argued for the view that the utilitarian theory is a "substantive," rather than essentially "analytical" or "meta-ethical" theory. In the present, I shall narrow down the sense of what this theory is about by insisting that we do not confuse the question it is answering with a number of others that are often conflated with it. The general question to which the Principle of Utility is an answer is: "What is it about an act that makes it morally right or wrong?" or more generally, "What is the criterion of moral value?"

On the other hand, it does not provide an answer to the following questions: (1) What is the (general) criterion of value? (2) How ought I (anyone) to live? (3) What is intrinsically good? When I say that it "does not" provide an answer to these questions, however, perhaps I should say instead that we should not think of it in that way. Undoubtedly, Mill did say that "Pleasure, and freedom from pain, are the only things desirable as ends."[15] It is debatable how this remark was meant to be interpreted. In any case, I shall propose (in Chapters III and IV which follow) that it is quite unnecessary to make this statement in the context of utilitarian theory. In order to lay down a general foundation for determining the questions with which utilitarianism properly deals, we need a reasonable characterization of the distinction between moral and non-moral evaluative questions. Fortunately, a fair amount of good work has at last been devoted to this question. In the main, I shall need only to summarize it here, hoping (no doubt unrealistically) to avoid the begging of any serious questions. To a certain extent, I am going to restrict the sense of the word 'moral' in what some people will consider an artificial manner. However, I hope to do so without hocus-pocus, and to provide good reasons for the limitation.

It is easy to generate examples of evaluative questions that are not, *as such*, ethical questions. Judgments of the value of works of art, mechanical devices, or of a person's performance at a special type of task are typically non-ethical. All such matters can, of course, be connected with others in such a way as to raise ethical questions. For instance, an artist in his garret may be on the point of completing a master-stroke when he hears a scream emanating from the neighboring room. Does he drop

---

[15] Mill, *Utilitarianism*, p. 6.

what he is doing, possibly to lose the inspiration forever, or does he ignore the cry for help in order to forward his art? This we would obviously consider to be a moral question. But a question of whether to use blue instead of pink at a certain juncture in the production of a painting would clearly not be counted as a "moral" question, but as an aesthetic one.

Probably there would now be general agreement that the distinction between moral and non-moral evaluation is not to be sought in a distinction of meanings of words such as 'ought,' or even 'right.' Rather, the distinction lies in the context of their use, or the point of view from which they are used. We may, without prejudicing the issue, characterize the question as follows: What makes the use of 'You ought to do x,' say, on a particular occasion a moral use? What factors constitute a context as a moral one rather than some other kind? In particular, there is the question whether and to what degree factors other than "formal" ones are relevant. For example, some writers have held what might be called an "extreme protestant" position, according to which a judgment is a moral judgment if it is "a matter of authentic personal decision or commitment."[16] On this view, the range of actions which might be morally judgable is logically unlimited, since almost any act could conceivably be made the subject of such a decision. At the other extreme from this view is that of Toulmin, according to whom the moral judgments are those whose function is "to correlate our feelings and behavior in such a way as to make the fulfillment of everyone's aims and desires compatible so far as possible."[17] It seems to me and to many critics that such a view amounts to a sort of naturalism. If we took that view, it would be no great problem to defend utilitarianism as a moral theory, since Toulmin's view is all but a statement of that position. But then the danger of trivialization discussed previously becomes imminent.

There is evidence in favor of both of these extremes, certainly. On the one hand, the "protestant" view takes account of the undoubted motivational element in moral judgments. Socrates'

[16] William Frankena, "Recent Conceptions of Morality," in Castañeda-Nakhnikian, *Morality and the Language of Conduct*, p. 3.
[17] Stephen E. Toulmin, *The Place of Reason in Ethics* (New York: Cambridge University Press, 1953), p. 137.

puzzles about whether a man can voluntarily do evil have worried philosophers for centuries; and for ages, men have experienced the phenomenon of wrestling with their consciences. All of this would be inexplicable if we simply meant by 'moral' some such thing as Toulmin suggests. On the other hand, modern philosophers rightly make a serious and general distinction between prudential and moral questions. In a broadened sense, in which 'prudential' is applied to what is best for oneself, or any particular person, not taking others into account, it is often proper to contrast the moral and the prudential, even though they undoubtedly have many points in common.

Ultimately, so long as we realize what needs to be done and where, it may be that the present question is not of too great intrinsic importance as it stands, and is primarily a matter of organization. If one takes the "motivational" element of moral expressions as primary, and yet argues for a socially-oriented ethics, then one must show that such an ethics really does exhaust the content of morality. On the other hand, if one defines 'moral' in terms of the common good, or some such, then we have to raise a question which, on the "protestant" conception of morality, makes no sense whatsoever. This question is: But *why* ought we to be moral? We can sensibly ask whether we ought to have regard for people other than ourselves. It would not do to try to apply the "definitional stop," as Hart calls it, to this question by saying that morality is, by definition, social, and at the same time answer the other question by saying that morality, by definition, commits one to action.[18] You can't have it both ways, and so long as this is realized, perhaps it doesn't matter too much at which of the two points one faces this question.

On the other hand, it seems to me that the purely protestant view of morality is a dangerous one, for on this viewpoint it is too easy to answer the "social" question in the negative, or not to answer it at all. Given that moral judgments are those that we regard as committing us to action, there is a very real danger

---

[18] David Gauthier, in *Practical Reasoning* (New York: Oxford University Press, Inc., 1963), p. 173. (E.g., ". . . the acceptance of the wants of others as providing reasons for acting is of the essence of morality." This would make the question, "Why ought I to be moral?" a logically open one. However, Gauthier regards this question as unanswerable.

that we will come not to think of the question of our responsibilities to other people as terribly serious, or that it won't occur
to us to think that there are such responsibilities at all. There
is something absurd about this. Failure to have regard for others
is obviously a moral shortcoming, whereas failure to have sufficient regard for oneself is clearly a different matter. It "puts
the thing in a different light," as one might say, so that any view
collapsing the two must surely have gone wrong somewhere.
The question is, can one have an understanding of the word
'moral' that does justice to both the "protestant" and the "social"
aspects of morality, and at the same time does not beg the substantive question of the criterion of right and wrong?

Some suggestions are available that will get us reasonably close
to this goal. In the first place, there is the general feeling, recognition of which is doubtless due mainly to Kant, that morality
is a matter of the ends one ought to have, whereas prudential
values are due to the ends one happens to have. The limitations
of this distinction for our general question are ably discussed
by W. D. Falk in his essay, "Morality, Self, and Others."[19] He
points out that despite the truth of this claim, moral duties can
be slight and prudential "duties" very serious; that prudential
values are capable of being as serious, as binding, as real, and as
cogent as moral ones. He rightly emphasizes that we cannot
think of moral obligations as merely those which are in fact imposed by society. But, and here we come to the crucial point, it is
nevertheless true of moral values that they ought to be imposed
by society, while this is not so of prudential ones. This point is
easy to overlook, but of the greatest consequence, I suggest. We
would like to distinguish, not only between those decisions which
the individual may make for himself, and those which society
prods him about or forces him to make; but also between those
which individuals may or should make for themselves, and those
which society would be justified in prodding him about, whether
or not it actually does so. This general view, which is derived
in part from Mill,[20] has been advanced by T. L. Sprigge in a

[19] W. D. Falk, "Morality, Self, and Others," in Castañeda-Nakhnikian
Morality and the Language of Conduct (cf., n. 18, p. 59, and especially
pp. 61, 62).
[20] Mill, *Utilitarianism*, Ch. 5, and *Liberty*, Ch. 1.

recent article. According to Sprigge, "The ethical sense of 'X ought to do A' is distinguished from others by the methods which the speaker would favor for inducing X to do A."[21] Roughly speaking, "Moral issues are issues with which we are concerned that everyone should be concerned."[22] This seems to me to point in the right direction.

This view does not beg the question about the content of morality. Any kind of activity in theory could have been, and indeed has been, held to be morally praiseworthy or blameworthy in the above sense. For example, many beliefs, as well as private practices such as autoeroticism, have been held to be proper subjects of social concern. Moral matters are everyone's business, but some very strange things have been (and thus, can be) held to be everyone's business.

The above account might not be held to be the most fundamental one. It is possible, for instance, that we could derive it from some other account of a more "protestant" kind. At least, the above account is not incompatible with the "protestant" one. The most essential feature of that type of account is: that moral judgments take precedence over other evaluative judgments, in the following sense: If a particular act is thought to be morally wrong on the whole, then no weight of other kinds of reasons in favor of doing it should be permitted to count. Only after an act has passed the tests of moral permissibility may other considerations be brought into the picture. It follows that moral values are "absolute" or "ultimate"—they have to be taken into account no matter what else is taken into account. For this reason, a certain stringency or authority, a certain onerousness, has traditionally been associated with moral questions, and rightly so, I think.

This "protestant" account nevertheless tends to support the suggested "social" one as well. For if moral ends are absolute, then there can be no limitation on the means which may be used to achieve them, and thus, in particular, the methods of social, as distinct from merely personal, reinforcement can be appropriate to them.

[21] T. L. Sprigge, "Definition of a Moral Judgment," *Philosophy* (1964), p. 309.
[22] *Ibid.*, p. 322. See also Baier, *Moral Point of View*, Ch. 8, pp. 195 ff.

This matter of being an "absolute" end, to which no limitation of means is relevant, may also be a main source of the felt weight of moral considerations. Bernard Suits has suggested[23] that the essential feature of a game is that there are certain limitations of means to the end of "winning" or succeeding, which are adopted for their own sakes and not because the means in question will not work. This may account for that lack of complete serious-ness that we tend to associate with games; if the end in question were really important, we would feel that any means would be justified. The principle that "The end does not justify the means" is obviously false, I suggest, if the "end" is just that of being morally good.

That moral ends are supreme and precedence-taking should not, however, be confused with the assertion that they are the most important in an unqualified sense. Precedence in action is certainly a sense (or perhaps a criterion) of "importance"; but it seems to me quite wrong to suggest that morality is "intrin-sically" important, for instance. That is precisely what it is not. Consider the way in which a sensitive person might regard art. We can easily imagine a person who is extremely interested in art, and who would not want to live without it, although he could get along very well without other people, or at least without personal contact with many of them. Nevertheless, such a person could be a very moral person—honest, kind, responsible, and so forth—despite the fact that he doesn't regard other peo-ple as very interesting. In a sense, he regards art as much more important than people; yet, he responds to the scream for help across the hall from his garret.

If this person believed that intrinsic importance was the basic factor in morality—if, for instance, he subscribed to the Moore-Rashdall theory that our only duty is to increase the quantity of intrinsic good in the world—he would have no reason to heed the scream. Should the lives of a lot of ordinary clods be held of more intrinsic importance than the advancement of Art? Opinions would no doubt differ a great deal on this point. For the artist's part, the answer is obviously, No. To use a Mooreian fantasy for illustration: if he had his choice between pushing

---

[23] Bernard H. Suits, "Life, Perhaps, is a Game," *Ethics*, 1967.

two buttons, one of which would bring a lot of "peasants" into existence (even if they were perfectly happy ones, and quite good people, morally), and another which would bring another Beethoven's Ninth into existence, he would not hesitate to push the second button. A person whose moral principles were determined by considerations of intrinsic value would say that such a choice was dictated by morality. If, for instance, he were faced with a button which would make some presently existing people miserable if he pushed it, while bringing into existence a magnificent work of art, whereas, if he did not push it neither would happen, he might very well push it. Yet surely a *moral* artist would not push it, however sorry he would be at the thought of missing out on that masterpiece—however much intrinsic value would thereby be lost, in short.[24]

I am going to suggest that utilitarianism provides an explanation for this somewhat paradoxical status of moral values. According to it, moral values are logically derivative. They ride piggy-back, so to speak, on nonmoral evaluations. If there were no nonmoral values, then there could also be no moral values. Thus the notion of a "Holy Will" which had absolutely no interest in any but moral values is incoherent—a community of such beings would be logically out of business, a metaphysical Ghost town, only with no previous existence! Moral values are precedence-taking, because they embody whatever other values there are, as seen by the people whose values they are. But moral values are not additional intrinsic ones, unrelated to those which people already happen to recognize.

However this may be, the characterization of morality in terms of precedence-taking, with the understanding that it leads therefore to the justification of social action, seems to me the best one to adopt for our present purposes. It does not logically beg the question as to the specific content of morality; and yet, at the same time provides a reasonable sense of direction to substantive work. Relations among the different kinds of values are, of course, complex—which is what we should expect on the utilitarian theory, in view of the preceding paragraph. It is sufficient for the present to emphasize that they must not be identified with

[24] Further discussion of these matters is found in various places below, especially Ch. III.

each other, that the utilitarian theory is concerned only with moral value as distinct from the others, and that our characterization of the precise difference between them is useful only as a guide. If some readers think that this is an arbitrary limitation on the purposes of utilitarian theory, or that it does not wholly correspond to the intentions of various utilitarian theorists, I am quite willing to accept these criticisms. In that case, let us consider the following chapters as an account of a certain *part* of morality, that part of it that is distinct from the purely prudential part. Further reasons for such a restriction will be presented in the final chapter.

Formulation of Moral Principles

We now need to consider the criteria which must be met by any well-formed moral principle. By "well-formed," I mean "applicable"—to the extent that a moral principle is vague or otherwise ill-formed, we shall be unable to apply it. With very general ethical principles—especially one meant to be so general as to comprehend the entire area of morals—there is a grave danger of formulating them so ill that no application is possible. There are many examples of such ill-formed principles. For example, the general view that right action is action "in accordance with one's nature," or action "aimed at realizing one's nature," fails hopelessly on this score. To begin with, the words 'nature' and 'realizing' are essentially misused in these views. Given any quite ordinary senses of the words, it will either make no sense at all to suppose that we ought to "realize our nature," or it will be hopelessly implausible to suppose that we ought to do so. Is Jones realizing his nature when he murders Smith? Yes, says Jones, because his nature is that of a murderer and he is simply trying to realize it. But the philosophers who try to defend this view reply that that is not his "real" nature. His "real" nature, then, is what? We have no idea how to decide, at least none that is provided by the word 'nature' itself. Hence, the application of the view becomes quite arbitrary. Such views of ethical principles are philosophically useless; worse than this, their vague-

ness can lead to ethical disasters. Especially if the view is incul-
cated with the formidable apparatus of an establishment of
religion, the people who are fed this vague slogan will find that
they cannot apply it themselves, and being unable to do so, they
come to rely on authorities to do it for them. They blindly
follow the opinions of the authorities they accept without being
able to examine them to see whether they are any good. If, as is
natural, the authorities are fallible or, worse yet, have special
interests to defend, their "flocks" will end up regarding the most
bizarre things as morally sacred and persecuting other people
who disagree, and there will be no end of troubles.

Moral problems are (ordinarily) serious ones—as is inevitable
from the meaning of the word 'moral,' if the views in the previous section are correct. Accordingly, any shortcomings of
formulation of ethical principles are likely to result in moral ill
of one kind or another. The same holds true, of course, for
misunderstandings of the process of moral reasoning, if anything
about the latter is held to be distinctive. Thus, there are moral
reasons for being precise and intelligible in the formulations of
moral principles. That this is philosophically desirable in any case
goes without saying.

What conditions must be met to achieve this desired precision?
Clearly, the general condition is that we should know, for each
namable act, whether that act is right, wrong, or indifferent;
also, which act to prefer among alternatives. In other words, we
must be able to see what the principle we are examining says
about each case it is intended to cover. Since the Principle of
Utility is intended to cover all moral questions whatsoever, we
should ideally get a decision in each case. Moreover, it ought not
to be the case that the decision depends upon who is doing the
interpreting; this indeed, is implied by my previous remarks.
The uselessness of a principle will be proportional to the amount
of disagreement among interpreters as to what it says about particular cases. Needless to say, we shall not be worried if those
who are not acquainted with the principle, or who have no familiarity with the arguments on its behalf or interest in attempting to apply it, should "disagree" in this way. But if a person
who is familiar with the language in which the principle is stated
is unable to give any sense to some of its terms, or is able to apply

his own tastes to its applications, then the principle (or its statement, if we can distinguish between them) is to that extent at fault.

Any moral principle or statement, however general, attaches some moral predicate to an act, character, or intention, or to a class of any one of these. In Chapter IV, it will be argued that concern with acts is logically primary in morals; thus I shall limit my statement here, for the sake of convenience, to acts. Also, since we are dealing only with principles, which are general, we shall neglect singular moral statements for the time being. Thus, we may represent any moral principle schematically as follows: $(x) (Fx \supset Mx)$, where 'F' is replaceable by a "factual" predicate, and 'M' is replaceable by some moral predicate. The point I wish to make about formulations may be made by concentrating on the possible replacements for 'F.' What I want to say about this is that these replacements must not contain any evaluative language if our goal of objective applicability, and therefore of reasonably public and uniform interpretation and usability, is to be achieved. They may, of course, include mention of evaluative language, but they may not contain the evaluative language itself.

For instance, the "Ideal" utilitarians' view that what is right is that which is conducive to maximum good will fail of this test, since applying it involves making value judgments oneself. On the other hand, an "old-fashioned subjectivist" principle, e.g., that $(x) (y) (x$ *thinks* that y is wrong $\supset$ y *is* wrong) does not fail on this particular score, since the antecedent here requires only that we discover someone's opinion on a point, and not that the opinion in question be right. It does fail on a different point, for it requires x to have an opinion already, independently of the "principle," (which is why it is such a silly one). It also leads to contradictions, since we need but find two people who disagree about y, and we shall be able to infer that y is both wrong and not wrong. It "leads to" them only if there are people who disagree—but there are. To be perfectly applicable, however, a principle must not be able to lead to any contradictions.

Compare this with "$(Ex)(y)(if$ x thinks y is wrong, then y is wrong)," which would be true on the theistic voluntarist's position. There is nothing wrong with this on either of the above scores, provided that the person [or God] x does not contradict himself about y. But it suffers on the quite different score that there is no clear and generally acceptable way of discovering what God's opinions are. The restriction we need here is not easy to formulate, but I am inclined to suggest that it be couched in terms of "empiricism": Replacements of 'F' must meet the condition that it is applicable by empirical procedures.

There is, of course, no end to the complexity of the project of trying to specify in clear and precise terms just wherein clarity and precision consist, and I do not propose to do so here. Some of the above conditions, not very precise or clear themselves, are surely necessary but not sufficient. I think it safe to say that they represent goals toward which the ethical philosopher who concerns himself with formulating moral principles must work.

It is worth mentioning here that Mr. Smart's view of utility seems unsatisfactory on the first of the above counts; in his view, 'happiness' is a partly evaluative concept.[25] This seems to me a theoretical shortcoming; certainly, it is what Mill must have had in mind in insisting in the *Essay on Liberty* that a person's own good is not a sufficient warrant for interfering with his line of action. Smart's admission[26] that two utilitarians might advocate very different courses of actions if they differed about what constituted happiness, and that this difference between them would be simply an ultimate difference in attitude, seems to point up the need for eliminating the so-called hedonistic aspects of utilitarianism as essential ingredients. A moral system should not presuppose solutions to any first-order evaluative problems.

However, it is worth adding a point of sufficient importance to count as a general principle of interpretation of utilitarianism. This is the point that if the applicability of a predicate is sufficiently difficult or obscure, that in itself constitutes a reason for not placing very much weight on the outcome. It is surely

---

[25] Smart, *Outline of a System of Utilitarian Ethics*, p. 15. "To sum up so far, happiness is partly an evaluative concept, and so the utilitarian maxim, 'You ought to maximize happiness' is doubly evaluative." This is a result we ought to avoid if we can. Smart's reason for holding this rests, I think, on the assumption that utilitarianism requires us to have a general theory of intrinsic value and that happiness is this value. This assumption will be discussed in the following chapter.

[26] *Ibid.*

contrary to the general interest to require people to spend too much time trying to make precise calculations of happiness or unhappiness, so long as methods for doing this are not available.

Clarity Versus Precision

Utilitarianism is, of course, a theory *par excellence* in which the fundamental predicates are matters of degree. In order to be able to arrive at moral decisions on the basis of utility, we must be able to say, in the case at hand, whether alternative x would produce more utility than alternative y, or less, or an equal amount. But the measurement of utility is notoriously fraught with difficulty, and some of the difficulties may well be inextricable. It might be thought that this fact makes the ideals of objective applicability discussed in the previous section unattainable. For that matter, it has been held in some quarters that an ideal of objective applicability is itself inapplicable in the realm of morals. It is difficult to dispute Aristotle's dictum that a theorist should aim at no more precision than the subject admits of: the implication being, in the case of ethics, that it is not very much.

What we have here are two contrary objections, although it is not uncommon to hear both advanced against utilitarianism by the same critic. On the one hand, it is argued that utilitarianism should be rejected because it is not possible to measure precisely the variable which it holds to be basic; on the other, it is argued that utilitarianism should be rejected because the precise measurement of anything whatsoever is out of place in so unscientific and visceral a subject as ethics. When we contemplate these contentions in juxtaposition, we can formulate a rejoinder which surely deserves consideration: If morality is essentially imprecise, calling for judgment and sensitivity, and utilitarianism makes basic the estimate of quantities whose estimation is essentially imprecise and calls for judgment and sensitivity, then it is the more plausible that utilitarianism is barking up the right tree.

The issue, or at least one important aspect of the issue, may be put as follows: Can we claim that 'has more utility than,' 'has less utility than,' or 'has as much utility as' are clear predicates, if utility cannot be precisely measured? In what does precision consist, and is imprecision compatible with clarity and applicability in the sense required? It was suggested, in the preceding section, that the principal (or at least one principal) component in the notion of objective applicability is attainability of general agreement. Consider, then, the following parallel. Height, as it happens, is (often) very precisely measurable with the aid of measuring rods and rules. But even without the aid of these instruments, there is a considerable range of cases in which we get general agreement among observers. Goliath is obviously taller than David, Napoleon shorter than Wellington. But if two people are of nearly equal height, then we might get disagreement. On the other hand, we would not get disagreement as to whether the pair in question are roughly the same height. Such developments make it clear that there is a "quantity" being observed in these different cases. These pave the way for the establishment of units of measurement and rules or rods by which to make the measurements precise. Indeed, the agreement of the precise measures obtained with the obvious but imprecise measures made previously is a necessary condition of being sure that the new system is measuring that quantity which we want measured. If I introduce a system which makes David "taller" than Goliath, then my system is no good, at least as a system of measuring height.[27]

We may now suggest the following conclusions. In the first place, if it is sometimes clear and obvious, that x is of more utility than y, and sometimes not clear whether x is of more utility than y or less utility than y but clear that they are of roughly equal utility, then it follows that utility is, at any rate, a "quantity," in the general sense of being subject to variation in degree—something which some cases have more, less, or the same amount of as others. In the second place, it ought to be possible to decide whether *this* "quantity" is the one whose magnitude is the relevant factor in a given moral issue. If it is the relevant one, then it may also be the case that if we can think of no good reason to suppose in a particular application, that one alternative will in fact produce more or less utility than another,

[27] The discussion of Baier on this subject is illuminating. Cf., *Moral Point of View*, pp. 57–64. (The example of height is his.)

then in that application, the two alternatives are morally equal—neither is better than the other. If this decision is the one indicated, then the fact that we cannot measure utility with precision will, of itself, have been the deciding factor in the case.

As to the first point, it seems evident to me that we are sometimes clear as to which of two alternatives produces more utility; and that we are clear about this without having had to invoke precise metrics, precise instruments. What really is in question is the second point: *Is* utility the relevant factor or not? This book is devoted almost entirely to the discussion of this second question, and to the effort to answer it in the affirmative in all cases where the issue is a moral one. Sometimes, the method will be that of matching vaguenesses: If a case really is hard to decide, and if we can show that what makes it hard to decide in that case is that utility is involved, and that the utility in question is hard to measure, then that is a point in favor of the utilitarian view.

Certainly Bentham's language has led many people to extravagance concerning the aims of utilitarian theory. The question is whether the difficulties in a program of making precise measurements of utility are practical or theoretical. The reason for supposing that the difficulties are "practical" is that pleasure or happiness would presumably be an intensive magnitude, and these are notoriously difficult to measure. In Bentham's time, the measurement of such quantities was in its infancy. Since then, psychophysicists have devised measures of apparent volume, of light intensity, and so forth.[28] If pleasure or happiness were comparable to such sensory phenomena, then the difficulty of measuring them would be of the same kind, and thus presumably soluble.

The trouble is that pleasure and happiness are not comparable to subjective sensations. What we have to measure (when it comes to measuring such things), is the desire or preference with which the pleasure or satisfaction we are considering is correlated. These can be measured only in a comparative way. There seems something nonsensical about trying to measure the total quantity of desire in a person, as opposed to the degree to which he desires this or that. Even the latter, in turn, can be "measured"

[28] Cf., S. S. Stevens, "Mathematics, Measurement, and Psychophysics," in *Handbook of Experimental Psychology* (New York: John Wiley and Sons, Inc., 1951).

in any clear sense only by considering a person's "preference structure": The degree to which he desires x is the number of other things which he desires, but which would rank below x.[29] Finally, it is noteworthy that the only occasions on which we clearly need precise measures for ethical purposes are those on which the things to be measured are quantities desired, but not quantities *of* desire. If two small boys are given chocolate cake, it may be important to divide it precisely into equal pieces. If Jones' income is $100 per year greater than Smith's, then it is presumed that Jones' income is slightly more desirable than Smith's. But this is because it can be safely assumed in such cases that an indefinite amount of the things in question, or at least a good deal more than is available, is desired. When this condition is not satisfied, it is difficult to make precise measurements of utility; but this is because we don't know what, in the relevant sense, the "utilities" in question are. (Further remarks pertaining to this are to be found in the following Chapters III and VII.)

Apart from these problems, which are of genuine concern, there are two more of a spurious kind deserving some attention. First, the contention that since the consequences of our acts go off into the indefinite future, we can never know what the utility of a given act is; hence, we cannot use estimates of it as a basis for action. Secondly, there is the contention that the "general happiness" is too indefinite, too remote, or too obscure an object of pursuit to permit its being used as a guide to action. Coupled with the latter is an extremely curious argument advanced now and then by critics, to the effect that according to utilitarian principles, it presumably follows that there ought to be as many people as possible provided they are all at least slightly happy.

With regard to the first, we need merely to deny both the premise and the reasoning. That the consequences of each of our

---

[29] However, game theorists and decision theorists have devised various ingenious measures of these things. The literature in these new disciplines is by now immense. For an ethicist's appraisal, see, for example, Robert P. Wolff, "Reflections on Game Theory and the Nature of Value," *Ethics* (1962). For a rather ingenious general formulation, see R. McNaughton, "A Metrical Concept of Happiness," in *Philosophy and Phenomenological Research* (December, 1953). This system introduces a way of making interpersonal comparisons of utility as well as intrapersonal ones; but it is subject to the difficulties of application discussed in the text, which are such as to make one wonder whether the system is of much use other than as a purely abstract exercise.

acts go parading off into the indefinite future is, in the relevant sense, just not true. The supposition is founded on a mistake, I believe, or rather, on two mistakes. (1) First, there is the standard philosophical tendency to inflate local and isolated cases into vast metaphysical generalizations. If one sits back and tries to recall any act which there is genuine reason to believe will significantly affect the happiness of persons into the indefinite future, he will find that the number of such acts is approximately zero. The speculation that all of our acts have such effects is theoretical speculation in the bad sense of that expression. If we take a perfectly elastic ball and let it fall onto a perfectly solid surface, it will keep on bouncing forever—provided that it's done in a perfect vacuum and that nothing gets in the way (and provided that the laws of nature continue operating?). True, but these conditions are never realized. There is friction, and there are winds, and so forth. Human affairs are similar. The fact is that people forget, or lose interest. When Mrs. Smith's husband is killed in an accident, she wails and rends her hair for a day or two; but, in a year or two she has found a new and different, and perhaps better, husband. Or, she has discovered she's better off without one, or . . . indeed, we may oppose a maxim based on better evidence to the theoretical speculation in question: Everything is in flux. (2) The other error is simpler. It is forgotten that the effects of my acts on persons remote in time from myself generally depend upon the intervening actions of other people. How, then, is the "effect" to be attributed to me alone? Are not the acts of the intervening persons to be counted as well? Clearly, if I do something which will affect the happiness of Smith in a certain way, and which will have a different effect if I don't do it, then the fact that it would not have been possible to do it had it not been for an earlier act of Jones is not sufficient reason for requiring Jones to have taken the possibility in question into account. Most of the remote effects of our acts are of this kind. They affect the happiness of remote persons only in the sense that they alter the conditions under which intermediate persons can produce the effects in question. If, for example, I have a child, then this makes it possible for persons in the future to affect its happiness. Nevertheless, the things they do which affect its happiness are their responsibility, and not mine.

Thus, there is no good reason to accept the contention that

utilities are inestimable because our acts have remote effects which are unknown or unknowable. Even if we did accept this contention, it would not follow that we therefore cannot ever know the utility of any particular act. As Bentham pointed out, one of the dimensions of utility is propinquity or remoteness, and another is certainty or probability. Principles such as that a certain present evil is not justified by an uncertain future good are clearly utilitarian in foundation, and are sufficient to resolve many cases.[30] Finally, we may point out that any sensible system of principles for guiding action is going to require some knowledge of the future. The fact that this is difficult to obtain doesn't differentially affect utilitarianism. We must carry on as best we can in a difficult world on any realistic moral theory.

The other class of objections may be dismissed more shortly. To the objection that our acts do not, in general, have discernible effects on the general happiness, we can reply simply that no utilitarian has ever held that in order for the utility of an act to be appraised, it must have effects on everyone's happiness. As Mill points out:

The occasions on which any person (except one in a thousand) has it in his power to do this on an extended scale, in other words to be a public benefactor, are but exceptional; and on those occasions alone is he called on to consider public utility; in every other case, private utility, the interest or happiness of some few persons, is all he has to attend to.[31]

The principle of utility is always stated in terms of the effects of one's actions on whatever persons they do affect, and not merely in terms of its effects on everyone in general. Thus, we have Sidgwick's formulation as follows:

The conduct which, under any given circumstances, is objectively right, is that which will produce the greatest amount of happiness on the whole; that is, taking into account all whose happiness is affected by the conduct.[32]

[30] Strictly speaking, one might doubt that these are two separate dimensions; it seems preferable to say that a near good is only preferable to a remote one of equal quantity because of the inherently lesser certainty of its being attained, things being as they are in this world.
[31] Mill, *Utilitarianism*, p. 17.
[32] Sidgwick, *Methods of Ethics*, p. 411.

This point might seem to be too obvious to be worth making. Yet Sidgwick himself, as well as numerous critics of the theory, have failed to see what follows from this. Thus it has been held that on utilitarian principles, bringing into existence twice as many people who are half as happy is just as good as half as many people who are twice as happy, other things being equal. He contends that:

Assuming, then, that the average happiness of human beings is a positive quantity, it seems clear that, supposing the average happiness enjoyed remains undiminished, Utilitarianism directs us to make the number enjoying it as great as possible.[33]

This is entirely unsatisfactory, for reasons which are worth going into very briefly here. There are two related confusions underlying the inference drawn in the second quotation from Sidgwick, and in the objection advanced on similar grounds. The first confusion is between two interpretations of the phrase, 'produce the greatest amount of happiness on the whole.' One interpretation, which I fear may be the one most usually adopted, is that producing happiness is like producing milk: just as it is a matter of contingent fact that, as things stand, we have to have cows to have milk, so too, as things stand, we need to have sentient organisms to have happiness. Just as we can, under present conditions, increase the production of milk by increasing the production of cows, so too we may increase the production of happiness by increasing the production of people: Make people happy by making happy people. This is a fundamental error, involving as it does the supposition that utilitarianism is a theory of intrinsic value, coupled with the moral position that the moral value of an act is proportional to its production of intrinsic value. In the following chapter, I shall attempt to show what is wrong with both of these assumptions. For the present, I shall simply contrast this interpretation with the other one which, in my view, is the correct one. According to this interpretation, the important phrase in the first Sidgwick quotation above is the phrase, "taking into account all whose happiness is affected by the conduct." The principle of utility, on this view, enjoins us to in-

[33] *Ibid.*, p. 415.

47

crease people's happiness and to decrease their misery.[34] The question of increasing or decreasing a person's happiness cannot logically arise unless and until there is a person whose happiness is in question. It is nothing more than a silly play on words to ask the question: What effect on a person's happiness does it have to *bring him into existence?* Even if we have gotten over the first confusion, it will do us no good if we make the second one, which involves the supposition that such questions make perfectly good sense. If I do not have a child, then the question of how happy he is logically does not arise; a comparison between the state of his happiness if not born versus the state of his happiness if born is similarly absurd. Nonexistent people are not one kind of people any more than nonexistence cupolas are one kind of cupolas, or nonexistent gods one kind of gods[35] (and in the case of people, as things stand, an unborn person is a nonexistent person).[36] But this is the mistake which one must make in order to advance the objection above.

Now, if it were impossible to exercise any control over the birth of children, so that we could not deliberate on population policy, then there would be no distinction in practice between the two interpretations of utilitarianism distinguished above. But

[34] Smart, in his *Outline of Utilitarian Ethics,* p. 18, distinguishes these two interpretations under the heading of "average" versus "total" happiness. I don't like this choice of labels owing to the fact that it tends to cross the present question up with that of distribution, for one thing. This confusion infects Marcus G. Singer's discussion of the present point, for instance in *Generalization in Ethics* (New York: Alfred A. Knopf, Inc., 1961), p. 202. Also, Smart tends to discuss the present question in terms of "what a humane and sympathetic person would prefer," and this seems somewhat tendentious.

[35] Cf., the 1930's routine which went: "Do you want to buy a duck? Does your brother want to buy a duck? If you had a brother, would he want to buy a duck?" Compare also Anselm's Ontological Argument which, according to many interpreters, involves use of the premise that an existing thing is better than a non-existing thing of the same kind, other things being equal. It is generally agreed that if Anselm's proof really does turn on this step (although not everyone thinks it does), then that constitutes a *reductio ad absurdum* of it. The same should be true of analyses of utilitarianism.

[36] "As things stand," because presumably it is possible that people should be raised in test tubes. There is also an issue about whether embryos should be accounted persons, and if so at what stage. Disagreements on this point are not relevant here, although they are very relevant when it comes to discussing the moral legitimacy of abortion.

we can, and consequently there is such a distinction in practice. On the first interpretation, the fact that a child would, if produced, be happy would constitute a positive intrinsic reason for having it; whereas, on the second interpretation, it would not. The reason is as follows. If one has not yet conceived, then there is, as yet, no person whose happiness is in question, and nothing can be done either to increase or decrease it. Consequently, no utilitarian considerations arise from this source; any reasons in favor of having a child would have to stem from effects on other people, e.g., the parents. On the first interpretation, however, the fact that a child, if born, would be happy, constitutes a reason of itself for having one; since on this interpretation, the moral question is that of production of happiness *tout court*, rather than of increasing or decreasing anybody's happiness, which is the question on the second view.

On the other hand, on the second view as well as on the first, the fact that a child, if produced, would be miserable, is a sufficient moral reason for not having one. The reason for this is that once a child *is* produced, then of course moral questions arise which would not arise if it is not. And if one can foresee that a child, if produced, would inevitably be miserable, then one can avoid an increase in human misery by not having it in the first place.[37] The conclusion, then, is that there can be a moral reason (on utilitarian grounds, arising from hypothetical considerations about the happiness, or reverse, which would be the lot of children if produced) for *not* having children, but there cannot be such a reason for having them.

This conclusion might be thought strange at first; but the reason for thinking so is failure to see that the situations confronting us here are subtly, but importantly, asymmetrical. If you have a child, then the relevant population whose happiness or unhappiness is in question is different from the relevant population if you don't have a child. To see this, assume for purposes

[37] It remains the case that bringing someone into existence does not, as such, have any effects on his happiness, although the process of being born can. Generally, it is the various things which happen to a child after birth which have the relevant effects, and these can be prevented by not having a child to have them happen to. See an interesting discussion of a related matter by Jonathan Bennett in *Analysis* (1965–66), entitled "No Matter What."

49

of simplicity that we have but two persons in the world, Adam and Eva. If they remain childless, then this fact might make them unhappy, in which case it is a reason for them to consider producing a child if they can; but it does not do anything to the happiness of their child, there being no child the happiness of whom to consider. Nobody, other than Adam and Eva themselves, will be missing out on any joys or experiencing any sorrows as a result of their childlessness. On the other hand, if they decide to have a child, for whatever reason, then that would put a third party on the scene whose happiness or unhappiness is on the utilitarian view, to be accounted equally with those of Adam and Eva themselves. Thus, the size of the population to be considered will be greater if the action concerned (i.e., having a child) is taken than if it is not taken.

One must not be misled, in discussions of this type, by the temporal connotations of the word 'exists' in ordinary usage. The view being recommended here does *not* imply that the principle of utility "merely enjoins us to maximize the happiness of already existing persons." All persons who can be affected by our acts are to be considered equally here, be they presently alive or in the however distant future. If one knows that certain people in the future will be affected by one's actions, then effects on such people must be taken into account. It's just the peculiarity of the present subject that it concerns actions whose effect is to increase, or not to increase, the population. The fact that persons other than those who presently exist must be taken into account is precisely why it is possible to have a utilitarian reason (arising from hypothetical considerations about the well-or ill-being of persons presently unborn) for *not* having children, but not for *having* them.

By way of a footnote to the above discussion, it should of course be remembered that there can be plenty of non-moral reasons for having children, and also sometimes moral reasons, such as when an area's population is too small to afford a good life for all. Most people enjoy having children, and this is sufficient reason to have them, provided that the resulting children will not be miserable or burdensome to others.[38]

[38] I discuss these matters more thoroughly in "Utilitarianism and New Generations," *Mind* (1967).

CHAPTER III

Utility

Hedonism

Utilitarianism is generally described as a species of "hedonism," a subject which is popularly divided as follows: On the one hand, there is "psychological hedonism"; on the other, there is "ethical hedonism," which in turn has two main species, "egoistic" and "universalistic." Psychological hedonism is the view that everyone actually does "seek" only his own pleasure. The two variants of the ethical theory are egoistic hedonism, according to which one ought only to "pursue" one's own pleasure (or happiness?); universalistic, that one ought to "pursue" the general happiness (or pleasure?). It would be logically possible to extend this classification in various directions. For example, "psychological" hedonism could be broken down analogously to the classification of "ethical" hedonism, into "egoistic" and "universalistic," the former being the theory that everyone in fact pursues his own pleasure; the latter, that everyone in fact pursues the general pleasure. We could also add a third category to both theories, that of "altruism." Its "psychological" version would be the view that we, in fact, pursue only other people's pleasure, and in its "ethical" version, that we ought to pursue only other people's pleasure. For very good reasons, I think, these three logically possible additions are regarded as uninteresting because they are too implausible to be worth discussion. It seems a matter of obvious common sense that not everyone pursues the general happiness, and still more obvious, that they do not pursue only other people's happiness; while on the ethical side, the theory that one ought only to pursue other people's happiness seems bizarre.

Why, and with what important implications is something we will consider in Chapter IX, but suffice it to say that I concur with these judgments of our three additional theories.

My concern in the present section is to complain about the principle behind this classification on the ground that it is seriously misleading. The picture of utilitarianism which it suggests seems to me an incoherent one. We shall go far toward understanding what utilitarianism has to offer as an ethical theory by exposing these sources of error.

Let us consider, to begin with, what "hedonism" is, or is supposed to be. In ordinary life, if we were to classify someone as a "hedonist," what would we be saying about him? We would surely be describing certain aspects of his behavior. We would, for example, be denying that he was a spartan, a puritan, or a masochist. We would also probably be implying that he was not an altruist. We would tend to think of a hedonist as a person who is not likely to be very responsible or even terribly prudent. The so-called "paradox of hedonism" can be cited in this connection: A very calculating sort of person, we would feel, is to that extent less of a hedonist than one whose actions were spontaneous or not terribly well-planned. Finally, we would most likely be implying something, in a rather general way, about the nature of his tastes. We would, for instance, be implying that he *has* some. A business executive who devoted all of his time to his work, seventy hours a week, and professed either to have no time for, or no interest in, the arts, good food, interesting company, and so forth, would not naturally be classified as a hedonist.

It may be that none of the above implications are of the sort for which we can be held strictly to account. A hedonist doesn't necessarily like olives, nor does he necessarily like and have a developed taste in good food. But what if he doesn't like music, art, women, sports, conversation, etc.? What would we say of a person who claimed to be a hedonist, but whose "hedonism" manifested itself in his sleeping on beds of nails and sitting for hours at a time, contemplating his navel? He might claim that he gets a unique pleasure out of resting on beds of nails and contemplating his navel, and this would be extremely odd, to say the least; it is safe to say that we wouldn't believe him. These are not the activities which one would normally be attributing to someone in describing him as a hedonist. But it is obvious that these are not the things with which utilitarians have been concerned, either to condemn or to recommend. Indeed, Mill makes it abundantly clear in the *Essay on Liberty* and elsewhere, that he regards the choice of style of living as up to the individual, and not a proper matter of concern for the moral theorist.

It is vital to the understanding of utilitarianism to see that it has *nothing at all* to do with this sort of thing. Nor is this merely because the utilitarians were using the word 'pleasure' in a more general sense, or perhaps because they were recommending that we seek happiness, rather than merely pleasure.[1] There are indeed a few passages in Mill which suggest this sort of thing. For example, there is the celebrated dictum that "It is better to be a human being dissatisfied than a pig satisfied . . . and if the fool, or the pig, are of a different opinion, it is because they only know their own side of the question."[2] Again, there is the discussion in the *Essay on Liberty* of "Individuality, as One of the Elements of Well-Being," in which it sometimes seems that he is in favor of being different for its own sake. But to regard these as central to his moral philosophy would be a mistake. Mill was not recommending that we seek happiness, because he believed that we do seek it, in the nature of the case. That ". . . human nature is so constituted as to desire nothing which is not either a part of happiness or a means of happiness . . ."[3] i.e., the principle of "psychological hedonism" is the main interest of Mill on this point. If this is true, then there is no need to *advocate* that people seek happiness because there would be no point in it. What Mill obviously thought needed advocating is that people have regard for other people's happiness, i.e., the general happiness. Those passages in which he seems to be telling us how to live our lives must surely be viewed in the light of the many passages in which he insists, often with great passion, that this is entirely our own business. Take, for instance, the two mentioned above. Certainly Mill is not saying that pigs or fools are

---

[1] This view is advocated in diverse places, e.g., in Aristotle and the Stoics, and occupies a central place in W. T. Stace's book, *The Concept of Morals* (New York: Macmillan Co., 1962), Ch. 6. From the present point of view, all of these efforts are beside the point.

[2] Mill, *Utilitarianism*, p. 9.

[3] *Ibid.*, p. 36.

immoral, insofar as they prefer slop to filet mignon, or pushpin to poetry. What he is saying, obviously, is that they are being piggish and/or foolish, and that people who know both in fact prefer the filet and the poetry. What has this to do with ethics? What has it to do with the "criterion of Right and Wrong," which is the avowed subject of *Utilitarianism?*

The truth is, of course, that a person who believed that the desire for happiness is already the sole motive of all that we do would not be advocating anything in particular by advocating that we seek it. Consider questions like this: Is it better to be happy and poor, than unhappy but rich? Powerful and unhappy, or weak and happy? Beethoven unhappy, or Hugh Hefner happy? Socrates dissatisfied, or a pig satisfied? These questions are devoid of clear sense. As Mill says, "If the sources of pleasure were precisely the same to human beings and to swine, the rule of life which is good enough for the one would be good enough for the other."[4] He plainly does *not* mean, by the phrase 'the rule of life,' the rule "seek happiness!" for this is the "rule" which both of them, according to Mill, are already following. His point is that pigs do not know what it is like to practice philosophy or to listen to Mozart, and so are not in a position to choose. In supposing that the life of a Socrates is preferable to that of a swine, Mill is speaking from the standpoint of a human being, and indeed, of a particular sort of human being, a polished, erudite, and cultured nineteenth-century Victorian human being; and such a person just isn't going to find any happiness in attempting to live the life of a swine. This is the crux of the matter. No particular sort of life is necessarily going to be a happy one—it depends on the individual in question.[5]

Certainly, some interesting and puzzling questions can be asked along these general lines, and, significantly, are barely touched upon in Mill's ethical writings. For example, consider gaiety. If a person is gay, does it follow that he is happy? There seems

[4] *Ibid.*, p. 7.

[5] Of course, some descriptions of lives imply that the lives in question are unhappy, e.g., "neurotic." It's just that we can produce relatively neutral descriptions of ways of life which would clearly be such that the ways of life described by them would make some people happy and others unhappy, let alone people happy and pigs unhappy, if pigs could live them at all.

to be some logical connection here. But then if a person wants
to be happy, shouldn't it follow that he would want to be gay?
And if somehow faced with a choice between being always gay,
versus living, say, the life of a Beethoven, which was generally
rather somber, shouldn't it follow that he would have to choose
the gay life? Yet, it is clear that Mill would not have thought
so. Why not? It is difficult to say. He might have taken the line
that Beethoven's life was, after all, happier than a life of continual gaiety would be. If so, this would evidently involve a shift
of meaning in the term 'gay.' Consider the view, often heard
among "intellectuals," that Heaven must be terribly dull—nothing but one continuous round of joy. Intolerable! Taken literally, this surely would be nonsense; it is contradictory to speak
of "joyful boredom." What they must mean is that they would
not get much joy from the sort of activities popularly associated
with the idea of "heaven," e.g., continually singing the praises
of God (which might be very distasteful to avowed atheists for
example!). The point remains that if we try to give any particular content to the idea of a "gay life," or even a "life of
pleasures" (cf., Mill's definition of 'happiness' as 'pleasure, and
the absence of pain'), we find it quite sensible to suppose that
we would prefer the kind of life that was lived by Beethoven,
Lincoln, or Socrates, despite the fact that their lives were not
apparently notable for the "quantity of pleasure" contained in
them. To repeat, it is perfectly obvious that Mill realized that
this was so.[6]

What follows from all of this? It follows that it is misguided
to think of utilitarianism as one species of the same genus of
which "egoistic hedonism" is the other species, if we think of
"egoistic hedonism" as a (supposed) "philosophy of life." According to this classification, egoism is one "way of life," viz.,
seeking one's own pleasure, while utilitarianism is another "way
of life," viz., seeking the general pleasure. The only difference
is that in one case you are seeking one person's pleasure, in the
other everyone's. But this doesn't make sense. What, after all, is
the ground on which we can advocate a "way of life?" Surely,
it is of the following sort: You will (we might say), get more

---

[6] If proof is needed, see the early portions of Mill's *Autobiography*.

real satisfaction out of life if you think of other people besides yourself. Selfishness is narrow, stultifying, restricting; the selfish life lacks richness and fullness. This is absurd because these are precisely the grounds which the "egoist" is recommending that we employ: We should seek the general happiness because it will make *us* happier. No doubt Mill, like many others, thought that this was true, as it may well be. But this is not relevant. For utilitarianism is out to show that we ought to have regard for the interests of other people on *moral* grounds. There is nothing wicked about choosing one way of life as against another, although it may be in bad taste to do so. But there is something wicked about killing other people when it happens to serve your interest to do so, regardless of the value of the "way of life" which recommends it.

"Egoism" could, perhaps, be advocated as a moral theory as well. If so, it would be a very peculiar one. It might, for instance, consist in the principle that we ought to disregard and suppress our benevolent impulses, however painful we find it to do so. A person acting in this way might be described as being selfish as a matter of principle (if a rather bizarre principle). In fact, "egoistic hedonists" do not advocate this. What they advocate, I take it, is that we should be concerned with other people only insofar as we happen to like or to be interested in them. Which is in turn equivalent to saying that one should do as one pleases. Critics have observed that this seems equivalent to having no moral theory at all. As Baier puts it, "[The egoist] does not have *principles*, he has only an aim."[7] The egoist's position is rather similar to that described by Bentham as the "principle of sympathy and antipathy," which is (as he says), "the negation of all principle, [rather] than anything positive."[8]

One *could*, then, advocate utilitarianism as a "way of life"; likewise, one *could* advocate egoism as a moral principle. But to

[7] Baier, *Moral Point of View*, p. 191.
[8] Bentham, *Principles of Morals and Legislation*, Ch. I, sec. XII. The strongest statement on this point, with which I think Mill would have agreed, comes from Kant, who held that "one's own happiness is an end which, to be sure, all men do have (by virtue of the impulse of their nature) but this end can never without contradiction be regarded as a duty . . . because a duty is a constraint to an end that is not gladly adopted." Immanuel Kant, *Metaphysical Principles of Virtue*, trans., J. Ellington (New York: Liberal Arts Press, Bobbs-Merrill Co., Inc., 1964), p. 43.

do either would be unnatural (and to do both would be quite bizarre). This is what makes it so misleading to regard them as species of the same genus. Properly understood, these may not be incompatible "views" at all. The way to appraise a "way of life" may well be by considering what's in it for you; the way to appraise the moral value of a course of action by considering what's in it for everyone. But to confuse the two is to get into trouble, and the standard classification sanctions the confusion. The term "hedonism" ought to be confined to the "egoistic" form, whether taken (more naturally) as a principle for appraising "ways of life," or as a moral principle; the man who is controlling his actions in the light of their effects on the general happiness is *not* "seeking happiness" or "seeking pleasure," in any natural sense of these expressions. He may not be acting in this way merely on the ground that this way of life happens to be intrinsically desirable or satisfying. He most likely would be doing so as a matter of moral principle, i.e., because this kind of action is morally best. At any rate, this is the way in which we are going to regard the principle of utility in this book, although it seems clear to me that Mill and Sidgwick, if perhaps not Bentham,[9] shared my views on the matter.

Psychological Hedonism

The theory of "psychological hedonism" has loomed large in the classical utilitarian literature, although it has not been quite clear just what role it is supposed to play. It seems to be a psychological theory, that is to say, a theory whose statements pur-

[9] It is very difficult indeed to determine just what Bentham's view on this matter was. The "official" doctrine is that everybody always pursues his own pleasure; that people are moral because they happen to enjoy it, or because they fear the sanctions attached to immoral actions; that the sanctions in question have been attached to them either by community custom (which is unreliable) or by legal imposition. Good laws, in turn, exist because people like Bentham who happen to enjoy being moral, and who like to see other people being so as well, press their adoption. It is not all that clear that my account is incompatible with this. It depends mainly on the doctrine of "sanctions," which has its obscurities as well. Does he, or doesn't he, allow the "internal" sanctions to be self-imposed as a result of reflection? We don't know.

port to describe human behavior in general in a non-tautological way. *Prima facie*, at least, it is plausible to say that ethical theories cannot be deduced from psychological theories. If this is so, then it is small wonder that the frequent occurrence of sentences of an ostensibly psychological hedonist kind raises the eyebrows of critics. The spectre of fallacy hovers over the entire operation. Yet, it does not seem altogether plausible to saddle the likes of Mill with this fallacy, as recent critics of Moore's destructive chapter on hedonism have been pointing out.[10] We have a problem, then, of historical interpretation, and simultaneously (and more to the present point) a problem in conceptual analysis. Just what does psychological hedonism amount to? And why bother with it for purposes of ethical theory? These are the questions that concern us in this section. The answers are, briefly, that "psychological hedonism" is not, as recent writers have correctly pointed out, a psychological theory at all, and that the reasons for bringing it up are two: To formulate the principle of utility, and to assist in the proof of it. So far as the proof of utilitarianism is concerned, we will defer this topic to the final chapter of this book, in which the reader will also find my reflections on the celebrated question of the "naturalistic fallacy."

To begin our consideration of these questions, let us turn to some points about the general formulation of "psychological hedonism." In the first place, it is never put flatly as a theory about what people do, but rather about what they desire or aim at. Clearly, no one would go so far as to maintain that people always actually do maximize their pleasure. They hold, at most, that people *intend* to maximize it, or *want* to. In the second place, the theory has never been intended to cover absolutely all behavior of a human being, but only that portion of it in which the subject knows what he's doing, has a conscious view of his situation. For instance, take even this extreme statement by Bentham:

On the occasion of every act he exercises, a human being is (inevitably) led to pursue that line of conduct which, according to his

[10] Cf., for example, Henry D. Aiken's article, "Definitions, Factual Premises, and Moral Conclusions" in *Reason and Conduct*, Essay III.

58

view of the case, taken by him at that moment, will be in the highest degree contributory to his own greatest happiness.[11]

Clearly, this statement is otiose if applied to those occasions when the agent does not *take* a "view of the case." This is an important point, on which we will reflect further below. It is closely related to a third general point, that its proponents have found it essential to distinguish ends and means, or ultimate and subordinate ends, and to put the theory in terms of ultimate, rather than secondary or subordinate ends, or of means. All three of these points are well illustrated in the formulations in Mill's *Utilitarianism:*[12]

1) Whatever is desired otherwise than as a means to some end beyond itself, and ultimately to happiness, is desired as itself a part of happiness, and is not desired for itself until it has become so.

2) Desiring a thing and finding it pleasant, aversion to it and thinking of it as painful, are phenomena entirely inseparable.

The section above goes further than my point (3), and distinguishes "parts of" happiness from "means to" it; there is a further expansion later on (which some would regard as more hedging in the face of difficulties), where he distinguishes "will" from "desire," saying:

3) Will, like all other parts of our constitution, is amenable to habit, and that we may will from habit what we no longer desire for itself, or desire only because we will it. It is not the less true that will, in the beginning, is entirely produced by desire . . . habit is the only thing that imparts certainty; and it is because of the importance to others of being able to rely absolutely on one's feelings and conduct, and to oneself of being able to rely on one's own, that the will to do right ought to be cultivated into this habitual independence. In other words, this state of the will is a means to good, not intrinsically a good; and does not contradict

[11] From Bentham's *Constitutional Code,* quoted by Sidgwick in *Methods of Ethics,* p. 41.
[12] All passages from Mill in this section are from Ch. IV of *Utilitarianism,* unless otherwise noted.

the doctrine that nothing is a good to human beings but insofar as it is either itself pleasurable, or a means of attaining pleasure or averting pain.

This suggested separation of will and desire, with the assertion that the "desire" for pleasure is "original," and the independence of the two "secondary" as a matter of later cultivation and training, is also employed in the earlier passage alluded to above, in which he develops the theory of "parts" of happiness:

4) There was no original desire of [virtue], or motive to it, save its conduciveness to pleasure, and especially to protection from pain. But through the association thus formed, it may be felt a good in itself, and desire as such with as great intensity as any other good.

A number of points strike me as being highly significant about all of this maneuvering. First, as a methodological observation made through hindsight, note the wavering between talk of causes and talk of reasons. Psychological hedonism might be thought to be a theory about the causes of human action. But Mill's account here is inconsistent with this view, for in selection (3), he clearly implies that there are causes of human action other than desire, namely habit. When it comes to discussing habit, and the significance of the fact that people can through habit do things other than seek their own pleasure, Mill does not offer evidence to show that people never do out of habit things which conflict with the pursuit of pleasure. Instead, he talks about the *point* of cultivating habits, and offers the utilitarian criterion, in effect, as a justification for such actions, or rather, as an account of what justification people might give *if* they were "motivated solely by a desire for pleasure." Another manifestation of this is in his discussion of virtue as a "part" of the "end." Here it is argued that the desire for pleasure was "original," i.e., came first in time. But note that the conclusion he actually argues for is that virtue may, through association, be *"felt as a good."* This leads me to my second point, a general observation about the substance of Mill's theorizing here. This is that he is trying to prove throughout that happiness is the only thing regarded as good in itself. This is what comes out in quotations (3) and (4), wherein Mill is trying to account for apparent objections to the views laid down in (1) and (2), which are couched in terms of "desire." Clearly, this implies that Mill believes that desiring a thing means *regarding it as good, or regarding it as desirable* [13]

A further observation: Mill does not take up a kind of objection which a modern reader acquainted with Freud and contemporary literature would want to raise immediately; namely, what to do about compulsions and drives? Mill only discusses habit, which he admits to be distinct from "will," as he calls it; but in fact, what he is distinguishing it from is, again, desire, or better yet, from "regarding it as pleasant." Clearly, he is correct to make this distinction. Doing something from habit is not doing it because one regards it as pleasurable, even though, as Mill quite properly observes, a "desire for pleasure" might very well recommend the cultivation of certain habits. The point is, neither is doing it from a compulsion, which is clearly not a matter of habit; nor, for that matter, is doing it as a primitive response, or (perhaps) out of sheer whim. Clearly, there are a number of causes of apparently non-hedonistic behavior. What do they have in common? Surely what Mill would say, judging from his account in *Utilitarianism*, is that what they all have in common is that behavior from such causes is non-rational, irrational, or anyhow a-rational. The thesis of psychological hedonism is surely meant by Mill as an account of how people behave when they are aware of what they are doing, when they are acting voluntarily, intentionally, and on purpose —when they are thinking about action.

Even about such action, it would be at least misleading to represent it as consisting entirely in calculations of pleasure. In general, we think in terms of the achievements of various "local" ends, as we might call them: e.g., marrying Jill, getting a job with Jones, seeing Gielgud do *Hamlet*, and so forth. The reason why the psychological hedonist represents pleasure as an "end" which we are ultimately "seeking" is this, I take it: If it could be shown that we would not enjoy it if a particular end were

[13] The Scraggs: "If Daisy Mae is the most desirable girl in the world, then we desires her!" ("L'il Abner," Waterloo *Record*, ca. January 20, 1966).

brought about—moreover, that it in turn wouldn't cause any-thing else that we would enjoy—then that would be sufficient reason for not pursuing that end.[14] Sufficient, that is, except in one important case—that in which there are moral reasons against it. For the present, we are not interested in a description of the moral behavior of people, because we are interested in discovering the foundations of a moral theory, i.e., reasons for regarding something as morally good, right, wrong, etc. Thus, what we must say, if we are to be psychological hedonists and utilitarians, is that what people "naturally" do, if they are ra-tional and before the onset of any moral considerations, is to "seek their own pleasure." What does this mean? It means, so far as I can see, that they use the consideration that they would, or would not, enjoy doing something as a standard for appraising it (or courses of action leading to it); and as *the* standard for appraising it in non-moral contexts.

It seems to me that we are forced to the conclusion that in Mill's account, psychological hedonism is, in fact, an attempt to state what people regard as good. That this is so is evidenced not only by the various statements quoted earlier from his account, but by the very terms in which he summarizes his effort to "prove" the principle of utility. "If the end which the utilitarian doctrine proposes to itself were not, in theory and in practice, acknowledged to be an end, nothing could ever con-vince any person that it was so. . . . we have not only all the proof which the case admits of, but all which it is possible to require, that happiness is a good: Each person's happiness is a good to that person, and the general happiness, therefore, a good to the aggregate of all persons."

Is it plausible to suppose that even this is true, i.e., that people do in fact regard conduciveness to their own pleasure (enjoy-ment, happiness, satisfaction) as the ultimate standard of ap-praisal for actions, is non-moral contexts? On this very important question, I have two principal things to say. (1) If the misleading words 'in fact' are eliminated from the last question, then per-haps the answer is 'yes'; (2) that in any case, from the utilitarian

---

[14] In *Moral Point of View*, p. 267, Baier argues that pleasure is not an "end" at all. His argument for this seems to show only that ends are not principles; how it shows that pleasure can't be an end is obscure to me.

point of view we may take an affirmative answer to this question as a completely uninformative one, because, for utilitarian purposes, we may regard 'conducive to x's happiness' as meaning no more than 'conducive to whatever x regards as intrinsically good.' Both require explanation.

1) Clearly the question here is, just what *is* "pleasure"? This is no easy question, and I do not intend to answer it in a precise way. Instead, I wish to point out a few facts about the way in which various theorists, especially utilitarian ones, have dealt with such questions. To begin with, it is obvious that Mill and Bentham use this word in a very broad sense. Bentham, indeed, goes so far as to say that "By utility is meant that property in any object, whereby it tends to produce benefit, advantage, pleasure, good, or happiness (all this in the present case comes to the same thing.)"[15] Mill, in turn, says the following:

Those who know anything about the matter are aware that every writer, from Epicurus to Bentham, who maintained the theory of utility, meant by it, not something to be contradistinguished from pleasure, but pleasure itself, together with exemption from pain; and instead of opposing the useful to the agreeable or the ornamental, have always declared that the useful means these, among other things.

Pleasure in some of its forms; of beauty, of ornament, or of amusement . . .

No intelligent human being would consent to be a fool . . . even though they should be persuaded that the fool . . . is better satisfied with his lot than they are with theirs . . . A being of higher faculties requires more to make him happy . . . than one of inferior type . . . We may attribute [this sort of preference] to pride . . . to the love of liberty . . . or to the love of excitement . . . but its most appropriate appellation is a sense of dignity . . . which is so essential a part of the happiness of those in whom it is strong . . . Whoever supposes this preference takes place at a sacrifice of happiness—that the superior being, in anything like equal circumstances, is not happier than the inferior—confounds the two very different ideas, of happiness, and content.[16]

---

[15] Bentham, *Principles of Morals and Legislation*, p. 18.
[16] Mill, *Utilitarianism*, pp. 5. 6, 8.

A later section will be devoted to the question of 'quantity versus quality' which is raised in these passages; they are sufficient to demonstrate that Mill was hardly concerned with the concept of pleasure in any narrow sense, and certainly not one in which it is opposed to satisfaction, enjoyment, appreciation of beauty, and so forth. If we turn to later theorists, we shall not find the story much altered in substance. For example, take the view of Sidgwick, who is rightly regarded as a sober, judicious, and careful thinker, often specifically (if with questionable justice) contrasted with Mill in these respects. Sidgwick concludes, after lengthy consideration, as follows:

> I propose, therefore, to define Pleasure—when we are considering its "strict value" for the purposes of quantitative comparison—as a feeling which, when experienced by intelligent beings, is at least implicitly apprehended as desirable or—in cases of comparison—preferable.[17]

> Meaning by 'desirable' not necessarily 'what ought to be desired' but what would be desired, with strength proportioned to the degree of desirability, if it were judged attainable by voluntary action, supposing the desirer to possess a perfect forecast, emotional as well as intellectual, of the state of attainment of fruition.[18]

This, I take it, does not come to very much more than the much-discussed view of Gilbert Ryle:

> To say that a person has been enjoying digging is not to say that he has been both digging and doing or experiencing something else . . . it is to say that he dug with his whole heart in his task, i.e., that he dug, wanting to dig and not wanting to do anything else (or nothing) instead . . . to enjoy doing something, to want to do it and not to want to do anything else are different ways of phrasing the same thing . . .
> (It should be mentioned that 'pain,' in the sense in which I have pains in my stomach, is not the opposite of 'pleasure.' In this sense, a pain is a sensation of a special sort, which we ordinarily dislike having).[19]

---

[17] Sidgwick, *The Methods of Ethics*, p. 127.
[18] *Ibid.*, p. 111.
[19] Gilbert Ryle, *The Concept of Mind* (New York: Barnes and Noble, Inc., 1949), p. 108.

We can also compare the recent view of Baier on this matter:

Both the claim that something is (or is found) painful or pleasurable and the claim that it is (or is found) pleasant or unpleasant have this important point in common: they indicate a person's positive or negative response or attitude to something (a pursuit, activity, etc.). What the response or attitude is can be said in general terms. The positive response consists in a tendency to continue, to make efforts to repeat the activity, etc., to be disappointed, sad, or annoyed when it is interrupted, and so on.[20]

The net purport of this is summed up very well in the observation of Francis Sparshott:

It does seem difficult to deny that if one asks a person, 'Why did you eat those strawberries?', the answer, "Because I like them" calls for no elaboration, whereas the answer, "Because I don't like them" does.[21]

The point is, that when writers attempt to define the notions of pleasure and enjoyment, invariably they end up saying, in one way or another, that they consist of a pro-attitude or positive evaluation of some experience on its own account. If this is so, then small wonder that "psychological hedonism" was so popular at one time, it being the theory that only pleasure is regarded as desirable on its own account. If this is true, then it is vacuously true.[22] If we can discuss anything about this theory, it seems to me that it can only be, how useful is it? And if at all, then for what? Perhaps we can go on to discuss whether "immediate experience" is a broader term than "sensation," and propose to confine 'pleasure' to 'desired sensation,' leaving some other term to cover the more global experiences to which people attribute intrinsic value. Such a discussion, while it might be of interest for its own sake or in some other context, is

---

[20] Baier, *The Moral Point of View*, p. 272.

[21] F. E. Sparshott, *An Enquiry into Goodness and Related Concepts* (Toronto, Canada: University of Toronto Press, 1958), p. 284.

[22] For the rest, the reader may be referred to Mr. Nowell-Smith's account in his useful book, *Ethics*, Chs. 8–10, wherein the thesis of the vacuity of "psychological hedonism" is well argued.

unnecessary here. The kinds of arguments used to support "psychological hedonism" surely demonstrate that it is not, as it was represented as being, a psychological theory which in a helpful way explains or generalizes about human action. Instead, it is a truism, if true at all.[23]

2) This takes us to my second point. We may by-pass these perhaps interesting questions about the exact differences between pleasure, enjoyment, satisfaction, "fulfillment" and the rest by simply admitting that we are trying to express, in some compact and general way, the standards which people employ in appraising courses of action in non-moral contexts. The purpose of this, in turn, is to specify the "utility" predicate. We want to say that moral value is proportional to utility; and utility, say Bentham and the rest, is pleasure and the absence of pain. But then it turns out that "pleasure and the absence of pain," after all the qualifications, interpolations, and interpretations are in, means "whatever it is that people seek for its own sake, when they are rational"; which is equivalent, in turn, to "that by reference to which people appraise courses of action" ("naturally," i.e., apart from moral considerations); which is, in turn, tautologically, what they regard as intrinsically good.

In sum, we can conclude that the generating idea of utilitarianism is a concern for the values that individuals adhere to. Whether or not this is precisely in accord with Mill's intentions, it is the idea that will be adopted here. An act's utility, then, is its productiveness of what those affected by it believe to be intrinsically good. Utilitarianism will be the principle that moral value (i.e., that by reference to which we are to appraise acts morally), is utility in that sense.

Since this formulation involves the notion of intrinsic value, it will be useful to comment on that subject, and on the theory

[23] Mill, in writing about Bentham, saw through the sort of "psychological hedonism" advocated by the latter. He observes that, "In laying down as a philosophical axiom, that men's actions are always obedient to their interests, Mr. Bentham did no more than dress up the very trivial proposition, that all persons do what they feel themselves most disposed to do, in terms which appeared to him more precise." "Remarks on Bentham's Philosophy" in J. S. Mill, *Ethical Writings*, ed. J. B. Schneewind (New York: Collier Paperback Edition, The Macmillan Co., 1965), p. 56. It is interesting to note that Mill's perception of this point did not prevent him from trying again in *Utilitarianism*.

of "ideal utilitarianism" advocated by Moore, Rashdall, and others. We turn, therefore, to these matters before producing our final version of the utilitarian formula.

"Ideal" Utilitarianism

Shall we concur with G. E. Moore, Hastings Rashdall, and some subsequent writers, and simply identify maximum utility with maximum good? Why should we bother with such qualifications as "What Jones thinks is good," or "Everyone's good"? Many writers would, I think, regard such a change as so subtle as to be nearly inconsequential. This may be true in practice, but so far as pure theory is concerned, the difference is fundamental. The most striking effects of the difference are brought out in Chapter IX, wherein an argument for utilitarianism is constructed making use of the "premises" supplied by psychological hedonism (or rather, what's left of it at the end of our foregoing considerations on the subject). But other differences are serious from the beginning. They all follow from one central fact: If we say that the moral value of an act is proportional to the absolute intrinsic value of its consequences, then there is no logical connection between the principle and a concern with other persons as such. Whereas, I have argued, a concern for other persons as such is precisely the hub of utilitarianism. To identify "happiness" with "utility" is automatically, logically, to raise the question, "whose happiness"? And to make "the general happiness" the predicate of the principle of utility answers it. But, if we take the "ideal utilitarian" viewpoint, we should have to subjoin to it either a hedonistic *analysis* of value, which most writers would agree is untenable, or we would have to add normative premises to the effect that pleasure is good or happiness is good; or, to take my suggested version, that experiences which anyone thinks are good are good. None of this will do. I have insisted that we must distinguish between moral value, or evaluation from the moral viewpoint, and non-moral value or evaluation from some non-moral viewpoint. We shall have to ask of the "Ideal" utilitarian principle, whether the "absolute intrinsic value" of the consequences is to be understood as moral value or non-moral value, i.e., as value from the moral point of view or from some non-moral point of view. If his answer is "non-moral," then it seems to me that there is no moral reason to do anything if the value produced by it is merely non-moral. If he says "moral," then I would be inclined to agree; only now we need to know just what things he thinks *are* morally valuable. But is this not precisely what a moral principle ought to tell us? It ought, that is, to tell us what to do. If it only says we should do what is best, then this answer is uninformative unless and until we know what is best.

Perhaps brows may be raised when I say that "There is no moral reason to do anything if the value produced by it is merely non-moral." I do not mean that there is no relation whatever between moral and non-moral evaluation, but I do mean that insofar as something is thought to be (non-morally) good, this by itself may imply nothing about what we (morally) ought to do. If x is a good bicycle, then what has this to do with morality? As such, it has nothing whatsoever to do with it. But, if Johnny *thinks* that it is a good bicycle, then I am doing a morally good thing in giving one to Johnny, other things being equal. Johnny can think that it is one, whether or not it is one. What is objectionable about Ideal Utilitarianism can now be brought out by showing that it appears to want us to be concerned with what is valuable, rather than whether it is thought valuable. Thus, if I believe that Picassos are intrinsically good paintings (which is an aesthetic judgment), then if the phrase "absolute intrinsic value" in the Ideal Utilitarian principle is understood as including non-moral values, then on the Ideal Utilitarian principle I might very well think that it would be a morally good thing to cause people to see Picassos. If I believe that abstract impressionist art is intrinsically bad, then I may believe that I have a moral reason to suppress such art. In fact, this is exactly what happens in some places. The Communists, for example, appear to believe that if the aesthetic value of a kind of painting is negative, then people who produce that kind of painting should be thrown in prison, their canvasses burned, and spectators prevented from going to see them.

If people disagree about the value of such painting, they may, on the "Ideal" utilitarian view, disagree about whether or not it should be suppressed. But, on the view advocated here, the aesthetic question is simply irrelevant. We may argue about the absolute intrinsic aesthetic value of abstract painting until we are blue in the face, if we are so inclined, but no conclusions arrived at in the course of it will have any moral significance as such. What matters for moral purposes is not whether it *is* good painting, but whether anybody *thinks* it is. If they do, then to that extent we have a moral reason for assisting, or at least not hindering, the activities which they perform on account of that evaluation.

The reason, I think, why "Ideal" utilitarianism and utilitarianism per se tend to be equated in recent literature is because of an assumption that "Ideal" utilitarians will tend to have utilitarian values in fact, as I shall document below. I am pointing out here only that what Ideal Utilitarianism implies about morality will depend entirely on one's evaluative assumptions, and that this is totally unsatisfactory because that is what a moral theory ought to provide or make explicit—the evaluative assumptions. Hitler could have been an "Ideal" utilitarian, and probably was. He probably believed that the quantity of absolute intrinsic value brought into being by killing millions of Jews, and wresting millions of people from the activities they enjoyed in order that they might go out and die on the field of battle, was greater than if everyone had been permitted to live as he pleased. *Ex hypothesi*, this would be a dispute about intrinsic value. How is it to be resolved? This will simply raise all of the old questions over again, which shows that ideal utilitarianism is unsatisfactory as a moral theory. On the classical utilitarian view, on the other hand, questions about the absolute intrinsic value of anything are irrelevant, as such.

We must not fall into the mistake of inferring that according to the present account, "value" is "subjective." It is important to bear in mind that, according to the view I am advocating, no "theory of value" is implied at all. We can quite consistently allow that intrinsic values are "objective," whatever this may mean. I take it to mean at least that if two people are of different opinions about the intrinsic value of something, then at least one of them is wrong. This can be cheerfully admitted by the utilitarian. On the other hand, some will take the "subjec-tivist" position, and claim that such quarrels are made of thin air. The utilitarian may likewise admit this, if he is so inclined. What he denies is that statements about intrinsic value per se may be admitted among the premises of moral arguments. (Statements about intrinsic *moral* value are, of course, another matter. We shall take up this subject in Chapter IV.)

Intrinsic Value

A teleological moral theory, of which utilitarianism is cer-tainly an example, holds that the moral value of acts is due to the value of their consequences. It follows that some account has to be given of the value of consequences. That aspect of consequences, on account of which the acts producing them have the moral value they do, according to the view taken in this book, is their utility. The foregoing sections of the present chapter have been devoted to the subject of what we are to regard as constituting utility. At the same time, I have been going out of my way to avoid the identification of utility with "intrinsic value" per se. To some, this may seem paradoxical. Frankena, for example, *defines* the "teleological" view of ethics as follows:

A teleological theory says that the basic or ultimate criterion or standard of what is morally right, wrong, obligatory, etc., is the non-moral value that is brought into being.[24]

If this were correct, then it would presumably follow that the teleological view of ethics must be Ideal Utilitarian; thus, that the preceding account of utilitarianism is logically ruled out.[25] Why does Frankena define it in this way? His reason is stated thus:

It is important to notice, here, that for a teleologist, the moral quality or value of actions, persons, or traits of character is dependent

[24] Frankena, *Ethics*, p. 13.
[25] Ross, for example, says of the "Ideal" utilitarian theory that "Not only is this theory more attractive than hedonistic utilitarianism, but its logical relation to that theory is such that the latter could not be true unless *it* were true, while it might be true though hedonistic utilitarianism were not." (*Right and the Good*, p. 17.)

on the comparative nonmoral value of what they bring about or try to bring about. For the moral quality or value of something to depend on the moral value of whatever it promotes would be circular.[26]

This is a mistake. There is no reason why the appraisal of acts from the moral point of view cannot involve reference to the *moral* value of consequences, as opposed to their nonmoral value. Frankena evidently supposes that since the phrase "moral value" applies primarily to "acts, persons, or traits of character," any value had by anything else (*viz.* consequences), must be nonmoral. The reason for not distinguishing morally significant consequences from consequences whose value is morally irrelevant would then be inappropriate because merely vacuous—namely, that consequences are not (generally) acts, persons, or states of character. This is beside the point. To say that something is good as a means is, of course, to imply that something else, namely that to which it is a means, is good "as an end," or "in itself." But the fact that something is good in itself from one point of view does not prevent it from being a means from another point of view. Similarly, the fact that something is morally intrinsically good does not mean that it is intrinsically good, period. It is often held that there must be such a thing as intrinsic good in an unqualified sense—goodness from no point of view whatever. This may be true, but I am questioning its relevance to ethics. Some consideration of this matter is therefore in order here.

It is common to make a distinction between intrinsic and extrinsic value, for the very good reason that despite occasional attempts to question the validity or utility of the distinction, we need it in practical discourse. The general idea is that something is said to have "intrinsic" value if its having that value does not depend upon its relations—especially, its causal relations—to other things. If it does so depend, then its value is "extrinsic."[27] Thus, Moore employs as a definition of intrinsic

---

[26] Frankena, *Ethics,* p. 13.

[27] Actually, the situation is a bit more complicated than this. See Moore's *Principia Ethica,* Ch. I, for an interesting discussion of the "principle of organic unities." See also Clarence I. Lewis, *An Analysis of Knowledge and Valuation* (La Salle, Ill.: Open Court Publishing Co., 1947), for Lewis' multiple distinctions of "instrumental," "extrinsic," "intrinsic," "inherent," and "ultimate" values. We may neglect these for the present. The knowledgeable reader will note that a good deal is owed to Lewis in this section.

value, that value which a thing would have, if it existed by itself "in absolute isolation." This definition tends to raise hackles, as though the existence of intrinsic values in that sense were a questionable, metaphysical matter. If we consider the argument by means of which it is concluded that there must be such things, we find that this is not so. This argument (which stems, at least, from Aristotle),[28] is as follows: Suppose we say that A is good "on account of" B (e.g., because it produced B). Clearly, the words "on account of" have the logical function of shifting the weight of accountability, so to speak, onto something about B. If, in turn, we ask "And why is B good?," then either we shall have to give an answer in similar form, "on account of C," or we shall have to give an answer equivalent to, "Well, just because it is the sort of thing it is." (Moore, and the Russell of "The Elements of Ethics" tend to say that there is literally no reason why what is intrinsically good is good—it "just is.")[29] It is important to see in this conclusion, that something or other must be held to be good "in itself" if anything is held to be good at all, is argued for on *purely logical* grounds —the ground, namely, of the logic of the phrase "on account of" or whatever equivalent is used. If we employ such a phrase, we imply that our evaluation is incomplete. Thus, I find this hoary argument entirely convincing: Unless something is "intrinsically" good, then nothing can be genuinely good at all. (We may, I take it, dismiss the use of 'good for' in which it is synonymous with 'efficient at' as secondary and uninteresting.)

It is important to see that this argument does not have any efficacy whatsoever regarding another matter with which the word 'intrinsic' has for centuries been connected, namely the dispute concerning "objectivism" versus "subjectivism." Such early moralists as Clarke, Cudworth, and Price share with G. E.

---

[28] *Nichomachean Ethics*, Book I, i–ii. Aristotle, however, is trying to establish that there is a single Supreme Good, and the argument notoriously fails to establish this conclusion. It is not unreasonable to cite Aristotle's model argument as the prototype of arguments about intrinsic good. Nevertheless, many excellent philosophical arguments have not proven what their authors wanted to prove with them, although they may prove something else of equal interest.

[29] Moore, *Principia Ethica*, p. 143. See also Bertrand Russell, "The Elements of Ethics," *Readings in Ethical Theory*, ed. Wilfrid Sellars and John Hospers (New York: Appleton-Century-Crofts, Inc., 1952), p. 2.

Moore the tendency to suppose that "intrinsic" values *must* be
"objective." Thus Moore, in his essay on "The Conception of
Intrinsic Value," begins by saying that he is going to talk about
"the most important question, which . . . is really at issue when
it is disputed with regard to any predicate of value, whether
it is, or is not, a 'subjective' predicate"; he maintains that "from
the proposition that a particular kind of value is "intrinsic," it
does follow that it must be "objective."[30] Now, if this is true,
then it is so only if the word 'intrinsic' is used in a different
sense from that in which the aforementioned argument stemming from Aristotle uses it. It is obvious that regardless of what
analysis we offer of evaluative predicates, we can and must always distinguish between valuing something for its own sake
and valuing it because of its contribution to something else.

Discussions of this kind tend, in fact, to assimilate three distinct
issues. On the one hand, there is the question of whether "value"
is "subjective," in the sense of being in some way mind-depend-
ent. Secondly, there is the question whether the truth-value of
an evaluative sentence necessarily varies with the person utter-
ing it. Thirdly, there is the question whether any values are
"intrinsic." There is certainly considerable tendency to run
these together, as in Moore's essay mentioned above. The tendency is to suppose that 'intrinsic,' 'absolute,' and 'objective'
are, if not altogether one and the same in meaning, at any rate
necessarily connected. This is not so; indeed, it is to be accounted
among the achievements of recent ethics to have clarified this
point.[31]

Now Moore convinced himself, mainly by means of the "open
question" test, that 'good' was not definable in "naturalistic"
terms. Having inferred from this that 'good' was a "non-natural"
property, it then appeared to him to be logically possible that
some things should have this property whether or not there is
anyone around to notice the fact. In his discussion of Hedonism,

[30] George E. Moore, *Philosophical Studies* (London: Routledge and
Kegan Paul, 1960), pp. 253, 255.
[31] On the first question, see Paul Edwards' *The Logic of Moral Discourse*,
Chs. 1, 2. On the second, see C. L. Stevenson, *Facts and Values* (New
Haven, Conn.: Yale University Press, 1963), e.g., "Relativism and Non-
Relativism in the Theory of Values." On the third question, see Lewis'
An Analysis of Knowledge and Valuation.

he goes on to argue that there (perhaps) actually are a few. By way of countering Sidgwick's view that "if there be any Good other than Happiness to be sought by man, as an ultimate practical end, it can only be the Goodness, Perfection, or Excellence of Human Existence," he offers the celebrated "two worlds" argument, in which the question is posed whether we should be "entirely indifferent" as between a world which, though "exceedingly beautiful," was entirely unpopulated and unobserved, and another which was as foul and ugly as the first was beautiful, but equally unpopulated. Moore asks, "Is it irrational to hold that it is better that the beautiful world should exist, than the one which is ugly? Would it not be well, in any case, to do what we could to produce it rather than the other?"[32]

Despite this result, we find Moore asserting, in his chapter on "The Ideal," that "by far the most valuable things, which we can know or can imagine, are certain states of consciousness, which may be roughly described as the pleasures of human intercourse and the enjoyment of beautiful objects."[33] What is more, we find that similar results were arrived at by practically all of the best-known ethical writers of this century. When they come to consider the question, what general kinds of things really have "intrinsic value," the answer is almost uniformly that they are "states of mind" of the general kind mentioned by Moore. A few cases are worth citing. Rashdall regarded Virtue and Happiness as the only intrinsic goods, adding that other

[32] Moore, *Principia Ethica*, p. 83. Although the immediate aims of this discussion is to establish that there are some things other than states of mind which actually have intrinsic value, I think there can be no doubt that Moore supposed that the result of this experiment would be to give additional weight to his analysis of value as an objective, but non-natural, property. Thus, at the outset of the chapter (p. 60), Moore remarks that "It is very difficult to see that by 'approving' of a thing we mean *feeling that it has a certain predicate*—the predicate, namely, which defines the peculiar sphere of Ethics . . ." I agree with Nowell-Smith that if this is what Moore supposed he was doing, then the experiment is a failure. What the experiment does prove, of course, is that we can have evaluative attitudes *toward* things other than minds. Cf., Nowell-Smith's *Ethics*, p. 74. Thus, later writers who wished to bring this argument to bear against emotivism are off the track. Independently of this, I am also inclined to agree that it would be pointless to exert any effort to bring such a world into existence; the important point for the purpose of this book, however, is that this simply is not a morally significant question.

[33] Moore, *Principia Ethica*, p. 188.

states of mind besides pleasure go into the latter, and that virtue is a state of mind too, only concerning "thought and volition" as well as feeling.[34] Ross finds that virtuous disposition, pleasure, the apportionment of pleasures, and knowledge exhaust the list of intrinsic goods, adding that "It might of course be objected that there are or may be intrinsic goods that are not states of mind or relations between states of mind at all, but in this suggestion I can find no plausibility."[35] C. I. Lewis regards the "realization of positive value-quality in experience" as the only intrinsic good.[36] Frankena finds that although pleasure in the narrow sense is not all that is intrinsically good, yet "the broader and somewhat similar thesis that nothing is intrinsically good unless it contains some kind of satisfactoriness seems to me to be clearly true," adding that "knowledge, excellence, power, and so on, are simply cold, bare, and valueless in themselves unless they are experienced with some kind of enjoyment or satisfaction."[37]

There is something impressive about the unanimity with which the best ethical theorists have regarded various states of mind or experiences as the only (or most important) intrinsically good things. Why shouldn't other things be allowed to be intrinsically good, one might wonder? Beethoven Quartets, for example? Surely the answer, in part, is that these theorists have not meant their thesis to be incompatible with the attribution of value to such things. But "intrinsic value" is special. Why?

Consider how parallel to this is the treatment accorded to the question, "What is it that people desire, *really*?" The tendency is to answer, 'satisfaction.' This satisfactory answer is a function of the logic of the case. After all, to say that a desire had been satisfied is to say that the person in question got what the desire is a desire *for*. The fact that people often get what they desire, and are still dissatisfied is due to the fact that they have other desires as well. If you desire an x and I give you an x, you are not entitled to complain on the score of dissatisfaction with *that* action of mine unless you've changed your mind meanwhile.

[34] Rashdall, *Theory of Good and Evil*, I, 63–80.
[35] Ross, *The Right and the Good*, p. 140.
[36] Lewis, *An Analysis of Knowledge*, p. 392.
[37] Frankena, *Ethics*, p. 74.

But the same consideration that shows that "satisfaction" is a natural answer to the question, "What do we really desire?" shows also that it is vacuous. As we saw above, "pleasure" falls into the same category.

Similarly, if we ask "what is good in itself?" we are apt to go through a sequence such as this: If I think that Beethoven Quartets are good, it is because I enjoy them; if I didn't enjoy them, then I wouldn't think they were good. What it is to be good is to be a means of enjoyment; so enjoyment must be good in itself. Compare this with: If I think that something is good, then I am in favor of it; and if I weren't in favor of it, I wouldn't think it is good. So what is good in itself must be "favoring." What's wrong?

It isn't so much that the conclusion in each of these sequences doesn't "follow." What's wrong is that the word 'good' seems to be used in different senses in premises and conclusion. The conclusion, one might say, is vacuous. What does it mean to ask, in the same tone of voice throughout, "Which is better: Beethoven's Quartet in C♯ Minor, or the pleasure of listening to Beethoven's Quartet in C♯ Minor?" Moore presumably regarded this as a sensible question. But is it?

Consider the following:

(a) "Jones enjoys playing the oboe."
(b) "Jones plays the oboe for its own sake."
(c) "Jones thinks that playing the oboe is intrinsically good."

What is the difference between any two of these? Certainly they could be used interchangeably in many cases. If there is a contrast, it is probably on incidental points. For instance, (c) could be true, even though Jones himself doesn't play the oboe, but not (a) or (b). Or, perhaps (b) or (c) could be used to describe the case where Jones suffers intensely from playing the oboe, and he doesn't expect to gain anything by it, and he doesn't expect to entertain others. But in this case, (b) or (c) would be equivalent to "Jones is a compulsive oboe-player," would it not?

At any rate, it seems clear that "he does it because he enjoys doing it" is not alternative to "he does it for its own sake," but ordinarily is just another way of saying the same thing. If so, then it is misleading to talk about the "intrinsic goodness" of pleasure.

Does it make any sense to "evaluate" pleasure? What are we doing when we do this? Principally, I think, we are pointing to the connection between pleasure and the evaluation of things which are pleasurable. Philosophers have been suggesting, in recent years, that, in the words of Baier, "everybody must agree that the fact that he would enjoy doing something is a reason for him to do it; that he would not enjoy it, a reason for him not to do it."[38] This, I suggest, is equivalent to the intent of "psychological hedonism" as discussed above. As such, it is perhaps, a logical comment on the concept of enjoyment, or at most, a comment on the way people do, in fact, evaluate things. It seems to me otiose to make such statements about oneself.

But if I say that the fact that Jones enjoys having something done is a reason for *me* to do it, I do make an intelligible, normative remark. I am not implying that I do it for Jones because *I* enjoy doing it, or even because I enjoy doing it for Jones; for I may dislike Jones personally. When people contribute money to help relieve starvation in India, it is not because they *like* Indians. Most likely, they don't know any Indians, and certainly not the ones who will be helped by their contributions. Such actions are usually, or at least often, done from a feeling that one ought to help people who are starving, whether one happens to know and like them or not. One might say that they contribute because the Indians are people in need. One might make such contributions even though one would much prefer, *intrinsically*, to spend it on things one enjoys.

To try to sum up the results of this complicated discussion, I want to suggest that to talk of "intrinsic value" in the abstract, without regard to any special point of view or context, is most naturally to draw analogy to evaluation of the aesthetic sort. "I do it for its own sake" is typically like "I enjoy it." If asked why one enjoys it, one replies, if one can, by indicating those features of the experience which attract one. Immediate experience is the natural home of "context-less" evaluation. This is

[38] Baier, *Moral Point of View*, p. 111.

shown by the fact that philosophers of art invariably begin by
pointing out that art objects are contemplated for their own
sakes, and not because of their connections with anything else.
Moral evaluations, I suggest, are more complicated than this.
They are not "contextless" in the above sense. It doesn't particularly matter how the prospect to other people's interests
"immediately strikes" me. To suggest that moral evaluation is
assessment of the intrinsic value of something is to suggest that
I am doing the same sort of thing in asking why I ought to help
old ladies cross the street, help relieve starvation or avoid harming people as I am doing when asking why "Don Giovanni" is
a good opera. Surely not. If I have a native sympathy with other
people, a natural desire to forward their interests, then no doubt
some of my moral evaluations will be like this. The interesting
cases, however, are those in which I do not particularly *share*
the interests of the people affected by my actions. Such people
are people whose judgments of intrinsic value may be in conflict
with mine, whose way of life may be quite different. To say
that the moral evaluation that nevertheless they have a right to
pursue the interests they have is based on another judgment of
"intrinsic value"—namely, a judgment of the intrinsic value of
Jones' thinking that such-and-such has a high intrinsic value,
where in *my* opinion its intrinsic value is very low—is to put a
great strain on the notion of "intrinsic value."

On the other hand, it is not true, either, that the judgment
that we ought to respect other people's values is itself merely
"instrumental" or "extrinsic." As moral philosophers have been
pointing out, to take such a view is inevitably to try to justify
morality on non-moral grounds, usually of self-interest. They
tend to agree that such justifications will not work. What to do
about this will be considered in my final chapter, but meanwhile, I have been trying to make clear that we need to compli-
cate the picture of evaluation for moral purposes, by introducing
a category which might be labelled "intrinsic moral value," or
perhaps, "intrinsic value for moral purposes," or "intrinsic value
from the moral point of view." If my analysis of utility is correct, then I can point to the overwhelming agreement of recent
moral philosophers that only states of mind or experiences have
"intrinsic value" as support for it. What they must have been

talking about was "intrinsic moral value." Surely, they were not endorsing the tastes of people who enjoy what the philosophers themselves would not enjoy. Rather, they were agreeing with me, that the fact that other people enjoy something is a good reason for helping them to procure it, or at least for letting them do it unimpeded, regardless of what one thinks of their taste. The generalization of this would be to say *prima facie*, that if someone regards doing x as an intrinsically (non-morally) good thing, then it is a good thing (morally) to assist him in doing x (regardless of the "real" intrinsic value of doing x).

Qualities and Quantities

Since Mill wrote *Utilitarianism*, there has been dispute about his contention that "quality" as well as "quantity" should be taken into account in determining utility. Some have held that this is flatly inconsistent,[39] others that it is only inconsistent with "pure" hedonism,[40] and still others that it is not inconsistent at all.[41] My own view is that this entire question has been enormously muddled, and could have been avoided by making a few rather obvious distinctions. Moreover, I am inclined to think that Mill comes out reasonably well on this score—more of the muddle is in the critics than in Mill.

Let us consider the passage in which this matter arose. Mill is discussing the "superiority of pleasures of the intellect, of the feelings and imagination, and of the moral sentiments" over "mere sensation." He remarks that

Utilitarian writers in general have placed the superiority of mental over bodily pleasures chiefly in the greater permanency, safety, uncostliness, etc. of the former—that is, in their circumstantial advantages rather than their intrinsic nature. And on all these points utilitarians have fully proved their case; but they might have taken the other, and, as it may be called, higher ground, with entire con-

[39] Moore, *Principia, Ethica*, Nos. 47 and 48, pp. 79ff.
[40] Frankena, *Ethics*, pp. 68, 69.
[41] *The Philosophy of John Stuart Mill* ed. Marshall Cohen (New York: Modern Library, 1961), pp. xxii, xxiii.

sistency. It is quite compatible with the principle of utility to recognize the fact, that some *kinds* of pleasure are more desirable and more valuable than others. It would be absurd that while, in estimating all other things, quality is considered as well as quantity, the estimation of pleasures should be supposed to depend on quantity alone.[42]

It seems clear that Mill is thinking of "pleasures" as experiences which one desires on account of their immediate character, as one would expect from our reflections above. If we count permanency, safety, and uncostliness as "circumstantial" (as seems reasonable), then we must turn to the "internal" character of these experiences when we are estimating their desirability in terms of variables which might reasonably be accounted their "intrinsic nature." How many such variables are there?

G. E. Moore plainly thought that there could be, in the nature of the case, but one:

If you say 'pleasure' you must mean 'pleasure': you must mean some one thing common to all different 'pleasures,' some one thing, which may exist in different degrees, but which cannot differ in kind.[43]

Moore thought of the term 'pleasure' as if it were comparable to, say, 'height' or 'water.' It would indeed be natural to think of just one measure appropriate to height and water—altitude and volume—although even here one might point out that there could be differences (e.g., height above sea-level, or from the base, or from the ground?) Of water, sometimes one is more interested in feet-below-flood-tide than in volumes; sometimes in area covered, etc. Neglecting these, however, the point remains that 'pleasure' need not be construed in this fashion. I am not sure that it is even natural to do so. Surely, Mill is thinking of 'pleasure' as analogous to 'color' rather than to 'height.' In the case of 'color,' it won't do to argue that there must be "some one thing common to all different colors, which may exist in different degrees, but which cannot differ in kind." If we do (say, "being visible"), then the common property in question is by no means incompatible with variations other than

---

[42] Mill, *Utilitarianism*, p. 7.
[43] Moore, *Principia Ethica*, p. 80.

in 'quantity.' In the case of color, there are, for instance, intensity, hue, and saturation. Just as one might prefer different colors on account of their hue, as well as their intensity, so one might prefer different experiences on account of their specific feeling-tone as well as their intensity. This could reasonably be called "rating pleasures in quality as well as in quantity." In fact, reflection shows that we do just that. The pleasures of wine-tasting are not, I suppose, nearly as intense as those of whiskey-guzzling, or taking a hot shower, or of sexual activities. But a person might very well prefer them, on account of their greater subtlety and delicacy.

The reason, I suppose, why there has been so much fuss about this is that the words 'quantity' and 'quality' both have several different senses; philosophical critics are prone to picking the worst at their disposal when they interpret an author they are resolved to ridicule. The utilitarian—and any other moral theorist, for that matter—must have some method of rating different acts, such that one is preferable to another. The word 'value' is obviously susceptible to adjectives like 'more' and 'less,' and one has to find something with which to correlate it, in order to have a theory at all. The "quantity" in question for utilitarians is 'utility,' and this is taken to be identical with 'happiness,' for example, (or, in my case, "what people put a value on"). We have seen, in Chapter II, the point, and the difficulties, of speaking of "quantities" in this connection.

The word 'quality' is doubtless the greatest source of trouble for the question of "quantity versus quality"; the trouble is probably due again to ambiguity. Sometimes the word 'quality' has an evaluative ring to it, as in 'quality versus price,' or 'a person of quality.' In such cases, we may speak of "high quality" and "low quality," because the word 'quality' has an evaluation built into it. ('Quality,' in this usage, is in fact a quantity.) If one says, "courage is a good quality of character," then it makes no sense to ask, "Yes, but is it a high or a low one?" In the phrase "good quality," 'quality' has to be taken in a neutral sense (although not the phrase as a whole, obviously, nor the word 'good' in it). The phrase, "a good, but low, quality" makes no sense as it stands. Most people, I think, have the evaluative sense of 'quality' in mind when they read Mill or Moore on quantities vs. qualities of pleasure. Since Mill is using 'quality' here as an index of *value* of pleasure (i.e., of its preferability or desirability), it would be circular for him to be using it in the evaluative sense. Mill says explicitly, in our quoted selection above, that "some kinds of pleasure are more desirable and more valuable than others." In the next sentence, he uses 'quality' in precisely the same location as 'kind' was used in the sentence preceding. He could not easily have made it more evident that by 'quality' he meant 'kind.'

If understood in this way, what Mill says is in no way dubious or contradictory. How could one conceivably prefer one experience to another if not on the basis of its being the *kind* of experience it is? Is it not absurd to suppose that hedonists are maintaining that *only* the "quantity" of a pleasurable experience *as distinct from its quality* is relevant in evaluating it? (As if pleasure *had* only "quantity," whatever that would mean.)

However that may be, my formulation in terms of 'degree to which x thinks y desirable' has no ambiguities of that kind in it. However, there are parallel questions which can be raised and which we need answer in specific cases. If, for example, a person is very fond of something of which I am very unfond, while another shares my tastes, I am likely to prefer the second's pleasures to the first. But the whole bent of the utilitarian outlook is toward toleration of other people's tastes. It is precisely in the belief that other people must be free to have their own values that utilitarianism is distinctive—it is austerely neutral in the matter of choosing the kind of life one wishes to live. *Prima facie*, then, it requires us to rate only the degree to which other people are interested in things, rather than the particular things they are interested in, as morally relevant. This implication, understandably, runs contrary to the grain of some moralists; accordingly some discussion at this point is called for.

"Apparent" Versus "Real" Satisfactions

The aforementioned moralists will accuse me at least of being excessively naïve. Surely, we can distinguish between what a person *thinks* is good, and what is *really* good for him? Ought we not prefer the latter to the former? My answer is that there are two ways of doing this. According to one interpretation, the present view is in consonance with making such a distinc tion, and thus, in some circumstances, of preferring the "real" to the "apparent" good of some (other) individual. In another way, or perhaps another set of ways, this distinction is either illegitimate, or morally irrelevant; if it is made, we are obliged to prefer the "apparent" to the "real" good of an individual.

Let us begin by taking an example. Suppose that Johnny (who is twelve years old) has a very high mathematical aptitude, but hates mathematics. He wants to be a used-car salesman, for which his aptitude is not obviously exceptional. In these circumstances, conscientious parents will have to decide how far they should push him in mathematics. They might reason that the life of a mathematician is preferable to that of a used-car salesman, and that they are therefore justified in pushing him to take mathematics courses and work very hard at them, despite the fact that he dislikes this very much and would prefer to go out and play ball, or read back issues of *Autocar* magazine. Are they justified? It depends on what we are to regard as the determinants of "preferability," when it is alleged that the life of a mathematician is preferable. If this is a judgment of the intrinsic value of such a life, then certainly the parents have a right to make this judgment; but Johnny has a right to disagree with them, and in the present case, he does. It might be objected that Johnny is not in a position to know, and there is also something to be said for this. However, what if he were to study as a mathematician, very much against his own will, and find it quite unendurable, as is possible? This, I suggest, is the heart of the matter: The judgment that the life of a mathematician is preferable to that of a used-car salesman is irrelevant, unless there is evidence that Johnny will come to share this view. If it can be foreseen, at least probably, that he will do so, then there might be justification in setting him on the path to that end, rather than countenancing a temporary aberration of his inexperienced youth.

The adoption of a person's own view of his good rather than, flatly, his good, as the measure of utility does not, then, automatically countenance the satisfaction of merely momentary views of it.[44] People can and do change their minds about what is good for them. All that is required is that we make the view of the individual the ultimate test of what is "his good," for moral purposes. Bentham, as we know, held that every man is the best judge of his own interest. Taken as it stands, this simply isn't true. Very often other people are better judges of our interests than we are, and we can know this to be true. Obviously, that is why we often seek out advice on subjects related to our own interests. But, from the fact that other people might be better judges of our interest than we are, it does not follow that we are not in a position of "epistemological primacy," as one might call it, with respect to our own interests—for we are. This, I take it, is what Bentham either meant or should have said: Each person is the ultimate arbiter of what is in his interest. It is Jones who, at some time, must be satisfied if something is satisfactory for Jones. If something is in his interest, then he must eventually find it to be so.

None of the above is to be construed as denying that there might be a real question as to which of two kinds of lives is really, intrinsically, better. What meaning might be attached to this predicate, if the person's actual satisfactions are regarded as irrelevant, is not presently in question. Intuitionists will find it meaningful, hedonists meaningless, and others one way or the other; as I have tried to make clear, a judgment on this point is not needed here. The question is whether the supposed real, intrinsic value of a way of life is the relevant standard in moral matters, when and if it diverges from the standard of the individual's own view of the matter, in the long run. The utilitarian view is that it is not. But in all of those senses of the phrases "real vs. apparent interest," (satisfaction, advantage, or good) in which they are compatible with the use of the subject's own feelings or appraisals as the ultimate test, these contrasts are perfectly meaningful and useful on the present account of utilitarianism.

Moreover, I believe that I can claim the support of enlightened popular opinion on this matter, if this is thought to carry any particular weight.[45] These are halcyon days for utilitarianism,

[44] See Ch. VIII for further discussion.
[45] It may not be much, since popular opinion, even "progressive" or "enlightened," is subject to change of fashion, generally without notice.

in the large-circulation "family" magazines, the daily advice col-
umns in the newspapers, etc. Nearly all agree, for example, that
it is the child's own satisfactions and not those of the parents
which ought to be made the ultimate standard of appraisal in
determining how to treat and guide him. The standard, in other
words, is individual autonomy. To this, I am proposing, the utilitarian can say only "amen."

Three Puzzles: Unrealizable Satisfactions, The Rights of Animals, and Mr. Smart's Electrodes

The foregoing discussions allow us to add something on some
particularly thorny questions of a rather specialized kind, among
which I find three of special interest. The first, which will become important in connection with promising (discussed in its
own right in Chapter VI), concerns the question of how, or
perhaps I should say whether, to attach positive value to the
production of states of affairs which are regarded as good by
some persons who, for whatever reason, will never experience
the states of affairs in question. The second one concerns the
question of the moral status of animals. The third is the question
whether we should think that certain rather exotic sources of
experience, such as drugs or artificial stimulation of the nerves
by means of electrodes, count as goods. The special interpretation of utility which I have been arguing for above will, I
think, cast some light on these matters.

(1) It would presumably be self-contradictory to talk of un-
experienced pleasures. Similarly, if perhaps not quite so obviously, it seems strange to attribute happiness to nonexistent
persons. Nevertheless, people do go out of their way at times
to do things for people who are dead or otherwise not in a
position to know that the things in question are being done. We
can question the rationality of desires whose fulfillment cannot
be experienced by the persons having them; or, we can question
the rationality of our taking them seriously; in any case, we
need to do something about them. The present formula, I suggest, helps by showing how this might be brought under the
umbrella of utilitarianism. If our moral criterion is productive-

ness of things valued by anyone, then we can argue plausibly what we could not argue plausibly using the "pleasure" formula, that there is value in carrying out the wishes of persons now dead. It does seem that people can put a high value on states of affairs which they will not be able to experience, e.g., posthumous fame. There is another source of support in the fact that unquestionably it is precisely the fact that x was valued *by Jones* and not the fact that x is "intrinsically" valuable, which is very often at stake. 'Jones would have liked that' is advanced as a credible reason for doing things by friends, admirers, or well-wishers.

The effect of the present formula is, however, merely to bring both sides of these disputes within the utilitarian framework, not to settle them. The question whether it is rational to want things one won't be able to experience is certainly an open one; so is the question how much, if any, weight is to be put upon such wants when it comes to weighing them against the wants of living people who will be able to experience their fulfillment. The question becomes interesting only in fringe cases.

(2) The second question is whether animals are to "count for one," along with people, in our moral concerns. If we were to define utility in terms of pleasure, it seems reasonable to suppose that many animals would have to be counted in on the principle of utility. Moreover, it is obvious that to *some* extent they do —it is surely wrong to inflict gratuitous suffering upon animals. But what about eating them, for example? We do not suppose that if we murder a man with the purpose in mind of eating him—bearing him no ill will, you understand—that is sufficient to justify the act. Yet, people invoke this argument on behalf of the justifiability of killing animals. Is there a real diffierence?

One consideration is evident, at least. If animals were able to talk with us, it would make a striking difference in most of our opinions about them. Imagine a cow not only looking at her approaching butcher with that sad and reproachful expression cows have, but also able to say to him as he approaches, "You brute! Have you no humanity at all?" Certainly if animals could employ moral language, as well as act as if they experienced pain or pleasure, that would put them into the category of "moral persons." This does make a difference, but *should* it? Should it, especially, on the Principle of Utility?

As I have said, if we define utility in terms of pleasure, it should make no difference. But if we define it as I have suggested, perhaps a more satisfactory explanation is forthcoming. We cannot expect to infer from an animal's apparently having a pro-attitude toward something any willingness or ability to defend its view as a sound one. Since animals are unable to talk,[46] we can only suppose that they are unable to "have moral concepts"—if indeed this amounts to anything other than being able to use moral language anyway. Therefore, we suppose that the reason we have no obligation to respect the animal's point of view is that animals don't really *have* "points of view."

It still doesn't follow from this that we are right in killing animals for food; but it does seem to move us several steps in that direction. Rawls' suggestion that we owe the duties of justice only to those who have the concept of justice[47] is much in accordance with my view, and his view would surely account for the disparity here. At the same time, I suggest, we can not say that we owe the (less stringent) duties of charity only to those who have the concept of charity. Thus, we can be said to have a (weak) duty toward animals, which consists in not inflicting gratuitous suffering on them; and at the same time we do not owe the (strong) duty of justice to them, which would involve treating them as moral persons.

My purpose here has not been to solve fully the problem about animals, but rather to point out the kind of difference made by defining utility in the present way rather than in a narrowly hedonistic manner. We shall find similar advantages of this view at some of the later stages of my exposition.

(3) Mr. Smart, in his interesting account of utilitarianism, mentions a psychological experiment carried out on rats, in which some electrodes were attached to their brains and attached to

---

[46] Perhaps I should have said 'if,' rather than 'since.' I gather that psychologists (as opposed to rhapsodizers) do not, at present, attribute the use of language to animals, in any serious way. The lack in animals, moreover, is not merely physiological, in many cases. Parrots and minah birds can mimic, and thus can pronounce words. Yet we don't think that they *talk*.

[47] John Rawls, "The Sense of Justice," *Philosophical Review* (1963).

levers such that the rat "would neglect food and make straight for this lever and start stimulating himself. In some cases he would sit there pressing the lever every few seconds for hours on end." So the question arises: if some such apparatus were invented for humans, would the resultant enjoyment be part of "the sort of life that all our ethical planning should culminate in?" Smart's ensuing discussion of this is incisive and illuminating, by and large, and the reader will want to consult it. I shall add only a small point to his remarks. This point is in reference to Smart's suggestion that the notion of happiness is "partly evaluative." To call a person 'happy' is

> To say more than that he is contented for most of the time, or even that he frequently enjoys himself and is rarely discontented or in pain. It is, I think, in part to express a favorable attitude to the idea of such a form of contentment and enjoyment. That is, for A to call B 'happy,' A must be contented at the prospect of B being in his present state of mind and at the prospect of A himself, should the opportunity arise, enjoying that sort of state of mind.[48]

It is not clear that this is true, though there is doubtless some tendency in the direction Smart mentions. But we might reflect on whether our own valuations ought to enter into the picture at all. It may be true that we cannot, psychologically, believe that someone else really has a value which we cannot share, but to permit it to enter into the picture in any sense in which we can control this tendency is to run the risk of altering the utilitarian view. At any rate, the question in the case of electrode-operating is not how we feel about it, but how the people who indulge feel about it. So much Smart recognizes. But the further question, which Smart presumably would not put much weight on, is whether the people in question think that the states of mind induced by electrode operation are good ones. This is a question which might, and perhaps in most cases would (as we observed in the section above), be identified with the question of enjoyment. Clearly, those of us who haven't tried it are not in a good position to carry on the argument about its intrinsic merits, as Mill pointed out in his remarks about Socrates and the pig, as discussed in the second section above.

[48] Smart, *An Outline of a System of Utilitarian Ethics*, pp. 13, 14.

A question of a type which in some cases could be very serious is raised in Smart's penetrating observation that very often we are not contented at the prospect of doing x, even though we would be contented if we were doing x, and perhaps even though we know now that we would. "If Socrates had become a fool he might thereafter have been perfectly contented. Nevertheless, if beforehand he had been told that he would in the future become a fool, he would have been even more dissatisfied than in fact he was."[49] The question is: Under such circumstances, which fact do we go by? Do we take steps to put him in the future state of contentment, contrary to his present wishes, or do we go by his present wishes, thus lowering his overall contentment level? The formula I propose puts the weight, *prima facie*, on the side of the present wishes. Not unless I can convince the agent that the future state would be a good one am I justified in counting it a positive utility that he be put in that state.

However, in extreme cases, this rule must be broken. I suggest that the condition which would justify this, other than the condition when the agent's present preferences are immoral,[50] is that in which the agent's rationality is genuinely in doubt. In that case, there is a doubt that the agent's preferences are founded on evaluations at all. My formula suggests that the preference is for the agent's assessment until really good grounds for doubting his sanity are at hand (which, unfortunately, are notoriously difficult to spell out).

We normally assume that if Jones likes something, approves of something, prefers something to something else, loves it, desires it, wants it, orders it, tends to go after it, or in general, shows that he has a pro-attitude toward it (either behaviorally or by applying pro-expressions to it), then he thinks that the thing in question is a good thing, or would be good for him to have or to get, or is better than the other thing (in the case of the relational expressions employed). By this I mean that we are normally expected to *defend* our pro-attitudes, so that if we

[49] *Ibid.*, p. 13.

[50] See Ch. VI below. The chief defect in traditional discussions of utilitarianism is neglect of the fact that it provides a criterion for evaluating desires.

have a desire which we regard as a bad one, we must qualify statements to the effect that we have them, so as to let people know that we do not regard these desires as providing good grounds for acting. The basic point remains that we cannot expect people to satisfy our desires if we do not ourselves think them worthy of being satisfied. This "assumption" *may* perhaps be defended on broadly logical grounds,[51] but for whatever reason, it is normally made. It is for this reason that we will, in general, assume that what a person enjoys, what pleases him, or what he prefers, likes, wants, desires, etc., are likewise measures of utility. In the cases where the assumption does break down, we shall morally prefer the alternative to which he applies explicitly evaluative language, if any.

In the event of the subject's unwillingness or inability to use evaluative language in connection with the things in question, if he otherwise expresses pro or con attitudes toward them, we shall assign utility (positive or negative) to them until further notice. If a man is faint with pain, he is unlikely to take the trouble to formulate evaluative sentences about it. We obviously would have no reason to expect him to, or to require him to, under normal circumstances. But what if a person is in a state which we would normally assume he regards as undesirable, but he insists that he regards it as desirable? This could conceivably happen, and when it does, we regard it as relevant. The fact that the fakir on his bed of nails is uncomfortable does not automatically mean that we'd be doing him a good turn by getting him off of it. He knows he's uncomfortable, but he regards that as a good thing. Unless we can convince him that his reasons for wanting to suffer are bad ones, we will just have to leave him alone.

These observations give us further criteria of weighing utilities. The values which a person holds more deeply and strongly count as higher utilities than those he holds as secondary. Indeed, the criteria of measurement, for each individual case, are provided by his own evaluative scheme. Again, it is necessary to remember that discussion of his values is possible. Indeed, we can produce an abstract argument to show that it is, in a

---

[51] Nowell-Smith's *Ethics* (p. 99) offers interesting support here.

90

sense, a *prima facie* good. For if A has a certain value which B regards as bad, and B convinces A that A is (was) in the wrong, so that A adopts some new value instead, then *prima facie* this is an increase in utility, since A's reason for adopting it (and the hypothesis is that he had a reason, i.e., that B convinced him, rather than, say, drugging him) must be that the new value is higher than the old one.

Thus, there seem to be some advantages in our new formulation, even though it was adopted primarily on the ground that it was the view underlying the old formula. Further advantages, I hope, will be shown in Chapter IX, wherein the question of proof is taken up.

Final Formulation

We are now in a position to suggest a precise statement of the principle of utility. The concern of this chapter has been to understand what utility consists in; the view taken is that it consists in the bringing about of whatever is thought to be intrinsically good by those affected, except, of course, for what is thought to be morally good.[52] We have not paid very much attention to the evaluative predicate, which is to figure in the principle. This is a matter which deserves attention for, as pointed out in the Introduction, we do not want to ride roughshod over the distinctions which need to be made between the "teleological" and the "deontological" vocabulary of ethics, for example. To say that an act is one we are morally obliged to do, have a duty to do, or are bound in justice to do, is generically different (as well as having finer differences with each other) from saying that it would be a good thing to do from the moral point of view. It would not do at all, for example, to settle for Moore's formula, that x is a duty if and only if x produces more good than any other alternative.[53] This would appear to imply the ludicrous result that if I would like strawberry jam better

[52] The extent to which moral views count as utility will be considered later.

[53] Moore, *Principia Ethica*, No. 17, 89 ff.

than peach on my toast for breakfast one morning, then it is my duty to have strawberry rather than peach.

In later chapters, especially Chapter VI and onward, I shall try to give an account of the differences in meaning between 'morally good' and 'morally obligatory,' in order to give an account of the moral principles making use of the differences. Meanwhile, it is enough to observe that we need a formulation which is neutral as between these sets of expressions. For this purpose, we may use the word 'value' to good effect.

Mill and Bentham put the matter in terms of 'right' and 'wrong,' Sidgwick adding that what is meant is 'objectively right' and 'objectively wrong,'[54] thus giving us a formula such as this: Acts are objectively right insofar as they increase utility, objectively wrong insofar as they diminish it.[55] This is rather satisfactory, except that it might be thought that 'right' and 'wrong' are themselves in the "deontological" set; it might also be held that these expressions are not naturally thought to be matters of degree. Therefore, we shall say that the single fundamental predicate is a relational predicate, 'is of greater moral value than.' Thus, the objective moral value of x is greater than that of y if, and only if, x has greater net utility than y.

For moral purposes, of course, we are concerned to appraise human acts, intentions or motives and characters. To many people it seems unnatural to think of comparing the activities of volcanoes and babbling brooks with that of moral agents. This is fair enough, in a way. We could, therefore, restrict the formula further so as to apply it only to acts; intentions and motives will be considered in the next chapter, and seem to depend for their appraisals upon the previous existence of standards for appraising acts. Thus, our narrower version will run as follows: Where our variables range over any set of acts which are alternatives to each other on any particular occasion of choice, x has more objective moral value than y if and only if x has more utility than y.

We may then define 'x is morally good' as being equivalent

[54] Sidgwick, *Methods of Ethics,* p. 411.
[55] Bentham talks of "tendencies" as well, in the Introduction to *The Utilitarians,* p. 18: "By utility is meant that property in any object, whereby it tends to produce benefit, advantage, pleasure, good or happiness."

to 'the net moral value of x is positive and exceeds the net moral value of doing nothing at all'; in parallel fashion, 'x is morally bad' as equivalent to 'the net moral value of x is negative and is less than the net moral value of doing nothing at all.'[56]

Finally, we may substitute our definition of utility in the formula to obtain the following: One alternative has more objective moral value than another if and only if it produces a greater net amount of what is valued by those affected than the other produces.

In Chapters IV and V, we shall take up general questions of method in the application of this rather abstract principle. Then we shall be in a position to take up the more concrete issues which are, in a sense, the heart of the matter.

[56] Perhaps "doing nothing at all" might be felt to be a vacuous description on the ground that in a situation of choice, whatever you do, including refusing to make a decision, is "really" a choice. I think this is slightly sophistical; better to say that one can be held responsible for not making a choice as well as for making any particular choice, in some situations.

CHAPTER IV

"Formalism"

The Distinction Between Formalism and Teleology[1]

Traditionally, the most fundamental division of theories on the "normative" question of ethics is doubtless that between "teleology" and "formalism" or "deontology."[2] According to this division of the subject, teleological theories are those according to which there is a single criterion for making moral assessments of acts, namely, their productiveness of good or evil consequences, while "formalist" theories hold that something besides the consequences is also relevant. This "something-else" is the "intrinsic nature" of the acts in question.

In this section, I shall contend that this distinction is misleading and unsatisfactory. We have not been told much about the meaning of the phrase, "the intrinsic nature of the act," other than that it is something besides the "consequences"; unfortunately, the term 'consequences' seems to be in some important way relative to the term 'intrinsic nature.' A close inspection of these expressions will reveal that the dichotomy fails to divide theories in the ways intended. The application of utilitarianism, which is supposed to be (and surely is) a "teleological" theory, requires a distinction between acts which are right or wrong on account of their "intrinsic natures" and those which are right or wrong on account of their "consequences," as indeed would any theory.

---

[1] A longer discussion of this subject is to be found in my article, "Utilitarianism and Formalism," *Australasian Journal of Philosophy* (May, 1965).

[2] We will confine the term 'formalism' to the present matter, reserving 'deontology' for the subject of duties and rights, which will be discussed later.

Let us, then, take a look at this term, "intrinsic nature." Clearly, it is used in rather the way in which "essence" is used. Just as the "essence" of anything is what makes it what it is, so the "intrinsic nature" of an act is what makes it the kind of act it is. Now, what is the sense of the word 'makes' here? Usually, it is to be understood in a logical sense: an act's "intrinsic nature" 'makes' it the "kind" of act it is, in the sense that any act having that "nature" is thereby said to be of that kind. On this understanding of the term, then, the intrinsic nature of act F is whatever about the act follows logically from its being F. In short, its "intrinsic nature" is simply its defining characteristics. On this usage, "formalism" would be the view that the basic criterion of the moral value of an act is something about what follows from its defining characteristics. But it follows from this that *every* ethical theory is ultimately "formalist." For if a theory could not specify any kinds of acts which are right just because that is the kind of acts they are, obviously it could never specify any act to be right. The reasoning is the same as in the argument for intrinsic values.[3] Thus, for example, suppose that I say that all acts which produce Q are right. Then, consider an act F, where "F" means 'productive of Q.' If Q-producing is what makes an act right, then act F will have to be said to be "intrinsically" right, on pain of nonsense. For act F doesn't, of course, *produce* Q. In order to say of something that it "produces" something, we must understand the thing produced to be distinct from what is doing the producing. Mills produce flour; but they do not "produce" mills: they *are* mills. Similarly, acts of Type F do not *produce* Q—they *are* Q-producers. Producing Q is their "intrinsic nature" (i.e., their defining property).

It is sometimes supposed that no line can be drawn between acts and consequences. This simply is not true. It is true that the term 'act' can apply to a tremendous range of different things. Sometimes our descriptions of acts, for instance, include a great deal of what would be accounted consequences, relative to another and narrower description of the events in question. For example, Jones starts a revolution. This is an "act"; but perhaps he started the revolution by starting a riot. The riot, perhaps,

---

[3] Cf. Chapter III, Intrinsic Values.

caused the bringing up of troops, which in turn led to bloodshed, which led to the collapse of the government. Relative to the act of starting the riot, the bringing up of the troops was a "conse-quence," but relative to the act of starting the revolution, this was part of the act. Given any specific description of an act what is to count as the range of "consequences" follows: It is merely all of those events, causally connected with the perform-ance of the act, which lie outside the logical boundaries drawn by that description. It is true that no one description is "the" description of "the" act. Did Jones start the riot or the revolu-tion? Well, he did both: the one by doing the other.[4]

As a point of ordinary language, we may observe that we can draw useful distinctions between 'act,' 'circumstance,' and 'con-sequence.' Roughly speaking, we describe as his 'act' the events which the agent saw himself as producing. Thus, if Jones killed Smith, we call this an act of "murder" if Jones' intention was to kill Smith, and if it was not his intention simply to defend himself from an assault of Smith's, or to carry out a duty as State Executioner, as a soldier, or the like. Let us suppose that Jones hit Smith with a crowbar, in consequence of which Smith died. If we say that Jones murdered Smith, we imply that if, for instance, there had been a wrench instead of a crowbar, he might have used that instead, or might have shot him if he'd had a gun. The specific act he can be said to have "done" is de-termined by his broader intention. In turn, "consequence" is usually confined to events which are not only caused by the act in question, but also such as could, within reason, have been foreseen by the parties acting, or at least by observers. Circum-stances, finally, are part of the "background" of the act, in the sense that they are the conditions which prevailed in the neigh-borhood of the act. It is not necessary for us to go into these fine distinctions for our purposes. It is enough to point out that some descriptions are ordinarily classified as descriptions of the act, others of the consequences, and others of the circumstances, but that unusual ones are sometimes possible; in any case, that these distinctions are relative, so that to classify a certain description under the "act" category automatically implies that some other

[4] G. E. M. Anscombe makes a similar point, in her book, *Intention* (Oxford: Blackwell Press, Ltd., 1957.) Cf., especially sec. 23, pp. 37ff.

97

descriptions will be classified as "consequences," and perhaps still others will be put into the "circumstance" department.[5]

Now to apply all this to utilitarianism. Suppose there is a type of activity which, by definition, consists of producing something which is reckoned by utilitarians to be (morally) a good thing to produce. An example is "entertaining," which by definition produces pleasure or enjoyment (entertainment) in those to whom it is done. According to utilitarianism, enjoyment is "intrinsically" good. It follows (according to utilitarianism) that entertaining is an intrinsically good activity, since its being morally good follows from its intrinsic nature. On the other hand, an "extrinsically" good act is one in which the fact that it is good is *not* due to its intrinsic nature. Thus, if I happen to bring great joy into somebody's life by giving him a baseball bat, that is an act whose goodness is not due to its intrinsic nature. I might have given it to him, but he might not have derived any joy from it at all. Some people will dispute whether this was not a "good act" anyway, because of its *intention*, but this is another issue, quite different from the present one (as we shall see in the following section, Intentions and Acts.) Thus, there may be quite a few types of acts which will turn out to be not only right but intrinsically right, on the utilitarian view. In fact, I shall argue that virtually all of the kinds of acts brought up by formalists as supposed counter examples to the utilitarian theory are of this kind. Examples are promise-keeping, gratitude, and reparation, which turn out to be intrinsically morally good or obligatory; and lying, cheating, stealing, and robbing, which turn out to be intrinsically morally wrong.

Confusion on this question of formalism stems from two sources. The first is the assumption that if an act is intrinsically right, then there cannot be any *explanation* of why it is right. We have already accepted the argument that if anything is good at all, then something, or some things, must be good in themselves, rather than because of their consequences. This argument seems to me quite undeniable; but it only shows that the kind of explanation we have to give for a thing's being good in itself must be different from the kind of explanation appropriate to

[5] There is a clear and useful discussion of these matters in Eric D'Arcy's book, *Human Acts* (New York: Oxford University Press, 1963).

things not good in themselves. It does not show that an explanation of their goodness is impossible. There is no incompatibility between a teleological view, according to which the ultimate criterion of a certain kind of goodness lies in certain effects, and the assertion that some acts are good in themselves. The explanation is simply that some acts logically *include* the effects in question: it is logically impossible to kill someone unless the victim ends up dead, even though there is only a causal (hence contingent) connection between pulling the trigger and the victim's death, or between pushing him over the cliff and his dying. It is a pity that failure to make this elementary logical observation should cause so much confusion in the ranks of moral philosophers.

I take it as proved then, that utilitarianism (or any ethical theory whatever), holds that some acts are intrinsically good, some are intrinsically bad, and some indifferent. So the difference between formalism and teleology, or deontology and teleology, cannot be properly made out in this way.

The gimmick in this question, as we have seen, is the notion of "consequence." In effect, this word has been seen to be ambiguous: on the one hand, it means roughly, "result of *something* done by the agent." Elsewhere,[6] I have invented a name for this distinction. Suppose my act is murdering P, then the consequences are such things as the grief of his widow, setting up of the hue and cry by the local police, and so forth. But P's dying, which is logically a part of my having murdered him, is also a non-logical consequence of something I did—for example, pulling the trigger or shooting him. Relative to the description 'murdered P,' this is part of the act; relative to the description, 'shot P,' it is a consequence. But shooting P was part of murdering him. Then, let us call his death an "infra-consequence" of my murdering P. That is, "infra-consequences" will be those consequences of portions of my activity which are necessary conditions of applying some larger act-description.

If, we were to ask now, in a purely general way, what we would be left with if we were to try to exclude all consequences and all "infra-consequences" of acts in a moral theory, we should

---

[6] In the article, "Utilitarianism and Formalism" (see n. 1).

find ourselves left with the ghosts, so to speak, of the actions which have always been main concerns of moralists. For there is hardly anything a person does which might not have been "infra-consequential" in the sense in question. Is raising my arm, for example, something I do, or a consequence of something else I do, such as issuing some kind of internal volition? As we know, an answer to this question led Prichard to adopt the view that all we can be required to do is to "set ourselves" to do something, rather than simply to *do* it.[7] Thus formalism, pursued with fanaticism, leads to "subjectivist" or "intentionalist" views, which we will consider in the next section. It is enough to observe here that the only meaningful controversy there can be between utilitarians and others is whether utilitarians have the right kind of consequences in mind. If we include both "consequences" and "infra-consequences" in the scope of the utilitarian theory—which we obviously must—then the question whether consequences are relevant at all becomes absurd. That is, unless it is metamorphosed into the question of whether, and if so why, intentions are relevant.

Perhaps it is necessary to add a cautionary note at this point, stemming from the liberal employment of such words as 'definition' and 'nature' in the foregoing account. The language in which ethical rules and principles are formulated is, of course, ordinary language, and all of the appropriate clichés about such language must be duly invoked to avoid an unwarranted assumption of precision. Thus, when I say that I hope to establish, in the cases of nearly all of our "standard" moral principles, that the things said to be right or wrong in those principles are intrinsically right or wrong according to the utilitarian view, we must admit that we aren't going to be able to say, for instance, that "lying" is, by definition, precisely this or that, and hence . . . . What we do have to say is that the logically normal cases of lying (or whatever) are like this or that, and in those cases, such and such holds, and thus. . . . However, if we take a case

---

[7] Cf. Harold A. Prichard, "Duty and Ignorance of Fact," an essay in *Moral Obligation* (New York: Oxford University Press, 1949), pp. 31–36. Mr. Robert Imlay's paper, "Do I Ever Directly Raise My Arm?" also affords some interesting material for reflection (unpublished paper read before the meeting of the American Philosophical Association, Chicago, 1965).

far enough out on the fringe, perhaps it will be one of those rare cases in which the principle breaks down, but alternatively, perhaps it isn't *really* a case of lying. Thus, recall Austin's remarks about ordering and warning:

He did "order" me to do it, but, having no authority over me, he *couldn't* "order" me: he did warn me it was going to charge, but it wasn't or anyway I knew much more about it than he did, so in a way he couldn't warn me, didn't warn me. We hesitate between "He didn't order me," "He had no right to order me," "He oughtn't to have said he ordered me," just as we do between "You didn't know," "You can't have known," "You had no right to say you knew."[8]

This is, of course, merely by way of general caution. Specific cases will be looked into by turns in due course, and they are what really count.

"Rigorism" and the Status of Particular Moral Principles

It has been said that utilitarianism encourages moral laxity by always making us look for reasons for keeping promises, paying bills, and other obligations. The suggestion is that there are certain rules of morality which will lose their authority if we think of them as subject to exceptions in the light of the overarching importance of the general happiness. A theory like Kant's, on the other hand, puts its money on real moral rigor—whatever that is supposed to be.

Now, there are some people whose activity is excessively rigid: they are always so anxious to be doing their duty that they walk miles to repay a shortchanged penny, frown whenever anyone tells a risqué story, and always watch suspiciously for signs of moral decline in their neighbors. As Baier says, they ". . . hunger and thirst after righteousness as others do after food and sex. They are moral automata, in the clutches of their superegos."[9] Such people raise psychological, as well as moral

[8] J. L. Austin, "Other Minds," in *Philosophical Papers*, ed. J. O. Urmson and G. J. Warnock (New York: Oxford University Press, 1961), p. 70.
[9] Baier, *Moral Point of View*, p. 13.

101

problems. For our present purposes we have merely to note a by now well-exposed confusion: that is, between the truism that morality comes first, that where duty calls one must follow; and the "falsism," as we might call it, that there are certain types of acts which one must always do, certain specific ethical principles which cannot be overridden by anything. The latter might be called "rigorism." It is necessary to distinguish between this and what I have been calling "formalism" (or "deontologism"), since the one does not imply the other. A formalist holds that we ought to do something because of its "intrinsic nature," and not because of its "consequences"; it does not necessarily follow that if an act has a nature which is such as to render it a duty, we must always perform it when the circumstances make it possible to do so. In fact, as the previous analysis showed, to say that something is "intrinsically right" is equivalent to saying, in effect, that it is *"prima facie"* right. By now, I take it to be commonplace that it is one thing to say that a certain kind of act is one's duty, and quite another to say on a particular occasion that *this* act is your duty. Baier has put this very well in distinguishing what he calls "reasons *prima facie*" from "reasons on balance."[10] In any particular situation, we are faced with choices of action. We consider various acts, in each case noting that it is of various kinds, i.e., that each act has various characteristics. Some of these characteristics will be such as to count in favor of doing it, and some against. Then we have to decide whether the reasons for doing it outweigh the reasons against it. If the characteristics in question are such as to make for reasons of a moral kind, and in particular of a kind having to do with duties, then it may be that, taking all things into account, the act is a duty. Some of the characteristics will be "duty-making" (i.e., their presence is such as to suggest that there is a duty to do the act), but others may be such as to suggest there is a duty not to do it. In that case, these characteristics have to be weighed, and the result will be one's duty in the given situation. But there is no specific kind of act which it is always right to do, regardless, or always wrong to do, regardless. It is conceivable that

[10] The importance of such a distinction was emphasized also by Ross in *The Right and the Good*, but his account is not as clear as Baier's, and is linked too closely with Ross' brand of "intuitionism." Baier's account is found in *Moral Point of View*, pp. 102, 103.

any two particular moral principles might conflict. For example, we may find that in order to avoid stealing, we must kill, or that in order to help a friend, we must harm an employer. "Rigorism" of Kant's kind is impossible in these cases. Kant, as is well known, felt that if a particular kind of act is a duty, then it will always be a duty, come what may. He failed to see the distinction between "*prima facie*" duties, and duties "on balance."[11]

However, if one holds that there is only one ultimate moral principle, then it cannot be merely *prima facie*. In view of the suggestions in Chapter II, if an act is a moral duty on the whole, then it cannot "have exceptions"; and if there is but one moral principle, and it makes a certain act a duty, then there is no further recourse. It follows, then, that the Utilitarian, since he is a "monist" in this sense of claiming that there is but one ultimate moral principle, is necessarily a "rigorist" with respect to that principle. The typical "formalist," on the other hand, claims that there are a number of ultimate moral principles, so he cannot be a rigorist with respect to any particular one of them.

We can produce a general proof of this last point. To say that there are several ultimate moral principles is to say that there are several logically independent predicates, call them 'F_1', 'F_2' . . . 'F_n', each of which figures in a statement to the effect that for any act, if the predicate in question is true of it, then it has some moral value, V. Presumably, a moral system, to be nonvacuous, must have some principles specifying what is wrong as well as others specifying what is right; i.e., it must specify some things which ought to be done, and others which ought not to be done. Then, let us take any two of its principles, say those involving 'F_1' and 'F_2', for convenience, such that they specify opposite values for the acts respectively instantiating

[11] Baier, *Moral Point of View*, 191–95. Baier makes another distinction between "presumptive" and "*prima facie*" reasons, which, he says, Kant overlooks. I shall consider a similar distinction in the chapter on Justice, below. According to Herbert J. Paton in *Kant-Studien* (Cologne: 1953–54), Vol. 45, Kant wrote the famous piece in which this doctrine is most explicitly defended in a fit of pique. Nevertheless, he did publish it, and though it is inconsistent with some of his practice, it is quite consistent with many of his statements in the well-known Kantian works on ethics. The small essay in question, "On a Supposed Right to Lie from Benevolent Motives," is found in an Appendix to Thomas K. Abbott (tr.), *Critique of Practical Reason, and other works on the Theory of Ethics* (London: Longmans, 1909).

the predicates in question. The formulas of these principles will be '(x) $(F_1x \supset Vx)$' and '(x) $(F_2x \supset V_1x)$' (where 'V_1' is some value incompatible with 'V'). It follows that any act which is both F_1 and F_2 will be given incompatible values. Therefore, the system will lead to contradictions in some cases. Thus, at least most of the principles in the system cannot be held "rigorously" in the above sense, and under ordinary circumstances, none of them will. Most of them will have to be, as Ross saw, *"prima facie"* principles. It might be held that no act can ever have both of any two predicates whose correlated values are inconsistent, but this cannot be held on logical grounds, for to say that 'F_1' and 'F_2' are logically independent is to say that '$F_1x \cdot F_2x$' is consistent. The compatibility of principles in application can never be assured, except by reducing the number of principles to one. (Or by cheating, e.g., by saying that everything is good.)

Given a particular moral code, of course, it will be possible to live up to it well or badly. A person who lives up to it perfectly might be said to be a "rigorist" with respect to that code. But it is plain that "rigorist" is not a theoretical term at all as used in this way. Obviously, we ought to do whatever is right, and if a rigorist is simply someone who always does what is right, then we ought all to be rigorists. But this has nothing to do with moral theory. One can be a rigorous utilitarian or a lax Kantian, or vice versa, in this sense of the word. Objections to utilitarianism on this score are merely *ad hominem*.

It may be felt that even though we are not obliged always to keep promises, utilitarianism provides for more exceptions to them than it ought. This may be one source of the allegation that utilitarianism "cannot account for justice." "Rule-utilitarianism" is in part an effort to shore up the status of particular moral rules without altogether abandoning utilitarianism. I will deal with this in Chapter V.

Intentions and Acts

We commonly apply moral terms to intentions and motives, as well as to intentions with which they were performed. (This is not surprising, since 'act' is basically an intentional term in the first place.)

Some have gone so far as to hold that *only* motives or intentions have genuine moral worth, with Kant, of course, as the principal once in point.[12] This is understandably thought to be a great difficulty for the utilitarian, and it is sometimes thought to be the single blow that fells the whole theory. If the moral value of an act is proportional to its utility, then how can the intentions or motives behind it have any bearing on the matter? In the present section I shall argue, as usual, that there is a good deal of confusion surrounding this question. I shall further argue that the view that intentions are the basic bearers of moral predicates is incoherent. In the following section, I shall go on to argue that only a utilitarian point of view makes good sense of all the facts involved here.

The problem then, is as follows: If we are to take account only of the consequences of acts and not their intentions, then how can we account for the fact (as we may call it) that an act which turns out unfortunately but was well intended is more excusable than one in which bad effects were intended? Notice that the objection presupposes that the intentions of an agent *could* be appraised quite independently from the acts to which they are "directed." If it could be shown that this is not so, then we shall be well on the way to showing that the objection is incoherent. That is precisely what I propose to do.

Let us begin by recalling the primary functions of ethical principles: to tell us what to do, i.e., to guide action. Whatever else an ethical principle is supposed to do, it must do that, otherwise it could not (logically) be an ethical principle at all. Now let us consider the way in which we can appraise a person's intentions. In order to do this, clearly it has to be possible for some intentions to be better or worse than others: our criterion for appraising them, that is, must be such as to distinguish among them. In order to do this, it must make use of some of the aspects

---

[12] Kant usually says that only the "will" can be called good "without qualification"; an action which is done "from duty" *derives* its moral worth from the maxim of the act, and "therefore" from the "principle of volition." This, as well as other passages, strongly suggests that the moral value of acts derives from the moral value of the will behind them, and not vice versa. This is the issue which is discussed in this section. Although most interpreters would agree with Kant's view, I claim that it is upside down.

in which they can differ from each other. And if one reflects on it, it will shortly become evident that there are, in fact, only three ways in which intentions can differ. They can differ, namely, in their strengths, in their "sincerity" (if this is different from "strength") and in their "objects," that is, in what they are intentions to do: i.e., in the kind of act which will occur if the intention is carried out.

Now neither of the two first are differences which can enable us to rate intentions morally. For plainly, a person can have a very strong evil intention, and also a very sincere one. He may, for instance, be beating a heretic at a stake, and he may really and sincerely intend to do this. It follows that neither of these will do.[13] Since there is only one left, it must be the one we need. We must, then, appraise intentions by reference to their "objects," i.e., by what they are intentions to *do*. But it is logically impossible to do this without having criteria for rating the acts which intentions are directed at. Thus, criteria for rating acts independently of their intentions are presupposed in any effort to appraise intentions for their moral worth. The worth of an intention is not, and cannot be, due to anything else but the value of the action intended (i.e., which the action would have, if it occurred as intended.) It is this which the Principle of Utility provides: a criterion for evaluating acts quite apart from the intentions of the people who perform them.

Someone will say, but you have not yet shown us how it follows from the utilitarian position that we should rate intended acts by the utilitarian criterion, and not just acts apart from intentions. How can we do this? However, the foregoing argument also shows that the Principle of Utility does provide criteria for rating intentions. For, if we can rate acts apart from their intentions, then we can also rate intentions by appraising not the act which actually was carried out by the agent, but rather the act which he intended to perform, whether or not

---

[13] Oddly enough, some of the "existentialists" suggest that sincerity alone is sufficient. Sartre seems to be an example. "Authentic" living, with which the existentialists seem much concerned, appears to be the same as *sincere* living, although I suppose that this will not be thought profound enough by most of Sartre's adherents. Cf. Jean-Paul Sartre, *Existentialism and Humanism* (London: Methuen Publishing Co., Ltd., 1948), especially pp. 50–51.

he succeeded. Now I must show not only that we can do this, but also that the principle of utility implies that we must.

At this point, it is again necessary to remind the critic of something which he often seems to forget when he discusses the utilitarian theory. That is, the purpose of any moral principle. Utilitarianism, as I have insisted, is a fundamental moral principle. Moral principles, it is agreed, are for the purpose of guiding action. The reason why utilitarianism implies that we should appraise intentions as well as acts follows logically from this. It is simply nonsensical to pose the question, "ought I to *intend* to do this, or ought I merely to *succeed* at it?" Obviously, I can have no such choice. All I can do is to seek guidance, and then proceed to follow it to the best of my ability. Conversely, when I seek to influence someone else's behavior by offering him advice, I am, *ipso facto*, attempting to alter his intentions. That is what it is to offer advice. If I thought that advice would not do him any good, and it appeared that he intended to do evil anyhow, I should have to resort to force or to psychological trickery to bring him around. Obviously, it is sometimes necessary to do this. But that is to depart from the making of ethical statements, which is our primary concern here.

In short, this famous and ancient objection to utilitarianism is simply misguided. The answer to it is parallel to the answer provided by Baier[14] to the ancient problem about the "paradox of subjectivity": ought a man to do what he *thinks* he ought to do, or what he *really* ought to do? The answer is that he has no option but to try to figure out what he ought to do, and then to do it. If his deliberation is faulty, we can blame him for that; if he fails to do what he agreed he ought to do, we can blame him for that. But there is nothing else left to blame him for, and these are different shortcomings.

Actually, utilitarianism does better on this subject than merely to escape this ancient objection. It is, in fact, the only theory that makes sense of all the phenomena involved. For example, consider a theory such as Kant's, according to which the intention is the only thing that counts. We have already seen that this is logically incoherent, if interpreted so as to imply that

[14] *Moral Point of View*, pp. 143–47. Cf., also the following section of this chapter, entitled "Objective" and "Subjective."

criteria for appraising acts are unnecessary. Plainly Kant could not have meant that, since his Categorical Imperative enables us to appraise acts apart from their intentions anyhow. The Categorical Imperative enjoins us to act only on maxims which could be universalized; but people can act as if they had a certain maxim even if they don't have it, and such actions can be appraised by reference to the principle that if they were performed with that maxim, then they would be wrong. It would be nonsense to interpret this merely as enjoining us not to act with that maxim (though acts of the type which the maxim suggests are all right, so long as they are not done with the maxim in mind). On the contrary, the only point there could be in enjoining us not to have that maxim is not to act on it. This implies that it is really the act which, in the logically prior sense, is bad. We can admit, of course, that we might want to say that unintended acts of the proscribed type should be called "unfortunate" rather than "wrong," but the point is that we can use the Categorical Imperative's test to determine the class of unfortunate acts as well as that of wrong ones, and it would be quite incoherent to maintain that it can be used only to determine that of wrong ones, but not unfortunate ones.

What Kant may have meant[15] is that regardless of how frightful the results of what a man actually does, he cannot be blamed so long as he meant well. If this is what he meant, then clearly his doctrine is false. A man who intends to drop an H-Bomb on New York City but who "means well" by it is not to be praised (supposing that he is, in fact, unjustified in this, which is likely supposition). He should be locked up, or at very least, put under observation. What is true is that the kind of treatment which should be given to a man who knew that blowing up New York City is wrong, but who did so anyhow just for fun, and

---

[15] This is strongly suggested by the famous passage at the beginning of the *Fundamental Principles of the Metaphysics of Morals* (tr.) T. K. Abbott (New York: Liberal Arts Press, Bobbs-Merrill Co., Inc., 1949), p. 12: "Even if . . . this will should wholly lack power to accomplish its purpose, if with its greatest efforts it should achieve nothing, and there should remain only the good will . . . then, like a jewel, it would still shine by its own light, as a thing which has its whole value in itself." Unfortunately, Kant does not really face the problem of what to say when it not only accomplished nothing good, but through bungling, accomplished a lot of harm. Cf. Nowell-Smith's fine discussion of this in *Ethics*, Ch. 17.

the kind of treatment to be given to a man who thinks that New York City is Sodom and Gomorrah incarnate and that the world would be morally cleansed by its disappearance, are quite different. But why should they be treated differently? I do not see how this can be answered intelligently, except by considering the probable outcomes of the different kinds of treatment.[16]

The fact, of course, is that all of our acts can be appraised by the principle of utility, including the acts of praising and blaming, of punishing, and of deliberating themselves. It would make no sense to blame people for what they did not intend to do, because "blaming" them is not going to enable them to avoid mistakes in the future. Only if it is going to do this, can we properly blame them.[17] Consider, for instance, a three-year-old child who does something he does not know is bad. If one blames him for doing so, it may well cause him to reflect before doing so in future; and if so, then the blame is to that degree justified. The same is true of people who are always going about doing evil with good intentions. Blame may well make them realize that something is wrong, and in the extreme case, it could cause them to adopt the principle, "Whenever I have good intentions, I should avoid acting on them." This policy might save them and everyone else a lot of trouble, in some cases. I do not see how any other view than a utilitarian one can account for the fact that we realize that such things do happen.

"Objective" and "Subjective"

It is plausible to say that 'wrong' is sometimes used in a sense equivalent to 'morally blameworthy' or 'reprehensible' in a sense which implies the propriety of disapproval of the agent for his deed.

---

[16] Further discussion of this is found in the following section; also Ch. VI ff.

[17] This has been noted by Bentham, Mill, Sidgwick, and Smart, among others. Brandt's recent article, "Toward a Credible Form of Utilitarianism," in Castañeda-Nakhnikian (ed.), *Morality and the Language of Conduct,* will be discussed further below. It is surprising how little they make of it; and it is unfortunate that in the case of Smart, for example, the use made of it is sometimes wrong-headed. Smart holds that a utilitarian might be justified in advocating some other moral theory on the ground that the time isn't ripe for its reception. (Cf., *Outline*, p. 36, for example.) Perhaps this is not wrong-headed, but it is certainly misleading.

Now, if utilitarianism is understood as a theory about right and wrong actions in this sense, I believe it is indefensible in all its forms. For we have good reason to think that whether an act is wrong in this sense depends in part on such things as whether the agent sincerely believed he was doing his duty, whether the temptation to do what he did was so strong that only a person of very unusual firmness of will would have succeeded in withstanding it . . . If whether an act is wrong depends in part on any one of these factors, then it is hard to see how the utilitarian thesis that rightness or wrongness is in some sense a function of utility can be correct.[18]

This passage by R. B. Brandt may be taken as typical of this type of criticism of the utilitarian view. Brandt goes on to suggest that a utilitarian-like view, which he elaborates in the essay from which the above is taken, may nevertheless be acceptable as a theory of right and wrong in what he calls the "objective" sense. It is this sense, I have argued, that one *must* employ when considering what to do (and which is the basic sense for ethical predicates). When one is trying to make a decision, one is not in a position to "blame" or "praise" himself for what he is about to do, because that is what he is trying to decide. Neither can he excuse himself for having an inadequate sense of right and wrong, because he is supposed to be exercising it at that time, and then, if he suspects himself of an inadequacy, to be trying to rectify it; he cannot excuse himself because he was provoked, since his question is whether or not to respond, and if so, in what way, to whatever provocations there are.[19] According to the utilitarian view, he ought to determine which of the actions open to him would produce the most value, as measured by utility in the sense we developed in Chapter III, and then do that (subject to the qualifications elaborated below). One could appraise the value of an earthquake, or an accident, in the same way, of course. One earthquake is worse than another if it kills more people than the other, causes more suffering and property damage, and so on, just as the Nazi regime was worse than the Mussolini regime because it caused the deaths of more people, more suffering, more property damage, and so on.

Now, whether there are two *senses* of 'wrong,' as Brandt's

[18] Brandt, "Toward a Credible Form of Utilitarianism," in Castañeda-Nakhnikian, *Morality and the Language of Conduct*, p. 111.
[19] Sartre's "Existentialism" seems largely an inflation of this point.

passage implies, is a difficult and disputed question. It is certainly true that we make appraisals of right and wrong for different purposes, and that such appraisals seem inappropriate in some contexts, but not in others. For example, it would be odd to say that an earthquake did something "wrong," even if its effects were the same as those of a crime wave, where we would say that the criminals had indeed done wrong. This certainly suggests that the sense of blaming is intimately connected with the use of 'wrong'; but it also suggests that there isn't any "objective" sense of 'wrong' at all. On the other hand, 'good' and 'bad,' 'worse' and 'better' apply equally to earthquakes and human acts. This suggests that the vocabulary of evaluation (as Sesonske[20] calls it), or the "teleological" vocabulary (as Nowell-Smith[21] calls it), could be reserved for the "objective" sense and the vocabulary of "obligation," or the "deontological" vocabulary (as they are respectively called by the same authors), could be reserved for the "subjective" sense.

But this will not quite do, either. When we appraise characters, as opposed to acts, plainly the "subjective" considerations about intentions and so forth are relevant, and yet 'right' and 'wrong' don't apply while 'good' and 'bad' do. There is nothing for it but to proceed slowly, and to explain each set of cases in turn, without hoping too much for a systematic vocabulary.

To begin with, there is obviously a connection between "subjective" and "objective" uses. In the ordinary course, if I say to Jones, "That was very wrong," in reference to his action, I am indeed blaming him; but, I am blaming him because of what he did. Obviously, my sentence on such occasions normally has both the "objective" and the "subjective" senses. Saying to Jones that what he did was wrong blames him, and indicates that there was a reason for blaming him, viz., a reason of a moral kind. Moreover, the fact that what he did was wrong "objectively," if it occurs to Jones retrospectively, will very often of itself constitute a retrospective blaming. It does so when the agent realizes that he could have avoided the act if, for example, he had been thinking what he was doing at the time.

Whether or not we should call these two functions of ethical

[20] Alexander Sesonske, *Value and Obligation* (New York: Galaxy Books, Oxford University Press, 1964).
[21] Nowell-Smith, *Ethics*, p. 223 and elsewhere.

terms distinct "senses" of those terms, we can at least give a utilitarian account of why the difference is called for. The reason is not far to seek. The clue to the matter is that the principle of utility may be used to appraise any act whatever, including acts of praising and blaming, criticizing and censuring. Now, the "subjective" senses or functions of ethical terms in which, as Brandt says, they "imply blame," are clearly performative. If I tell somebody, "What you did was wrong," I am (normally) blaming him, and this is an act of mine. What considerations, now, are relevant in trying to decide whether to blame him? In particular, whether to blame him, as opposed to non-emotively informing him that he could have done better (for instance), or keeping quiet and forgetting it? I propose that we can use the principle of utility to decide this, and that doing so will show why considerations about the person's intentions, the state of his knowledge, the degree of temptation to which he was subjected, the degree of psychological pressure under which he was operating, and so forth, are relevant.

The basic consideration in all this, as urged above, is that the purpose of ethics is to guide action. What does this mean? Consider the difference between getting someone to do something by giving him a drug, by hypnotizing him, by threatening to put him in jail if he doesn't, by offering him a reward if he does, by commanding him to, by telling him to, by requesting him to, by suggesting that he do it, or by reasoning him into doing it. These are all different ways of controlling or influencing behavior. Corresponding to these differences, there are differences in the subjects whose behavior we are trying to control. (Notice that it might be our own; I am speaking generally here.) If a person is in a foaming rage, the last several methods are unlikely to be available. On the other hand, if he is perfectly calm, knows just what he's doing, and speaks your language, then several of the first methods listed will be inappropriate. Why? Because they cause the subject much more trouble than the later ones, in general, and also because they are, in a sense, not likely to *work*. Obviously, the Principle of Utility calls for the use of that method which will cause the subject the least amount of harm, discomfort, pain, damage, loss, etc. If he is a reasonable man, and I request him to do something, then he will do it if it's a reasonable request. Suppose that it's a request which I believe to be sanctioned by the principle of utility. If he regards the principle of utility as a reasonable principle, then if he agrees that it is sanctioned by that principle, he will want to perform the act in question. In that case, resorting to force, blame, or other means are unnecessary, therefore, their use would be wrong.

Now, consider a person who has just done something wrong, and suppose that we have reason to suspect that he didn't know it was wrong. We should point out to him that it was wrong, so as to put him on guard against doing that kind of thing in future. Blame is out of place, because it's more than is needed (so far as we can see) to correct his behavior. Suppose, however, that though he knew it was wrong, he couldn't help it. In this case, blame is out of place, but not because it's more than is needed: it's because it wouldn't do any good. If he couldn't help it, then in future cases of the same sort he won't be able to help it either, and the fact that his ears are ringing with the scolding we gave him last time will not succeed in preventing him from doing it again. This mental pain will be quite useless. What we need to do is to go into the circumstances and try to remove the compelling factors. Thus, if he did it because Al Capone was threatening him with death, we should go out and round up Al Capone. If he did it because there was a landslide and he was making a frantic effort to escape, we shall advise him to move to a safer area or to put up a retaining wall, or we shall conclude that it was just an unfortunate accident.

Suppose he did it because he thought he was perfectly justified, though in fact he wasn't. Now, a utilitarian is someone who believes that actions are justified by their utility; obviously, he is not someone who believes that we ought not to perform actions that are justified. We are not saying, "Never mind whether the act is justified: look only to its utility." This would be perfectly perverse.[22] Thus, if the individual thinks that it is justified, and that is why he did it, then there is no sense in blaming him,

[22] Cf., for instance, H. D. Aiken, "Moral Reasoning," in *Reason and Conduct*, p. 100. He remarks that the "ordinary utilitarian would have to disallow the claims of justice except insofar as the obligation not to act unjustly is derivable from that to maximize happiness or reduce misery." This is highly tendentious, since it carries weight only if the utilitarian can't derive the whole of the obligations of justice from his principle. Aiken, like so many others, treats it as self-evident that the utilitarian cannot do this. But I propose to do just this, in Ch. VI below.

just like that. For we want people to do what is justified, and
he thought he was justified. What we have to do is to consider
whether to blame him for thinking that what he was doing was
justified. And this is quite a different matter from blaming him
for what he did.[23] It might be a great deal less, or it might be a
great deal more than that. If the act was wrong, but not seriously wrong, whereas his justification was seriously, horribly
wrong, then blaming him for thinking badly in a fairly strong
tone of voice might be called for. It is called for because that
type of thinking could lead to much worse actions in future.

However, suppose that although his ethical thinking is shock-
ing, nevertheless there has been a lot of it. He is, let us imagine,
a thoughtful but misguided Existentialist, or even a theorist for
some fantastic fascist "ethics." This is an extreme case, and
there might be no hope; but if there is hope, then certainly the
proper thing to do, if we have the time and means, is to sit down
and reason with him. For if utilitarianism is a truly reasonable
philosophy, and his is really unreasonable, then we ought to be
able to show him this, if his mind is in working order. We shall
have to go into the material of Chapter IX with him, perhaps.

In brief: blaming people, criticizing them, ordering them,
and the like, are all ways of influencing people's courses of action. They are all, therefore, means which should be avoided
unless justified by overriding utilities. On the Principle of Utility, it follows that we should use the method which causes the
least harm in the form of mental or physical distress. Therefore,
we should inflict just that degree of blame which is necessary
to get the individual's behavior in line, and the kind of blame
which will do the job. Moral praise and blame occupy a limited,
but extremely important, spectrum of the methods of influencing
people's behavior. What is limited about them and what is important about them are due to the same thing, namely, that they
are verbal, "rational" methods. If I accost someone with words
in order to change his behavior, I am using a method which
won't work unless he is rational to some degree. There is no use
blaming mountains, because they don't understand the concept
of blame (nor anything else). There is a kind of "blame" which

[23] Baier, *Moral Point of View*, pp. 143–47.

works for horses and dogs, but not for mosquitos; and there is a kind of blame which works for people, because they are more intelligent than horses and dogs. Finally, we get to the point where a mere remark or proposition uttered without heat or fury, and indeed, one that gives something close to pleasure in a rational agent, is quite sufficient. Being able to sit down and coolly reflect on one's own behavior, without great agonies of conscience, indulgence in neurotic self-reproach or "existential anxiety," and still to effect important changes in one's future behavior by that means, is the mark of the rational being from the point of view of practice. The language of ethics is the language which such a person employs at its best. The principle of utility explains why we should employ that language in appraising the conduct of fully rational people who know what they are doing, whereas we must resort to successively harsher or cruder or more psychologically dynamic methods with other people, or, in the extreme case, with animals or even inanimate objects. The latter we just push around without a care for what they think, because they don't. The former are beings we do care for, morally, and therefore we want to use the least unpleasant methods with them.

This account also shows how absurd certain of the controversies about "free will" become in ethical contexts. The reason for using one or another kind of blame, in reference to this or that aspect of a person's activity, has to do with the likelihood that it will, in fact, bring his behavior into line with the requirements of morality, as opposed to the amount of disutility their use will cause. This involves consideration of "responsibility." At no point is there any sense in trying to determine whether the subject's behavior—and remember, this includes one's own behavior when one is appraising it—was or was not "caused" at all.[24]

Indeed, no decision on the subject of whether human behavior is predictable in principle or not, or whether some of it is gov-

---

[24] See Smart, *Outline*, p. 39. "The 'Act' utilitarian will quite consistently reply that the notion of *the* responsibility is a piece of metaphysical nonsense and should be replaced by 'Whom would it be useful to blame?'" It is better to say: The notion of who is responsible is the notion of whom it would be useful to blame. This view is well argued by Nowell-Smith, *Ethics*, Chs. 19–20.

erned by chance, is required for ethical purposes. In every case, we have only to look at the facts. Some behavior is apparently random and unpredictable (so far as we can see, at present), and one has to allow for this. We can, by the way, "predict the unpredictable," to put it paradoxically. Certainly many or most of us have had the experience of setting out to do one thing and finding ourselves doing quite another, and learning to avoid situations where we might find ourselves behaving quite randomly or irrationally, if the random or irrational behavior in question is likely to lead to harm. It is equally obvious that what a person thinks about his behavior often makes a difference to it. This has nothing to do with "metaphysics," but is a matter of plain observation, as Locke and Hume correctly pointed out.

This last point, incidentally, is the reason why fantasies about universes of people who are always trying to do the right thing but always fail are indeed "fantastic."[25] Beings who are unable to control their actions in the light of their beliefs cannot develop a language of ethics, for then it would be completely unteachable. If people did not frequently succeed in altering their behavior in the light of their beliefs, then the point of having a language of ethics would be lost, and they would be just as well off not having one as having one. In that circumstance, they not only would not try to develop one (if they were capable of "trying," which they obviously would not be), but they would be perfectly justified in not developing one.

Implications for the theory of punishment are readily available from the above account, and fortunately, are to some extent being put into practice today as well. In particular, this account emphasizes the continuity between procedures of criminal justice, such as incarceration, fining, probation, and capital punishment, and those of the psychiatric profession, right on down to abstract moral philosophy. A further advantage is the naturalness with which an account of the role of rules follows. The precise way in which rules are justified, the degree and limits of the justification, and the type of rules which can be justified, will be discussed below. But the general consideration is clear: a rule is promulgated, taught, or otherwise put into circulation

[25] Nowell-Smith, *Ethics*, p. 250.

in order to enable people to anticipate (and keep track) of occasions when blame would be in order and when it would not.
If, as I have urged, the essential feature of the language of morals is that it is designed to influence the behavior of rational
beings by giving them reasons for various courses of conduct,
then the purpose of such language is defeated if a rational agent
cannot predict when predicates of praise and blame will be applicable and when they will not. If we were all calculating ma-
chines and could appraise our actions in the light of the Principle of Utility with no reference to rules, then moral rules
would indeed be useless. Later, I shall show that this does not
apply to rules of games, contracts, implementational rules, and
many others.

To some theorists, talk of ethical predicates as essentially stimulative or performative is repugnant, or even appears absurd. Of
course, it is silly to suppose that in holding some general moral
belief (e.g., that murder is wrong), I am here and now addressing
commands, injunctions, and criticisms, to all murderers and
would-be murderers past, present, and future, and in all portions
of the universe.[26] This does not mean that an essentially different
account of the uses of these expressions is called for. Surely what
we mean when we use these expressions in general formulae is
simply that on all occasions when anyone is confronted with an
opportunity to issue such injunctions, criticisms, blame, and so
forth, he would be justified in doing so. In short, that we have
reason to do these things. But reasons for doing some of them
are different from those for doing others, as I have taken pains
to point out in the foregoing account. In some circumstances,
the appropriate thing to say is "That would be very wrong;
don't do it!"; in others, "That's O.K., but wouldn't this be even
better?" The meaning of a general moral principle, therefore,
is logically connected with the meaning of particular second-
person uses on specific occasions. And since all evaluative language, as theorists have recently argued, is reason-backing language[27] (i.e., carries with it the implication that there reasons

[26] Cf., Wilfrid Sellars, "Imperatives, Intentions, and 'Ought,'" in
Castañeda-Nakhnikian, *Morality and the Language of Conduct*, p. 180.
[27] See Baier, *Moral Point of View*. Also, A. E. Murphy, *The Theory of
Practical Reason* (La Salle, Ill.: Open Court Publishing Co., 1965).

licensing the use of the particular performative being employed), it follows that this relation is symbiotic. Use on particular occasions of moral predicates in a performative manner depends for its logical legitimacy on the supposition by the user of the existence of general reasons; but the general reasons, in turn, are reasons *for* the corresponding stimulative use of language.

I would argue for the further link between the stimulative use of language and stimulation of a non-verbal kind, by actual use of force. The strongest ethical predicates, I shall be suggesting below, may well have their force just because they suggest the appropriateness of the use of punishment or forcible restraint or stimulation. A rational agent can react to the verbal indication that punishment would be in order just as much as to an actual punishment; and indeed, the measure of his rationality as a practical agent is the degree to which (given that he allows the reasonableness of the particular moral judgment being addressed to him, whether by himself or others) he is able to react to these intellectual proddings without having to wait for physical proddings to set him in motion (or restrain him from moving).

Once we understand the essentially performative nature of ethical language, on the one hand, and its connection with reasons on the other, we are in a position to understand how the utilitarian theory is not confined to giving merely an account of the "objective" sense of ethical terms. Indeed, we are able to see why it is misleading to think of the "objective" and the "subjective" as essentially different meanings or senses of ethical words. Unless we make the mistake of literally identifying the "objective sense" of ethical expressions with their so-called "cognitive meanings" (and thus of lapsing into just that kind of naturalism which it was a chief accomplishment of ethics in the first half of this century to refute), we shall have to admit that the differences of dramatic situation[28] due to our remoteness or propinquity to the occasions when direct stimulatory usage is possible do not alter the basic meanings of these expressions. The relevance of "subjective" factors of the kind we have been

[28] John Dewey's theory of "dramatic rehearsal" is perhaps relevant here; cf., *Human Nature and Conduct* (New York: Modern Library, 1930), p. 190.

118

discussing becomes clear when one reflects on these same stimu-latory or "performative" functions of ethical language.

In sum, it seems to me that the scruples of Brandt and others on the supposed inability of utilitarianism to account for the "subjective" senses of ethical terms are unjustified. They are due to failure to distinguish between appraisals of the acts to which moral predicates are in the first instance applied, and appraisals of acts of criticizing, blaming, praising, and so forth. Once we make this important distinction, it rapidly becomes evident why the agent's intentions, motives, state of information, psycho-logical pressures, and so on, become relevant on the utilitarian view.

CHAPTER V

Tasks and Methods

Tasks

Thus far, we have been concerned with matters of formulation, and with presumed challenges to the utilitarian view in general. In this and the following three chapters, we turn to what might be called internal matters, which are really the most vital ones: that is, to the utilitarian analysis and defense (insofar as defense is necessary), of the general principles and rules which form the corpus of "common sense morality." Of course, this is a program which can lead into indefinite complexity of detail. Inevitably, we must be rather general and sketchy in our considerations of these matters. But I do hope to consider all of the main questions which have been thought to raise special problems for utilitarian theory.

Before going into these vital questions, however, it is necessary to discuss certain general methodological questions internal to utilitarianism. The present chapter will deal with these. Since our discussions of the problems we shall consider mostly take the form of defending specific rules or principles on the basis of the Principle of Utility, we shall have to make clear what this involves. This might be thought to raise no problems, were it not for the rise to prominence in recent years, of "Rule" utilitarianism, which some have thought a viable method for avoiding the absurdities of classical utilitarianism. On this view, considerations of utility are fundamentally of a different level than considerations of conformity to rules or principles. According to a variant view (or perhaps a view fundamental to the whole approach, depending on one's understanding of it), the basic consideration is not what would happen if I were to do this, but rather, what would happen if *everyone* were to do it. Something which may, or may not, be viewed as still another variant is what might be called the "logical" view. According to this view, certain rules are logically constitutive of the obligations which they are thought to specify, of which promising and game-like rules are the main examples. We shall study the first two views in the sections below, and take up the third in Chapter VI, because of its close connection with the subject of that chapter.

It is possible, even without recourse to the fundamental modifications which rule-utilitarianisms involve, to make mistakes of principle in applying utilitarianism. Some dangers of this kind will be outlined in the fourth section. To round out the general topics internal to utilitarian theory, I shall develop in the fifth section the general distinction between predicates of moral obligation and those of moral evaluation which, I believe, is vital to satisfactory application of the utilitarian principle. It is fair to say that the most serious objections to utiltarianism have to do with its account of justice and obligation. We have seen some reasons for this in Chapter III, above. In order to be able to understand and to deal with these objections, we must make a distinction of the kind in question.

In the succeeding three chapters, I have divided the main questions in the following manner. Chapter VI concerns what various authors, including Mill, call "duties of perfect obligation." This topic divides into two general departments, according to whether the duties in question are "natural" or "conventional." Utilitarians are concerned here with the justification of punishment, and the justification of the type of rules mentioned above as the third variant of rule-utilitarianism. Chapter VII is devoted wholly to the subject of distribution, which also has been thought by many philosophers to be the main sticking-point of utilitarianism. I append to this a brief discussion of the subject of "self and others," which seems to me to be the fundamental source of the troubles about distribution. Finally, in Chapter VIII, I shall take up the subject often described under the heading of "imperfect obligations," which in the view developed there will be argued to be duties "of society" in a sense to be defined. These include, especially, the area of relief of suffering and the provision of conditions under which people can provide for their own advancement. The second portion is what I will suggest is the completely non-obligatory, "sheer benevolence." In this area are those occasions on which we can do good to people who are not in a state of need, and to whom we have no obligations of any distinctive type. This will complete our general survey of morality, insofar as the adequacy of utilitarianism to account for it is seriously in question.

Having, as I hope, overcome the main obstacles on the score of adequacy, we will take up, in Chapter IX, the problem of whether, and if so how, we can "prove" that we ought to accept the principle of utility.

Rule-Utilitarianism

When a person is asked to believe that this morality *derives* its obligation from some general principle round which custom has not thrown the same halo, the assertion is to him a paradox; the supposed corrollaries seem to have a more binding force than the original theorem; the superstructure seems to stand better without, than with, what is represented as its foundation.[1]

In these observations, Mill has represented what is doubtless the chief motivating force behind the view now commonly known as "Rule Utilitarianism." All sorts of anomolous consequences are thought to follow from the assumption that on each particular occasion on which we act, we are to be guided solely by the utility of any choice; and yet it is allowed that there is, after all, utility in the practice of telling the truth, keeping one's promises, and refraining from murder, theft, and so forth; and so a compromise is arrived at, according to which we must distinguish between the supreme Principle of Utility, and the secondary principles (or "rules"; though accounts vary as to the precise significance of 'principle' versus 'rule'), such as that of promise-keeping. It is held that the relation between these, and

[1] Mill, *Utilitarianism*, pp. 24–25.

123

between the secondary rules and particular acts, is some such as the following:

(A) A particular action is justified as being right by showing that it is in accord with some moral rule. It is shown to be wrong by showing that it transgresses some moral rule.
(B) A moral rule is shown to be correct by showing that the recognition of that rule promotes the ultimate end.[2]

Without going too far into niceties of interpretation, it is worth observing that this formulation has some essential obscurities, obscurities which are, in fact, present in all accounts of this theory. For example, what is it for a "moral rule" to "exist?"[3] How much does it take for there to be *one* "moral rule?" Both of these questions raise serious and perhaps unanswerable problems in the theory of this kind of rule-utilitarianism. Instead of pressing these, we shall go first to what seem to me the fundamental objections to any "Rule" utilitarianism of the sort broadly characterized by Urmson. In order to bring these to bear, let us turn to the recent account of Professor Brandt, whose thought-

---

[2] This is half of the account found in J. O. Urmson's article, "The Interpretation of the Philosophy of J. S. Mill," p. 35. Urmson believes that his account describes what Mill was actually advocating, and that the "act-utilitarian" account is a distortion. He adds two conditions to those mentioned in my text, one to the effect that "Moral rules can be justified only in regard to matters in which the general welfare is more than negligibly affected," and another to the effect that "Where no moral rule is applicable, the question of the rightness or wrongness of particular acts does not arise, though the worth of the actions can be estimated in other ways." Neither of these additions affects my discussion of the main points. As to the historical question, I once believed that Urmson was right about Mill's views, but I now think that he is wrong, for substantially the reasons advanced by J. B. Schneewind (ed.) in the introduction to J. S. Mill, *Ethical Writings* (New York: Collier Paper Edition, The Macmillan Co., 1965), p. 34. Needless to say, I do not accept the criticisms of "act-utilitarianism" itself offered by either Urmson or Schneewind. The bibliography on "rule-utilitarianism" has by now become quite extensive.
[3] This question is raised properly in B. J. Diggs' "Rules and Utilitarianism," *American Philosophical Quarterly* (January, 1964), pp. 32–44. This article also contains an extended and subtle analysis of various types of rules. (The criticisms which Diggs believes to be supported by the distinctions he makes do not seem to merit special discussion. They are being answered by implication both above and in the discussion of promises in Ch. VI.)

ful labors on behalf of "Rule" utilitarianism are recorded in a recent paper, "Toward a Credible Form of Utilitarianism."[4]

After explaining the usual "catastrophic objections" to which "act-utilitarianism" is (he thinks) prone, Brandt proceeds to point out a difference in the programs of various "rule utilitarian ians." We must distinguish between those who hold that the cri terion of right and wrong is conformity to an ideal set of rules (i.e., a set obedience to which would ideally promote utility, whether or not the rules are presently in existence), and those who hold that the criterion of right and wrong is obedience to the rules, or some of the rules, which are presently observed or at least regarded by "conscientious persons" as worthy of ob servance. The first party can be disposed of quickly, for the ideal set of rules from the utilitarian point of view would contain just one basic rule: the principle of utility itself.[5] There are serious difficulties with the other party's view, too. Clearly, we don't believe that all existing sets of moral rules are actually good ones from the point of view of utility. Utilitarian or no, we must allow for the possibility of improvements in our moral practices.

Brandt proposes to fix this up by appealing to rules, the recog nition of which would have the best consequences. The set of rules in question would be limited to those "learnable" by "peo ple of ordinary intelligence."[6] We must allow for the fact that people are not perfect; thus, we must restrict these rules to those practiceable by people of "ordinary conscientiousness."[7] In par ticular, we must allow exceptions in cases of societies which have already "fairly decided moral convictions."[8]

There is also need to teach some second-order rules which would resolve conflicts of first-order rules. Finally, it would perhaps be necessary to allow for the possibility of different

---

[4] In Castañeda-Nakhnikian (eds.), *Morality and the Language of Conduct*, p. 123.

[5] It might be said that this would be true only in a population equipped with lightning moral calculators. The point is, however, that secondary rules would have no *independent* weight. (See the ensuing discussion.)

[6] R. B. Brandt, "Toward a Credible Form of Utilitarianism," in Castañeda-Nakhnikian (eds.), *Morality and the Language of Conduct*, p. 123.

[7] *Ibid.*, p. 125ff.

[8] *Ibid.*, pp. 129.

rules being the best for different societies, depending on temperament.[9]

Brandt evidently regards all of these restrictions as restrictions in *principle* on ordinary act-utilitarianism. But why must we so regard them? Obviously, an act-utilitarian will agree that if an individual cannot learn to apply the principle of utility without compromise, then he should do the best he can by learning a "code" of rules of the sort Brandt describes. This will also, no doubt, result in making allowances for different societies, and perhaps even for previously held moral convictions in the way indicated in principle in Chapter IV above. In order to explain the difference from utilitarianism in principle, let us consider how the "Brandtian" set of rules would have to be applied. We will concentrate on a particular example from our own "society," the rule of stopping at red lights.

Most of us have experienced the aggravation of sitting and waiting for a red light to change, when there is obviously no traffic coming from right or left. Suppose an act-utilitarian were to come along and propose that the law ought to be modified so as to permit people to proceed through red lights when this is the case. How would a "rule-utilitarian" react? If he is somehow different "in principle" from the "act-utilitarian," then presumably he might say something of the following sort: because stopping at red lights is "in general" conducive to utility, *for this* reason, we should always stop at red lights. If he says this, however, how is he a utilitarian at all? The reason why stopping at red lights is useful "in general" (in view of the fact that "green" is designated as the "go" light), is that it prevents a lot of accidents—chaos, in fact. Well, it does so when there is traffic. But obviously, it does not do anything of the sort when there is no traffic. So, of the infinite number of possible rules on this subject, surely the one supported by the principle of utility is the one that says you should stop at red lights if there is traffic from right or left (or turning traffic from straight ahead). Why not use this rule?

It would surely be irrational to argue in the way I have made my "in principle" rule-utilitarian argue above. What he, Brandt,

---

[9] *Ibid.*, p. 130–38.

and any sensible person would of course say is that they doubt that the average person in the community would have sense enough to look carefully before going through the red light. And this *might* be true. But how do we know? Have there been tests? As a matter of fact, a few places have made some steps in the direction of greater liberality without serious consequences. In Ontario, one may turn right on a red light if the way is safe; in Kansas, one may proceed through the light after midnight. What will the genuine utilitarian say? He will surely say that we ought to run tests to see whether the most liberal rule will work; and if not, then whether the next most liberal rule will work, and so on. But he will do more than this. He might claim also that even if a lot of people in the community are too stupid to make the liberal rule work (which is very doubtful), the "rigid" rule should still be "selectively reinforced" (as many laws actually are, often with quite satisfactory results). If, for example, after stopping a driver who has just proceeded through a red light when the way was clear, a policeman were to inspect the man's license, and upon seeing that the driver has had no black marks on his license for the past year or two, were to say, "O.K., you may proceed," would any disastrous consequences ensue? It's hard to see why they would. But the point is, we could try it and see. That is the trouble with Brandt's modifications if they are modifications in principle. Their net effect is inevitably to ossify prevailing moral rules, to inhibit experimentation in the interests of the general happiness. This is, in substance, the criticism of such writers as Smart, who accuse the "rule-utilitarianisms" of "rule-worship." These criticisms are justified.

It will be useful to summarize these reflections in a more abstract way. The position under consideration is that rules are justified by their utility, and acts only by their conformity to the rules in question. But what does it mean to say that a rule is justified by its utility? It can mean nothing but that actions of the type prescribed by the rule are useful. Now, if there is reason to suppose that every act, insofar as it falls under the rule, is useful *ipso facto*, then the rule will be justified well enough as a *prima facie* rule. As we shall see, the principal moral rules are precisely of this kind. What we want to know is, what if less than all of the acts in question have this property? In that case, the rule-utilitarian is saddled with the argument that because say, 95 per cent of acts of type F are useful, *therefore* we ought *always* to perform acts of type F (even when it can be foreseen that they will not be useful). It is essential to see that the "Rule" utilitarian must, if he is to be distinguished from an act-utilitarian, say "therefore" and not merely "and," in the statement of the argument. For this is precisely what makes him a rule-utilitarian. Rules, according to him, are justified by their utility, but acts are not. So there must be acts which are not useful which are justified by rules, in order to make his position logically distinguishable from "Act" utilitarianism. After all, it is the "Rule" utilitarians themselves who insist that it is distinguishable; how else could they put it forth as a solution to problems insoluble by act-utilitarianism? Yet it is justification of the rules via their utility which *makes* the position "utilitarian." Thus, the "Rule" utilitarian, if his position is to be, as he says it is, a plausible means of escaping the supposed objections to act-utilitarianism, is absolutely committed to both of the above. From these two conditions, that there are non-useful acts which are justified by rules, and that these rules in turn are justified by their utilities, it follows logically that the rule-utilitarian is committed to saying, as a basic moral position, that if *most* acts of type F are useful, then we ought *always* to perform acts of Type F, for at least some replacements of the predicate 'F.' In my view, this of itself is a sufficient refutation of this position. How can it possibly be maintained that every member of a set of acts is justified whenever 90 per cent of them have some property? Obviously, it cannot. The would-be rule-utilitarian must find some other conditions which supplement this argument. But what could these other conditions possibly be? Either they are of the general kind mentioned by Brandt, which are shown above to be further utilitarian conditions quite acceptable to the act-utilitarian, or they are some other kind of irreducibly non-utilitarian conditions. And if they are the latter, then we ought to call a spade a spade, and the view what it is: a species of formalism.[10]

---

[10] Subsequently, this point also was pressed by Professor Joseph Margolis.

In our forthcoming considerations of justice, promise-keeping, and so forth, I shall try to show that the objections thought to hold against act-utilitarianism are due to various confusions, and if these arguments are successful, then we can dispense with the only motive for holding an obscure and essentially incoherent theory. Meanwhile, however, the variant[11] of rule-utilitarianism which makes essential appeal to the question of what might be called "hypothetical utilities" (that is "What would happen if everyone did so-and-so?") needs separate analysis.

"But What if Everyone Did That?"

Many of our public obligations are of a type where the expectable disutilities of defaulting are very small, taken one by one, and yet, if everyone were to default, the damage would be very great. Reflection on such cases gives rise to the thesis that the fundamental reason for regarding some course of action as an obligation is not a direct consideration of the consequences of failure in each case, but rather of what would happen if everyone behaved in this way? The most influential and acute advocate of this view is Professor Singer,[12] and since he has also written some very caustic things about utilitarianism, it is worthwhile for us to consider his view.

Singer says that all instances of the generalized argument form, which he calls the "Generalization Argument," namely that "If everyone were to do that, the consequences would be disastrous (or undesirable); therefore no one ought to do that"[13] are valid. This is equivalent, I believe, to asserting the principle, "It is wrong to do anything which is such that if everyone did that kind of thing, the consequences would be undesirable." Singer believes that this principle follows from two other prin-

[11] Frankena, incidentally, makes this view not a variant, but the very essence of "Rule" utilitarianism; *Ethics*, p. 30. I take it, though, that the contention that acts of type F are justified if they usually have good results is different from the contention that acts of type F are justified if there would be good results if everyone did them.

[12] See *Generalization in Ethics*.

[13] *Ibid.*, p. 4. (He qualified this statement with the restrictions noted below.)

ciples, namely, that if the consequences of doing x are undesirable, then one ought not to do x, and that "what is right (or
wrong) for one person must be right (or wrong) for any similar person in similar circumstances."[14] We must accept both of
these latter principles, but the Generalization Argument's validity does not follow from them, as has been pointed out by F. E.
Sparshott, among others.[15] The role of the second "principle"
will be considered in my final Chapter, and the role of the first,
the "principle of consequences," is of course dealt with throughout the present one. The question is, does the special consideration that *if* everyone were to do this, then the consequences
would be disastrous, have any independent moral weight? It is
of the greatest importance to distinguish carefully the sense in
which this is a "special" consideration. Of course, wherever it
is the case that if I were to do this, the consequences would be
undesirable, regardless of whether anybody else does or did or
would, the "principle of consequences" takes care of things by
itself. This principle is obviously supportable by utilitarians,
whereas Singer's is not, I think.

Singer claims that Mill unwittingly succumbed to the generalization view, for Mill says:

In the case of abstinences indeed—of things which people forbear to
do from moral considerations, though the consequences in the particular case might be beneficial—it would be unworthy of an intelligent agent not to be consciously aware that the action is of a class
which, if practiced generally, would be generally injurious, and that
this is the ground of the obligation to abstain from it.[16]

[14] *Ibid.*, p. 5, and pp. 63 ff.
[15] *Philosophical Review*, January, 1963, pp. 97–99. This amazingly lucid
review of Singer penetrates to the logical heart of the matter in several
paragraphs. It is now possible to point to a thorough treatment of generalized utilitarianism in David Lyons' new book, *Forms and Limits of Utilitarianism*, which was published after my treatment above was written.
(New York: Oxford University Press, 1965.) If any doubts remain about
the inefficacy of Singer's view and its relatives after reading my necessarily
brief account above, Mr. Lyons' book will certainly put them to rest. In
his final chapter, Lyons produces some criticisms of utilitarianism of his
own with which, needless to say, I am not in agreement. In any event,
it is too late to go into his views, except to say that I think they are discussed by implication in my treatment of Justice in Ch. VI.
[16] *Utilitarianism*, pp. 17–18.

Singer says that this is an "obvious appeal to the generalization argument,"[17] but this is an overstatement. It is hardly obvious, especially since Mill says in the very next sentence:

The amount of regard for the public interest implied in this recognition, is no greater than is demanded by every system of morals, for they all enjoin to abstain from whatever is manifestly pernicious to society.

It is difficult to say what an author of the first passage means if he holds it on the basis of the second. The fact that if everyone were to do x the consequences would be disastrous usually has some significance, as we shall see; and thus an "intelligent agent" does need to keep an eye open for this kind of case. Whatever Mill may have thought, we shall find reason to reject the Singerian thesis.

Singer's view is made difficult to assess (as all views are which make use of phrases such as "and all similar acts") because of his ingenious covering arguments against what otherwise might appear to be decisive counter-examples. For example, consider the objection, often raised against Kantian ethics,[18] that it would be disastrous if everyone were a postman, since we would all starve for lack of farmers to raise food. Singer points out that disastrous consequences would also ensue if no one were a postman. Whenever this is the case, Singer calls the argument "invertible," and argues that invertible generalization arguments are invalid. They require one to restrict the reference class of performers of the type of act in question.[19] The other restriction on the generalization argument is on those which involve "reiterability." An argument is reiterable if it relies for its force on the fact that something is done on a particular occasion, place, time, or by some particular person. "If everyone ate at six, the restaurant would be jammed; therefore, no one ought to eat at six." But the same is true of five, three, or any other hour, so

---

[17] Singer, *Generalization in Ethics*, p. 196.

[18] Wrongly, I think, for Kant's views have no particular connection with Singer's, in point of fact.

[19] Singer, *Generalization in Ethics*, pp. 72 ff.

the argument would show, if valid, that no one ought to eat at all. Thus, it is also invertible; so it is invalid.[20]

It is not as easy as Singer believes to apply these restrictions. We need not bother to try to interpret them precisely, for if Singer's view is to differ essentially from the utilitarian view, there must be some arguments which are both valid (neither invertible nor reiterable) and which give different results from the rule of consequences alone. I shall consider two cases which allegedly illustrate these properties.

One, which Singer apparently regards as valid,[21] is this one about voting: if everyone refused to vote, the consequences would be disastrous; therefore, I should vote. Another concerns walking on the grass in public places. If everyone were to walk on the grass, it would die and there would be no grass; therefore, I ought not to walk on the grass. Singer regards most of the standard moral rules, such as that against lying, as founded on the generalization argument. I will show that this is not so, since they can be defended with just the required degree of rigor by the straight utilitarian principle.

We may begin by considering the two specific examples above. In the first place, the one about voting is suspect. It simply is not true, in general, that citizens in a democracy have an "obligation" to vote. In countries like Russia, where the government is trying to impress the world with how "democratic" it is, the citizens do indeed have an "obligation" to "vote," in the sense that the government jolly well sees to it that they go to the polls. Also, while they're about it, they see to it that they vote for the right people. In a real democracy, as opposed to a sham one, the reason for voting is so that people can get the kind of government they want, and the method is to offer a choice, by voting, for one among a slate of supposedly differing candidates. If a citizen doesn't care which candidate wins, there is no reason why he should vote. And, if the citizen doesn't know the difference between the candidates, there is a good deal to be said for suggesting that he stay home and let people who do know what they're doing determine the fate of their

[20] *Ibid.*, pp. 81 ff.
[21] *Ibid.*, pp. 74, 75.

country. If everyone were indifferent to the kind of government he has, then there would be no reason for having a democracy rather than some other kind of government, and it
would also be impossible to have a democracy (or, any other
kind probably). So what?[22]

Now very often, people stay home in elections because they
are pretty sure that their man will be elected, or defeated, anyhow. If one can know for certain that one's man will be elected
or defeated regardless of how one votes, then the most obvious
reason for voting, namely to help elect the man you want,
doesn't apply. In that case, the reason for voting reduces the
considerations of the size of majority the winner gets. You
might vote just to put on a good showing for your man and
thus encourage him to run again; or, for example, pile up the
majority for your man (if he's winning) in order to increase
his popular mandate. On the other hand, you might want your
man to win, but just barely, so that he won't get overconfident.
In that case, you might have a reason for staying home. Considerations about what would happen if everybody did this,
that, or the other, are irrelevant. But considerations about what
the others are likely to do are definitely relevant. Moreover,
just because other people may be reasoning the same way you
do, the situation can be very unstable. If they all stay home
because they're sure he's going to win, of course he will lose.
That's why it matters whether you have good reason to suppose
your man will win. If your only reason is an intuitive hunch,

[22] A popular argument invoked against various policies, especially governmental ones, follows this form: "The policy so-and-so would lead
ultimately to X, which would be disastrous; therefore, it should be rejected." ("X" is often replaced by "Socialism" in the United States; no
doubt by "Capitalism" in Russia.) This argument is irrelevant unless "X"
has been shown to be a bad thing. If nobody voted, then democracy
would come to an end, of course. But in that event, presumably nobody
would care, in which case the fact that democracy would come to an
end is irrelevant. Incidentally, the argument is also irrelevant unless it can
be shown that the tendency of the policy to lead to "X" is uncontrollable.
In fact, it never is. Arguments from "tendency" are exactly parallel to
this: Do you want to go to Philadelphia? It's that way; but you mustn't
go that way, because if you keep going that way far enough, you'll
inevitably fall into the Atlantic and drown. (See "Some Dubious Utilities" below.)

then you'd better vote. Game-theoretic considerations are sometimes needed here, but the "generalization argument," as such, is not.

We proceed to the "keeping off the grass" example.[23] If everyone in town always cuts through this particular corner in the park, soon an ugly path will be worn there. So, should I walk across the corner at this particular time? One person's walking on the grass will make no difference at all, and neither will six. On the other hand, several dozen people walking on the grass all at once might do irreparable damage. What is the solution? To jump immediately to the conclusion that no one should cut the corner is simply irrational. It depends on many factors. The "Ideal" utilitarian solution is to let as many people cut the corner as is consistent with the good appearance of the grass and no more. (We are supposing that most of the townspeople care how the grass looks; the appearance of the grass is not intrinsically a moral value.) How shall we accomplish this?

Suppose, to begin with, that only a few people want to cut the corner. In that case, it is not necessary to do anything. There is no point in requiring them to refrain (although self-righteous, puritannical policemen would doubtless make them do so, if they had anything to say about it). But suppose everyone wants to? Then we have to consider ways and means. Questions of the distribution of utilities will enter in (and these again we will defer until Chapter VII). It is clear that we need some way of restricting the number of people who are allowed on the grass at any one time. The worst way to do it is flatly to require everyone to keep off. The sensible way is to consider how much trouble it would be to find a way of controlling the number. There are several possibilities. A rule posted, "Keep off if oc-

---

[23] These examples are employed also by Lyons and indeed, have a long history. Lyons' account is by all means the best and most thorough, however. His concept of "threshold" (which is obviously at work behind the scenes in my discussion) efficiently marks out the difference between these cases and the income-tax case discussed further on. (Cf., *Forms and Limits,* pp. 63 ff.) Also, the distinction between ordinary and "contributory" causation formulated by Henry West in "Act and Rule Utilitarianism" (unpublished Ph.D. dissertation, Department of Philosophy, Harvard University, 1964), pp. 141 ff. His idea is that we "assign to each participating act causal responsibility for a fraction of those collective consequences, even if there is a surplus of constituent acts."

cupied by more than twelve persons," is one way to do it. This might work if no particular twelve persons always hogged it to the exclusion of others who wanted to use it, and everyone in the town tended to obey such signs. But if it's a great deal of work to enforce it, some other system should be considered. We must remember that in order to make these systems workable, someone has to think of them, someone has to enforce them, and these have to be taken account here. If someone in the community just happens to love solving this kind of problem, then well and good; if not, someone would have to be paid to do it, and this is expensive.

There are many cases in which the trouble is that a lot of people want to do a certain thing, but only a limited number can do it without undesirable consequences. The utilitarian principle does not give us any reason for singling out any particular subgroup to be given permission over any others, assuming that they all want to do it. The consideration that some might want to do it more than others would, of course, give a reason for preferring those; but who is to decide which ones do want it more than others? Critics of utilitarianism somehow seem to find it self-evident that this consideration of who would be more pleased is completely unascertainable. Of course, if it is unascertainable, then we just have to assume that all have an equally strong desire for it, and then we shall have to settle it by chance. But it is often ascertainable. An obvious way to ascertain it is to charge admission, making the admission high enough so that just the right number are admitted, with the profits to go to the general welfare. But this will not be a true measure of desire if they have greatly different resources. The techniques of game-theory are available in this kind of situation, and of course they are of an eminently utilitarian lineage.[24] Many things will have to be taken into account, and if there is absolutely no way of ascertaining relevant differences, then one must resort to chance. They can draw lots, for example. (Critics here will want to know why we should give everyone equal

[24] J. J. C. Smart works out an interesting example (pp. 42–44 of the *Outline of Utilitarian Ethics*.) See also R. B. Braithwaite's *Theory of Games as a Tool for the Moral Philosopher* (New York: Cambridge University Press, 1955).

consideration, other things being equal. We shall take this up in Chapter VII, pausing only to note that the question, "Why should we treat people equally if there are no relevant differences between them?" is one which does not ordinarily reflect the good sense of anyone asking it.)[25]

The truth is, then, that there are a host of ways in which problems of this sort might be dealt with, and there is no way to—and no need to—lay down any particular rule about them, other than the principle of utility. The way to handle it is the way that does the best job all around, taking into account all interests that bear on the case. In no case does the consideration that it would be disastrous if everyone did this show, by itself, that no one ought to do it. It only shows that not everyone ought to do it, and thus, that some way of deciding who should do it and who shouldn't do it needs to be found. If not everyone wants to do it, we can ignore those who don't, and then the work of finding a sensible method begins. But it does not end. That is what I object to about Singer's view. What he recommends as a fundamental principle of reason is, in fact, irrational. If it would be disastrous if everyone did it, but not disastrous if a few did it, only a malevolent or unintelligent person could take this by itself as a reason for saying that no one should do it. And actually, Singer realizes this. He makes the important qualification that "If not everyone ought to act or be treated in a certain way, then no one ought to act or be treated in that way without a reason."[26] This phrase 'without a reason' is a weasel-phrase. To begin with, any statement of the form 'if P, then q' is true, if the proposition symbolized by 'q' is necessarily true. Surely, for any given way of treating a person, it could be argued that we ought not to treat him that way

[25] Nicholas Rescher, in "Choice Without Preference" in *Kant-Studien* (Cologne: 1959–60) argues cogently that if the reasons supporting two alternatives are exactly balanced, then it follows that random selection should be employed: "Random selection is the only reasonable procedure for making choices in the face of symmetric preference" (p. 170). This principle is a self-evident part of the logical apparatus with which we apply the Principle of Utility, and is, in that sense, independent of utilitarian considerations. But so is the Principle of Non-Contradiction, whose "independence" of the Principle of Utility has never been alleged as a ground for criticism of the latter.

[26] Singer, *Generalization in Ethics*, p. 31.

without a reason. It depends on how much one builds into the word 'reason,' and what sort of reasons he has in mind. If, for example, one uses a randomizing procedure to determine who should be treated that way, is that a reason, or isn't it? If it isn't, then Singer's principle is false, even with this qualification; for, as we have seen, there are some cases in which not everyone can engage in some activity without undesirable consequences, but quite a few people can, and the best way to decide who should be permitted to engage in it is by drawing lots. In the second place, it is clear that the word 'reason' has a moral flavor in this qualifying phrase, and wherever this happens, it is necessary to indicate what would constitute a suitable reason. This cannot be done by using Singer's principle itself, which shows already that it cannot be the most fundamental moral principle. This was true anyway because of the use of the word 'undesirable' in it, which calls for principles specifying what, for moral purposes, is to be rated as desirable or undesirable. Utilitarianism supplies all of these lacuna and also supplies the Principle of Consequences itself.

The cases, I suspect, in which the consideration "What would happen if everyone did that?" seem strongest are of a rather different kind than the "keep off the grass" case. In the latter, there would be no undesirable consequences at all if I (and no one else) walked on the grass; the undesirability of the consequences depends entirely on having a considerable number do it. But let us take the example of paying one's taxes. Suppose I owe the government just $25, and the total government budget is fifty billions of dollars. By comparison, my contribution isn't even a drop in the bucket, and the government won't miss it. Only if a great number of people—say fifty million or so—should fail to pay will it be noticed much. So why should I pay?

It is true, of course, that the other people who are paying the same amount have no more reason to pay than I do. So one might say that I would be unfair if I argued that I shouldn't pay but that they should. In a sense this is true, and this again brings up the question of distribution, which I will take up in Chapter VII below. But 'unfair' isn't necessary here. If their failure to pay would diminish utility precisely as much as mine, then they have exactly as much reason not to pay as I do, neither more

137

nor less. The question is, do I have any reason to pay? Unlike the "grass" case, the answer here is Yes. How much reason? As much as I owe. If I argue that it's just a pittance and the public won't miss it, the government, of course, can point out equally well that it's just a pittance and I won't miss it. If I will miss it, on the other hand, so will the public. I could say, "But they won't miss it as much as I." But how do I know that? Of course it is true that if the government doesn't find out about my cheating, then the public "won't miss it" in the sense that it won't find out that I haven't paid it. But it will miss it in the relevant sense, which is that it will have $25 less than it would if I had paid.

I can, of course—and should, on the principle of utility— question whether the government's policies are just, and if they are not, then what? Well, if the government's policies are literally unjust, to the extent that it had no right to demand my money in the first place, then I have absolutely no (moral) reason to pay the taxes, and in fact a very good reason for refusing to do so. The question is, then, on what basis to argue that they are unjust? The answer, naturally, is the utilitarian basis. The question of how to apply utilitarianism to the justification of governmental policies is a very big one, and it will not be possible to go into it here. But I presume that the relevance of questioning the justice of policies one is paying to support, as a condition of paying for them, can hardly be questioned. Included in the objects of question, of course, might be the method of assessing the taxes, as well as the substantive policies they are used to support.

That this kind of case should have been supposed to constitute a special problem for utilitarians is due to the supposition that we are to be permitted to weigh the harm of a proposed line of action against the benefit we derive from the satisfaction of our desire to inflict it. Once it is seen (as we shall see in Chapter VI) that we cannot do this, the only remaining question is whether nonpayment of taxes really does harm anyone. It does, on two counts. In the first place, the particular public service which is a little bit curtailed because of the unavailability of one's particular little bit of taxes is harmed. This is admittedly small, but it is not nonexistent. To say that my $25 is very trivial set beside the public's $100 billion is a red herring. For each of those hundred billion dollars is worth precisely $1 (i.e., the price of a lunch, a movie, a sack of flour for some needy person on welfare or of a titanium bolt that keeps some rocket from exploding, and so on). The same amount of money is worth exactly as much to the public as it is to me, neither more nor less. In the second place, by nonpayment I am harming the chap whose taxes are greater on account of it. This counts as a harm if I acknowledge the justice of the imposition of the tax in the first place. If I don't acknowledge it, then of course I must be able to show that it is unjust.

In short, we have a reason for not doing small harms to anyone, even where (as with taxes), the "anyone" is everyone. The reason is not that if everyone did it, the harm would be even greater, any more than that if one did a lot more of it, the harm would be greater. The reason is that one does precisely the amount that one does—in the present case, $25 worth. Given that it is justly exacted and justly used, one cannot complain that no one will be harmed, for someone will be harmed, as we have seen. The fact that they won't be harmed very much merely means that one's crime if one defaults isn't a very big crime. Of course, it's not a very big crime, unless you owe a very great deal. But a little crime is still a crime. And the fact that utilitarians refuse to call a spade anything but a spade, or to employ an inflated and mysterious defense when a small but sensible one is available instead, is to my mind not to be counted too serious a defect of character.

It is impossible, of course, to examine in detail each of the countless number of specific cases which a critic might use in support of Singer's thesis. But I trust that this is also unnecessary. Once it is seen that his thesis does not follow from the two true and important principles he thinks it follows from, and that it is not intuitively sound as it stands, a few examples will show in detail that the principle of consequences is by itself capable of doing whatever needs to be done. This should surely be enough to make it reasonable to suppose that the remaining cases will not derive any further benefit from Singer's principle.

In sum, there are two types of cases in which the Generalization Argument might seem to be of use. One is where literally no harm is done in the individual case, but a lot of harm might be done if everyone, or a lot of people, did the deed in question. In this type of case, what we ought to do is to permit as many people to do it as won't cause harm, and no more, employing the best system we can think of for deciding who should be able to indulge and who should not, employing game-theoretic considerations where useful, and doing it by lot in the extreme case. Here, the prohibiting of everyone from doing it, far from exemplifying in its purest form the operation of practical reason, would be simply irrational. In the other type of case, where the amount of harm done is simply a function of the number of people who do it, the reason why I shouldn't do it is because of the amount of harm my doing it would cause, including where applicable the amount of trouble I would cause the public in tracking me down, given that they have just reason for doing so. In neither case does the rule, "If it would be disastrous if everyone would do it, then I shouldn't do it," have anything as such to be said for it.[27] I conclude that the Generalization Argument is a bad one, and should not play any independent part in a rational system of ethics.[28]

Some Dubious Utilities

There is often a good deal of confusion as to just what we need to accomplish in the way of deduction of particular rules or principles from more general ones. A word of clarification is therefore in order.

A satisfactory deduction of rules and principles which are intuitively acceptable (in the sense outlined in Chapter I), must consist in showing that the kinds of acts mentioned in them are intrinsically right or wrong, good or bad, according to the wording of the intuitive principle, where 'intrinsically' is used

[27] Incidentally, what if it would be disastrous if just about 47 per cent of us did it, but not if many more or less did it? Such things could conceivably happen, and it is not clear what the Generalization Argument would have to say on the subject.
[28] The use of certain notions of "generalization" will be taken up in Ch. IX.

in the sense elaborated in Chapter II, under Formulation of Moral Principles. Let us put this more precisely. A particular kind of act (if one is a utilitarian) will be said to be "intrinsically" of moral value V if, and only if, it follows logically from the principle of utility, conjoined with the description of acts of that kind and appropriate definitions of the terms of 'V,' that such acts have moral value V, other things being equal. By 'other things being equal' we mean, of course, that they are of value V insofar as they are of that kind, though whether a particular case of that kind is of value V "on balance" will depend on what else is true of that case. A complete system will enable one to determine, in all cases, whether or not the other factors which may be present are "equal" in the required sense, and if they are not, how they affect the case. Whether or not one can arrive at a satisfactory decision in each case will, of course, depend on whether one can get all the facts, and this one often cannot do. However this may be, the task of the theorist is to show what factors to look for, and to produce some reasonably sound method of weighing the different factors to reach an over-all assessment. If we can show, for each major type of act which we are likely to run across, whether it is intrinsically good, bad, or indifferent, we shall have accomplished the first goal; and if we can arrange them in an order of precedence, then we shall have accomplished the second in a general way. Detailed work will, of course, always remain.

A type of defense of a common-sense principle which will not do, however, is one to which utilitarians have often resorted hitherto, namely, that of appealing to some vague apprehension of "upsetting the general confidence" in some practice. Professor Singer, in his chapter on "Moral Principles and the Principle of Utility,"[29] has put his finger on the defects of this kind of defense. There are two specific shortcomings of this sort of argument, and one which involves a matter of general principle. In the first place, as Singer says, to claim that every act of promise-breaking, for instance, has "led to bad consequences" of the required sort is "as a general proposition simply false. It suffices to point to cases of wrong acts that no one ever hears about."[30]

[29] Singer, *Generalization in Ethics*, Ch. VII.
[30] *Ibid.*, p. 196.

Appealing to general consequences, if they really are consequences in the sense explained in Chapter IV, is an empirical
matter. One simply cannot assert with any confidence that there
is really a general lowering of public confidence every time one
breaks a promise, even when it is found out, let alone when it
is not. The same goes for other examples besides promise-
keeping. If this is the way such practices must be defended, on
the utilitarian view, then of course they are indefensible. Fortunately, as I shall show, we can do better. The second shortcoming is that if such appeal to "secondary consequences" were
acceptable at all, it would prove far too much. For, as Singer says:

If these "secondary effects" apply in any case, they apply in all, and
if they show of any act that it is not really "useful," no matter how
useful it may appear apart from them, then they would show this of
every act. It would follow that every moral rule holds without exception, or that no rule ought ever to be broken, and this contradicts
the view that rules "cannot be so framed as to require no exceptions."[31]

This is a trifle overstated, since the utilitarian can still reply
that in a particular case if a moral rule conflicts with another
rule, then they cannot both be justified "without exception."
The principle of utility can be used to decide which takes
precedence. This, in fact, is what Mill does.[32] However, this
reply would not touch the main point, for whenever there is no
such conflict, the proffered justification would prove too much.
This objection really boils down to the complaint that such
appeal to "secondary consequences" is entirely too vague to be
plausible, and would never have been appealed to in the first
place, except as a dodge.

The third point, which is perfectly general, is that appeal to
secondary consequences, such as the lowering of general confidence in a rule, is wrongheaded in principle. Why should we
pay any attention to the rule in the first place? The argument
that following the rule is "generally" useful is no argument at
all. It would show simply that we ought to educate the public
to see the difference between the cases in which following the

[31] Singer, *Generalization in Ethics*, p. 210.
[32] Mill, *Utilitarianism*, p. 24. "If utility is the ultimate source of moral
obligations, utility may be invoked to decide between them."

rule is useful and those in which it isn't, and not to be alarmed about cases in which the rule is broken in a useful manner.

It is fair to say that often the utilities supposedly associated with certain types of acts specified in moral rules are conjured up for the occasion by the would-be defender, as Singer charged. Appeal to the "general confidence" is a case in point. But whether or not the existence of the supposed utility in question is dubious, a question of principle needs to be raised about the status of the alleged utilities. Consider, for example, the general confidence in promises. Why should it be thought to be a bad thing, to have this confidence upset? If it is, then evidently this presupposes that the confidence in question is merited. But if it is merited, then this in turn presupposes, it would seem, that there is some *other* reason for keeping promises, apart from the supposed fact that breaking them would upset people's confidence.

In other words, confidence is something which is, in any given case, either justified or not justified, merited or not, legitimate or illegitimate. Only in those cases in which it is justified, merited, or legitimate should upsetting it count as a negative utility. Yet the moral criterion being proposed by utilitarians is supposed to be adequate for all purposes, and hence, for the purpose of determining whether the confidence in question is merited. The utility of the confidence is therefore what Bentham calls a "secondary" one, along with such things as "alarum," expectations, and so forth. The reach of such secondary utilities is quite broad. It includes, for example, the upsetting or satisfying of the moral opinions of others. But to include these among relevant utilities would be logically disastrous. Clearly we can get nowhere with a moral theory if among the effects to be taken into account we include consistency with contrary moral opinions. The purpose of a moral theory, presumably, is to say what those opinions ought to be; and if they are in disagreement with it, then the logical requirement on the upholder is simply to regard the contrary opinion as in error, or else give up (or alter) his own theory.

I conclude that we should take into account the fact that people would complain if a certain practice is engaged in, or a certain act performed, only in the sense that we should consider whether the complaint is justified. If it is not, then we should not. It is no use saying, as Brandt does, that our moral rules ought to be consonant with the opinions of the "intelligent" and/or the "conscientious." For in what does intelligence and conscientiousness consist, in the relevant sense? Surely these properties are tested, for the purpose in question, by seeing whether the persons alleged to have them live up to the principle of utility, if it is indeed true. If intelligent and conscientious people differ, then of course one is obliged to go into the merits of the theory—to write books on ethics, for example, offering arguments in support. But this is not an intra-theoretical consideration; it is, rather, a consideration of the type outlined in Chapter I, wherein we observed that a plausible ethical theory will inevitably have to square with a good many of our moral convictions held at the outset. It can hardly be a part of our theory that it be required to reckon such things as relevant utilities.

To summarize, the satisfaction of people's moral opinions, or in general, of expectations, confidence, and other sentiments which presumably are under the control of the persons experiencing them, is not, as such, a utility. Whether such satisfactions are to be reckoned as utilities depends on whether they are, under the circumstances, justified. To find this out, one must apply some criteria for appraising them. From the point of view of utilitarianism, these criteria must, of course, be provided by the principle of utility itself, or at least by something consistent with it. But this means that the acts or practices toward which these sentiments and expectations are directed must themselves have some other utility (hence, some "primary" utility) than their effects on these very sentiments and expectations; either that, or there must be some special reason for regarding these as the "primary" utilities for the case in question. We shall see, in the following chapter, how vital this distinction and the attendant considerations will be.

Distinguishing Moral Predicates

According to Brandt, a complete ethical system has a lower limit of economy in that "the system must contain at least as many distinct basic principles as there are different ethical concepts."[33] If this is correct, then if 'is morally obligatory,' for instance, cannot be defined in terms of 'is morally good,' then if our system is to be complete we shall have to have at least one distinct principle providing for the conditions of application of each predicate, and thus utilitarianism would be doomed.

Brandt's principle, however, is stated a bit too strongly. Surely there could be different ethical predicates which are nevertheless interdefinable in some way. When he says 'different,' he must mean 'irreducible,' and this is another matter. Ross has shown, I believe, that there is no hope of directly inferring 'x is obligatory' from 'x is good,'[34] and in some sense, this certainly shows that these are "different" ethical predicates. But this, as it turns out, is not the end of the matter. Nowell-Smith has produced an account according to which 'ought' and 'good' have different uses, but nevertheless are such that the usability of 'ought' is logically contingent on that of 'good.' What Nowell-Smith calls "pro-words," he says, "belong primarily to the language of 'I shall,' " and 'G-words' (deontological ones) belong "to the language of 'You ought,' and decisions never follow logically from imperatives."[35] Nevertheless, he points out that although it would be possible to have a world in which people used pro-words and no G-words, it would not be possible to imagine one in which they used G-words but no pro-words. "The reason for this is that all these words, both pro-, con- and deontological, belong to practical discourse; and they could not be used in the way that we in fact use them in a world in which people did not know what it is to choose; and this they could not know if they were indifferent to everything in the universe."[36]

What Nowell-Smith says is true, I think, but it does not quite solve our problem. We still do not know exactly how to interdefine them, and indeed, since Nowell-Smith denies that imperatives entail decisions (and could certainly deny the reverse entailment likewise), we seem to have to admit the logical distinctness required.

[33] R. B. Brandt, *Ethical Theory*, p. 295.
[34] W. D. Ross, *The Right and The Good*, Ch. 1
[35] Nowell-Smith, *Ethics*, p. 223.
[36] *Ibid.*, pp. 224, 225.

The clue to the answer here lies in the considerations I have advanced in Chapter IV under the topic "Objective and Subjective." The main point of using moral language is to *get* people to do what is right, and shun what is wrong. I tell someone that what he is doing, or is about to do, is wrong primarily in hopes of getting him to quit, or not to start.

Now, what of 'right,' and 'ought,' and 'duty,' (the so-called "deontological" words) versus 'good,' 'desirable,' etc. (the "teleological" group, which is perhaps ill-named—"evaluative" might be better)? Nowell-Smith's contention that the former, as a group, are primarily for 'advising, warning, commanding, exhorting, and admonishing,' while the latter are concerned with 'giving reasons for choice' seems to me to suggest the relevant distinction. Obviously, that something is one's duty, or is the right thing to do, gives us a reason for doing it, just as does the consideration that it would be desirable or would accomplish a good result. But it suggests something more, surely. What it suggests, I think, is that one can be held to account for nonperformance in a way, or to a degree, which is not suggested by the latter kind of reasons.

This analysis goes back at least to John Stuart Mill. In Mill's treatment of the concept of justice, he says, "When we think that a person is bound in justice to do a thing, it is an ordinary form of language to say that he ought to be compelled to do it."[37] Brandt, as we noticed above, indicates that there is a sense of 'duty' in which it "would imply that the person is properly subject to moral criticism or punishment if he fails."[38] There is a peculiar onerousness, amounting nearly to a kind of distaste, about moral considerations, especially those having to do with duty, justice, and obligation. We are "bound" by obligations; they interfere with the normal course of activity, and prevent us from doing just what we want to do. Moral considerations "intervene" and "impinge" on us, rather than occupying us in a perfectly natural and happy-go-lucky way.

Now, this trend of analysis seems to me a plausible one. The general distinction between saying that something is morally

[37] Mill, *Utilitarianism*, p. 44.
[38] "Toward a Credible Form of Utilitarianism" in Castañeda-Nakhnikian (eds.), *Morality and the Language of Conduct*, p. 111.

desirable, good, or praiseworthy (not meaning to imply that these three are precisely equivalent) and saying that it is morally obligatory, one's duty, or wrong not to do, is that the latter carry with them the suggestion that certain types of reinforcement are in order. There are two aspects to this. On the one hand, the words suggest that one could rightly be punished for nonconformance to a rule of right. On the other hand, the use of the words is itself a form of mild reinforcement. It is a bad thing to be morally censured; and the badness of it is part of the meaning of the words themselves. This is one reason why it is so strange for a person to say with a perfectly straight face that what he is doing is wrong, for his saying this not only implies that he does not approve of his own action, it also suggests that he is in a way already punishing himself for it. (This may be part of the reason why we think of criminals as abnormal.)

At the extreme end of the scale of deontological words are those having to do with strict justice. Justice and punishment are intimately related to each other: That it is just to prevent injustice by force if necessary is, I suggest (along with Mill) a strictly analytic proposition. At the other end of the scale, matters of right shade into matters of indifference, in one direction, and matters of good and bad, in the non-deontological sense, in the other.

Of course, we do not always feel that it is up to us to punish, or sometimes even to admonish or criticize, when we feel that someone has done something wrong. This can be accounted for by pointing out that there are second-level rules appropriate in some cases, rules about the appropriateness of criticism or punishment being applied by people with different relations to the person in question. Thus, for example, punishments for crimes should be inflicted by the community's agents, and not by private parties; children's discipline often should be left to their parents, and so forth. In every case, an implication that "negative reinforcement" of some kind is called for is present in the use of the deontological words. Surely this is why this group of words has a forbidding aspect lacking in such words as 'good,' 'desirable,' 'preferable,' and 'undesirable,' for example.

Another aspect of 'deontological' words which distinguishes

them, though not sharply, from the "evaluative" words is that they imply or suggest a notion of *rules*. Mill's account makes reference to this aspect as well:

There can, I think, be no doubt that the *idée-mère*, the primitive element, in the formation of the notion of justice, was conformity to law.... the sentiment of justice became attached, not to all violations of law, but only to violations of such laws as *ought* to exist, including such as ought to exist, but do not.[39]

It is evident that the idea of rules of one kind or another, and of laws in the extreme case, are closely related to the ideas of justice and of moral right and wrong, and this is amply attested to by the attention given to them in current literature. We can profitably ask what connection there is between these two major aspects of the notions of justice, right, duty, and obligation. On the utilitarian view, as I pointed out in Chapter IV above, this connection is quite intelligible. If our purpose in using moral words is to get somebody to do something which he might not otherwise do, and if the use of the expressions we are considering involves the suggestion that reinforcement is in order, then our purpose cannot be accomplished unless the subject is able to predict with reasonable accuracy if he can expect to be punished or not, and on just what occasions. A rule establishes a general criterion by which he can make this prediction, and thus be enabled to take avoiding action if he is so inclined. But if the threat of punishment is random, then he has no way of predicting when it will come and when it will not, and hence, there is no way of guiding his action accordingly. Thus, our purpose of guiding his action will be defeated, and we shall have introduced fear, apprehension, and frustration, as well as the pain of the punishment (whatever it may be when it is inflicted), into a person's life without adequate utilitarian reason. This is, obviously, the very reverse of utilitarian behavior on our part.

This is the only explanation of the relation of rules with justice that makes sense to me. The supposition that the rules of morality exist entirely for their own sakes must be classed as a

[39] Mill, *Utilitarianism*, pp. 43, 44.

neurotic symptom, at best.[40] And the idea that a morality might not involve an implicit suggestion of reinforcing procedures must be classed as fantasy. The institutions, and indeed the idea of morality, would not arise in a community of perfectly rational beings with no untoward passions, no inclinations to do anything wrong; they would have no purpose, and thus would make no sense.

We may now briefly summarize the range of words that have a use in morality. At one extreme, we have expressions such as "It would be best to do this, and not quite so good to do that"; "This is the most desirable policy, that one has its points, but isn't quite as satisfactory"; "This one is admirable, laudable, noble, and magnificent; that one is all right, sensible, satisfactory, within the line of duty." Here the "pro" words are highly commendatory, and imply praise and the desirability of reward, while the second members of each set, while they suggest a lower rating, do not admonish or criticize, but merely withhold reward or praise. Roughly, the positive words positively reinforce, while the negative ones do not negatively reinforce but only signify the absence of positive rewards.

At the other extreme, saying "This is a depraved, wicked, evil act, while that is justifiable, permissible, and within one's rights," are such that the negatives imply the appropriateness of the strongest kind of negatively re-inforcing action. They indicate that the business is serious indeed. The second class of statements indicates that a serious question has been raised, but that the subject has passed the tests and is not to be negatively reinforced. They do not imply praise in any particular degree, however. In fact, one might well say that a person was within his rights, but add that he was being rather ill-tempered, mean, rigid, or perhaps ill-advised in sticking to them. He should have to go several notches better to deserve praise. On the other hand, what he's done cannot be assessed as really wrong.

Statements of the form, "It is right to do so-and-so," or "It is just to do so-and-so," are rather ambiguous. Most often, I

---

[40] A person might, of course, regard conformity to some rule as worthwhile in itself. But this is his own business, and is not relevant for morality.

would say that to call some act "right" is not positively to praise it, but to clear the air: it implies that a question has been raised about the morality of the act, and that the party is not guilty. But it often suggests a certain praiseworthiness, because often it indicates that the subject has resisted temptations of some degree of force. If he didn't, then it would have been rather pointless to raise the question of the morality of his actions. The same goes for 'just': Once the question about an act is raised, then we are forced to say that it is either just or unjust; but very often, to raise the question would be out of place. If, for example, on a quite ordinary day, in my own kitchen, I am drinking a glass of water and somebody says, "Is that just?," my first inclination would not be to defend myself but to ask him, "What's going on?," with the implication that if there isn't some rather special circumstance of which I'm not aware, he must be kidding, or some kind of a crank. We are tempted to say that such actions are neither just nor unjust, in any serious sense; but they are certainly within one's rights.[41]

[41] Various writers have insisted that most acts are neither just nor unjust, taking a position analogous to that of Strawson on the truth-values of statements containing non-referring referring terms. Thus Stanley Cavell says, "A case can also be made out that it was failure to recognize such action which produced some of the notorious paradoxes of classical Utilitarianism: what neither the Utilitarians nor their critics seem to have seen clearly and constantly is that about unquestionable (normal, natural) action no question is (can be) raised; in particular, not the question whether the action ought or ought not to have been done. The point is a logical one: to raise a question about an action is to put the action in question." See "Must We Mean What We Say?" in *Ordinary Language*, ed. V. C. Chappell (Englewood Cliffs, N. J.: Prentice-Hall, Inc., 1946). How does this differ from saying to the doctor, "But normal people do not have cancer, and I am a normal person, so I can't have cancer?" The question is: Are any acts immune, logically immune, from raising a question? It is moot that raising a question *ipso facto* makes it an unusual case. 'Just' and 'unjust' are further cases in point. Frankena says that "I want to agree that beneficence is *right* and failure to be beneficent *wrong* under the conditions specified; however, I want to deny that they are, respectively, just or unjust, properly speaking." (In *Ethics*, p. 36). But why not? Perhaps we can come to agreement by allowing that in one sense, a just action is required by a consideration of justice, but in another sense, a just action is simply one that isn't unjust (neither required, nor its avoidance required, by a consideration of justice). We are not to the bottom of the analysis of "*presupposition*." This is Strawson's term in "On Referring" (*Mind*, 1950). I am hopeful that further research will uncover nothing gravely unsatisfactory about this account.

I shall take up more particular questions about justice, rights, and duties, as they arise. Meanwhile, my purpose has been merely to lay down the general framework within which the utilitarian view of these matters can be defended sensibly. Broadly, the difference between the performative functions of evaluation and obligation (with judgments of justice or injustice being the extreme case), is that between reward or praise and the withholding of reward or praise on the one hand, and punishment or blame, and exoneration from punishment or blame, on the other. If this is correct, then the charge of fanaticism and moral extremism laid against utilitarianism is unjustified. What follows immediately from estimates of utility is a license for judgments of evaluation, not of obligation. The question whether we are to judge an act wrong, and not merely undesirable, is another issue. Broadly, the way in which one decides it is by deciding, not just whether the act in question is, not conducive to utility, or productive of the opposite of utility, but also whether it would be conducive to utility to punish, blame, reprove, or admonish the agent. Of course, punishment, blame, reproof, etc., are intrinsically contrary to utility, since the imposition of strictures and punishments logically consists in the production of effects which are negatively valued by the subject. So, we must balance the badness of his act against the intrinsic undesirability of reinforcing action, and see whether the net results are desirable or not from the utilitarian standpoint.[42]

Notice that the question has to be whether the imposition of penalties is morally desirable and not whether it is "just," if this program is to succeed. For the Principle of Utility as it stands only affords judgments of evaluation, and not judgments about justice. The utilitarian must show that the latter are reducible to the former, and therefore must show that a judgment of value must underlie any properly made judgment of obligation.

---

[42] The point has been recognized by several writers (e.g., R. B. Brandt in "Toward a Credible Utilitarianism," in Castañeda-Nakhnikian, *Morality and the Language of Conduct*, pp. 118, 119; also, W. D. Falk, *Ibid.*, p. 56; William Frankena, *Ethics*, p. 58, in connection with free will and responsibility). No one has made enough of it, in my opinion.

At this point, some critics may be inclined to object. "You stand convicted out of your own mouth, for this is an impossible task," they will say. We shall see. Let us be clear about what I am maintaining. Briefly, I claim that where no one cares, nothing can be unjust. It is impossible to be unjust to a person who is absolutely indifferent to any mode of treatment. Judgments of justice and injustice must be justified by reference to people's interests in order to have any point and (therefore) any meaning. If this is thought to be self-evidently absurd by anyone, I can only urge the arguments in the remainder of this book.

Those who doubt the possibility of making judgments of obligation depend on judgements of value may perhaps be confusing two senses of 'justify.' Justice and justification are not the same thing at all. When we say that a person's action may be just or unjust, we are in a quite different line of work from what we are in when we say that a statement is justified, or even that an action is justified in non-moral contexts. 'Justification' has what we might call a "logical" sense when we speak of justifying a judgment to the effect that a certain action is wrong or unjust. 'Just' or 'unjust,' on the other hand, have a moral sense when said of actions. Justifying an action is one thing; justifying the statement that it is justified is another. There is no absurdity at all in supposing that the justification of judgments about the justice of actions consists in producing certain relevant evaluations.

CHAPTER VI

The Utilitarian Theory of "Strict" Obligation

In the present chapter, we will take up what many regard as the chief stumbling-block in utilitarian theory, namely the theory of what is strictly obligatory, meaning by this the realm of acts which one is specifically obliged to do or to avoid. Mill distinguished "perfect" from "imperfect" obligations in a rather similar way, applying the former label to those acts which we are to perform (or avoid) on each occasion when it is possible to perform (or avoid) them, and the latter for acts which one ought to perform sometimes but not on all occasions.[1] This is not so clear a distinction as it seems at first sight, unfortunately. But it goes some way toward catching a difference which we all feel to be important; that is, between acts which it would be wrong to do (or in the case of positive obligations, wrong not to do) and acts which it would be meritorious to do but the non-performance of which would not be wrong (or anyway, not wrong on most occasions).

At any rate, the theory developed here is that in order to qualify for the former status, an act must have, or be intended to have, the effect of "harming" someone, which is essentially the position of Mill's *Essay on Liberty*. Since it is closely con-

---

[1] Mill, *Utilitarianism*, p. 46: ". . . perfect and imperfect obligation; the latter being those in which, though the act is obligatory, the particular occasions of performing it are left to our choice . . ." Mill goes on to associate this distinction, as if it were simply an alternative but "more precise" way of saying the same thing, with the distinction between those duties which create a correlative right in some person and those which do not. I am inclined to regard all obligations or duties as creating a correlative right, and to deny that "imperfect obligations" are obligations at all. This rather obscure subject will be considered further in Chs. VII and VIII, in the latter of which I try to achieve a more satisfactory solution with a notion of "duties of society."

nected with this subject, the theory of punishment gets some consideration here as well; finally, an account of "institutional" obligation is sketched.

Some will feel that justice is more properly associated with the question of equitable distribution, but for various reasons I have reserved this for consideration in the next chapter, which also takes up the question of rights in particular.

Fundamental Justice and the "Innocent Man" Problem

In this section I shall develop a utilitarian theory of what might be called "fundamental justice," "fundamental duties," or "fundamental obligations." These are the chief "deontological" expressions, and the conflation of the three in the preceding sentence is intentional. Of course, they have specifically differing meanings, and it is not my intention to deny these differences.[2] But my present purpose is to consider what these expressions have in common, namely, as was suggested in Chapter V above, that they all suggest the appropriateness of "negative reinforcement," such as punishment and blame. If a person is bound in justice to do something, or if it is his moral duty or obligation, then (unless the circumstances excuse him or he has an overriding duty or obligation) it would be morally wrong of him not to do it. Thus the subject of the present section is the fundamental principle governing the application of 'morally wrong,' and hence of blame and punishment on moral grounds.

Problems associated with this area are undoubtedly the most influential, historically, in preventing acceptance of utilitarianism as an across-the-board moral theory. Virtually every critic who has touched the subject has insisted that the flat application of the principle would violate our sense of justice, or some obvious principle of justice, in one way or another. Some of these objections have to do with narrower aspects of the problem, such as the keeping of promises. These will be discussed below.

[2] See, for example, R. B. Brandt's "The Concepts of Duty and Obligation," in *Mind* (1964); and the discussion in Baier, *Moral Point of View*, pp. 215 ff.

Others have to do with distribution, in what I shall call the "special" sense, and this will be considered in Chapter VII. In a sense, all or nearly all problems of justice have to do with distribution, for nearly all aspects of justice have to do with fairness or equity of one kind or another. It is with objections to utilitarianism on the general problem that I shall be concerned here.

Before beginning my constructive remarks, it will be useful to describe some representative types of problems with which, it is alleged, utilitarianism has been unable to deal successfully. I shall list three somewhat different types which will adequately illustrate the difficulties needing treatment. First is the punishment of the innocent. It is almost universally believed, among the critics of utilitarianism, that the principle of utility would justify punishment of persons who have done nothing wrong in certain circumstances. Thus, for instance, E. F. Carritt claims:

If some kind of very cruel crime becomes common, and none of the criminals can be caught, it might be highly expedient, as an example, to hang an innocent man, if a charge against him could be so framed that he were universally thought guilty; indeed this would only fail to be an ideal instance of utilitarian 'punishment' because the victim himself would not have been so likely as a real felon to commit such a crime in the future; in all other respects it would be perfectly deterrent and therefore felicific.[3]

Of course, if this charge cannot be rebutted, then utilitarianism must be rejected. We must be able to show that such procedures would always be immoral. In fact, I am inclined to agree with Elizabeth Anscombe's contention:

If a procedure is one of judicially punishing a man for what he is clearly understood not to have done, there can be absolutely no argument about the description of this as unjust. No circumstances, and no expected consequences, which do not modify the description of the procedure as one of judicially punishing a man for what he is known not to have done can modify the description of it as unjust. . . . if someone really thinks, in advance, that it is open to question whether such an action as procuring the judicial execution of the

[3] E. F. Carritt, *Ethical and Political Thinking*, p. 65.

innocent should be quite excluded from consideration—I do not want to argue with him; he shows a corrupt mind.[4]

Or rather, I agree with the spirit of the thing. Of course, if in some incredible situation we should have our choice between judicially punishing an innocent man and, say, judicially punishing two innocent men, then it is not obvious what to say. In fact, the range of circumstances Miss Anscombe has in mind when she says "*No* circumstances" is almost certainly limited to certain *kinds* of circumstances; in particular, those brought about by human contrivance, where there is some possibility of prevention by someone, and of our doing something about it; and in which the reason for bringing it about has to do with someone's gain, especially that of the person bringing it about.[5]

A second representative type is where by inflicting some horrible harm on one person, we can increase the happiness of a great many other people. This, in fact, is a more general version of the "punishment" case above, for whether we inflict this harm on him by framing him before a jury or just go ahead and do it without any trappings of legitimacy doesn't really affect the matter very much, Miss Anscombe's intuitions to the contrary notwithstanding. Different kinds of harm will affect the situation differently here, and variations will be discussed below. Notice also that I am purposely taking a more interesting case than the simplest one. In the simplest case—suppose I just have a sudden desire to hit someone—it would give me great pleasure to do so, say. Critics could charge as follows: If it would really give me a great deal of pleasure, and it wouldn't hurt him very much, then why wouldn't it be perfectly all right for me to smack him? In fact, some could add that it would be my positive duty to do so! Even the most rabid opponents of utilitarianism don't seem to have considered advancing this bald example as a reasonable one, however. The case I have in mind is subtler.

[4] G. E. M. Anscombe, "Modern Moral Philosophy," *Philosophy*, 1957, pp. 16, 17.

[5] It has been said that utilitarianism doesn't really sanction the punishment of anyone. So long as we're sure the criminal will never do it again, we need only publicize his punishment without really doing it, according to this view. See "Punishment and Retribution," below.

Here, the benefit is not to the *agent*; he's behaving in a perfectly selfless manner. It's just that a lot of other people would benefit from his (say) torturing or stealing from someone. We can add salt to the case by supposing that the victim is an unpopular old so-and-so who is always being nasty to people, who has no talents or saving graces; he is just a general blot on the social horizon. Here, the critics will urge, we have a splendid case of utilitarianism in action. I kill the old man, nobody will miss him, he was miserable anyhow, and his vast fortune will greatly increase the happiness of the community.

The third case is somewhat different from the two above, and has already been answered implicitly in Chapter III. We will find it useful here as a means of comparison. This is the case of "involuntary euthanasia." For example, here is a man with a mortal case of cancer; his whole future life, which won't be very long anyway, will be filled with pain and unrelieved by any possibility of productive participation in the community life, or by amusements or spiritually enriching activities. Why not put an end to him and save a lot of trouble on the part of physicians, as well as taxpayer's good money which could be used for more worthy projects than maintaining him in being for a few miserable months? And what difference does it make if he doesn't go along with the project?

Here, then, we have a suitable array of difficult cases. In all of these cases, our intuitions are pretty clear, at least barring radically unusual circumstances not hinted at in the descriptions. Is there any general principle underlying these intuitions? Can it be supported on utilitarian grounds? I shall try to show that it can.

Actually, the principle we need has been around for a long while, since it is the one advocated by Mill himself in his *Essay on Liberty*, a book which the average critic of utilitarianism either ignores or sloughs off as a mere eccentricity of its author, or perhaps as an illustration of his preference for Nobility when it conflicts with the requirements of Consistency. This principle, as it is stated, is that "the sole end for which mankind are warranted, individually or collectively, in interfering with the liberty of action of any of their number, is self-protection. That

157

the only purpose for which power can be rightfully exercised over any members of a civilized community, against his will, is to prevent harm to others."[6]

Note that in this passage, Mill is equating 'exercising power over' with 'restricting the liberty of'; also, note that 'harming others' is treated by Mill as equivalent to these two phrases. It follows from the two sentences here (which Mill clearly regards as equivalent), that if an individual, x, restricts the liberty of another individual, y, then since the sole purpose for which this may legitimately be done is to punish y for harming someone, z, it follows that if y is not harming z, then x's action is illegitimate, and hence mankind are warranted, individually or collectively, in punishing x for this action. In other words, x's action is wrong in this case, and not wrong, in the sense in which 'wrong' implies 'punishable,' in any other case.

Unfortunately, we cannot take the amount of space here that would be necessary for thoroughly explicating Mill's view, and in replying to all of the specific criticisms which have been levelled at it. I shall proceed to develop what seems to me the appropriate interpretation and defense of this view, without further reference to the fact that it is Mill's. Suffice it to say that I think my view is substantially the same as (or at least consistent with) his; although the arguments which I shall employ to show that it is, as a whole, implied by utilitarianism are not, to my knowledge, to be found in his work.

In effect, the question posed by all of these problems has to do with the legitimacy of balancing negative against positive utilities in certain contexts. The principle we need to establish is roughly as follows: an action having negative utility (i.e., which harms someone) can never be justified merely by reference to other effects of the action which have positive utility (i.e., which benefit someone else). I propose to show that this principle is true (i.e., that all acts to which just the description above applies, without qualification) are morally wrong.[7]

If this principle can indeed be supported, then it will take care

---

[6] Mill, *Essay on Liberty*, pp. 72, 73.

[7] This is a bald statement, due, no doubt, to its being bold: we must always add "except when the harm is trivial and the benefit substantial." The criterion of triviality, however, rests primarily with the person harmed.

of two of the types of cases described above. Clearly, punishing the innocent is not justifiable on grounds of benefit to others, if the above is true; nor is killing someone for his money, or to benefit third parties.

The third case requires a note of explanation which will prove important in all of these considerations. The key to the third case is the assumption that we can know whether another person would benefit on the whole from an action of which he doesn't approve. This assumption is not normally justified. If utility consists in what any individual believes to be valuable, then the fact that he is suffering (for instance) or apparently miserable, and doomed to be so indefinitely, does not by itself show that we should do away with him. We might suggest that he do away with himself, though this would be a rather morbid thing to do, since the individual in question will surely have thought of it himself, without our assistance. The point is that if he likes to live under those circumstances, then that's his business. The fact that one would have decided differently in the same circumstances oneself is quite irrelevant;[8] in fact, this is a good case to remind us of what I have argued to be the central point of utilitarianism—not to project our own values indiscriminately on other people. Those who argue that if other people are suffering, then we should do away with them on "the" utilitarian view, are taking the thesis that everyone wants to be happy in a nonvacuous sense. That is to say that they give "happiness" some definite substantive meaning apart from the evaluative preferences of the individual whose happiness is in question. But if there is room in the utilitarians' writings for this interpretation, there is also room for the opposite. We can point, in particular, to Bentham's dictum that every man is the best judge of his own interests. As we have seen, if this principle is taken to be descriptive of prudential reasoning, it is as false as the thesis that everyone seeks nothing but pleasure would be, if that were a substantive psychological thesis. But neither of them are. Since

[8] I am thus taking sides, generally, on Richard M. Hare's question whether the agent's dislikes and likes are "part of the shoes" when I imagine what I would do if in his shoes. A tribute is due to Hare's discussion of utilitarianism in his book, *Freedom and Reason* (New York: Oxford University Press, 1963), which is well above the usual level. (More on Hare is found in Ch. IX.)

this is so, it will continue to be necessary to do what we all believe we ought to do, namely, to consult before we act.

Certainly, a utilitarian must admit the legitimacy of euthanasia in cases where we have consulted the sufferer, and knowing all of the facts as well as we, he insists on being put out of his misery. (There will be moralists who regard this as immoral because cowardly, or just intrinsically bad; these moralists are in disagreement with the utilitarians.) It is also true that the "ordinary moral consciousness" is not undividedly with him. The same is true of the legitimacy of suicide, which the utilitarian must also grant in principle.[9]

The first general principle of interpretation which I propose, then, is that utility is not measurable (for moral purposes) independently of the judgment of the person whose utility is in question. This principle, in view of Chapter III, may be regarded as analytic. A few further remarks on its application are in order here, for the sake of clarity, and in view of the importance of this principle in many of the contexts we will be discussing.

In the first place, we have to be confident, in important cases such as when the termination of a life is involved, that the subject really means it when he consents to be treated in a certain way. We have to be very sure that he knows all the facts which he would believe to be relevant, and has considered them carefully. The reason for this is that his total happiness (i.e., the worth of his whole life from his point of view), is in question, and not just the next day or the next five minutes. We know from experience that people have different evaluative views in an extremity than in a cool hour; if we can be pretty sure that the subject's view of the situation will be quite different tomorrow or next month from what it is now, then it follows that the subject's total happiness will in fact be different from what he now supposes it will be.

In the second place, it follows that we can only go on our own independent judgment of his probable welfare, if the subject's judgment is not available or known to be unreliable. Thus, if the subject is an animal, and has no opinions of his own welfare,

---

[9] Richard Robinson's views on suicide seem to me an excellent statement of the utilitarian's case. See *An Atheist's Values*, pp. 56 ff.

the considerations of the Three Puzzles in Chapter III come into play. If the subject is insane or deranged, we have to try to get him back into shape, before we can carry on; but if we can't, then we have to go on such behavioral cues as are available. To the extent that a person is like an animal, he will have to be treated like an animal; his opinions cannot be consulted if he doesn't have any.

In the third place, and most importantly, it follows that if you want to harm somebody in order to benefit yourself on the ground that the benefit is "greater" than the harm, there's only one way in which you can sensibly test this supposition—*ask* him. If he's perfectly willing to be harmed for your benefit, then it is all right. But if he isn't, then your position is untenable and you must desist. The significance of this third point is evident. In particular, it means that many of the theoretical problems about weighing and measuring utilities can be by-passed.

We are now ready to consider the general problem of the justification of the principle I have stated, which I shall henceforth refer to as the General Principle of Duty. This principle, we will recall, stated that no act of harming another person can be justified by reference to the benefit of others. In view of the first principle of interpretation laid down above, we shall assume for the sake of all future discussions except where specifically indicated to the contrary, that the "harms" in question are effects on the subject which *he* classifies as harms (i.e., where he does not consent to be treated in the way in question).

To begin our assessment of this problem, let us recall what it is to have a moral principle, and what the utilitarian principle says. The function of a moral principle is to guide our actions. This means that when we act, we don't just act, if we have a principle, but instead we reflect. To act is to act on the desire to perform this particular action. (Differences between "direct" desires to act, and action for the sake of other ends which are the direct object of desire, are irrelevant here; as of course are random, unintentional, or unmotivated "actions.") A person does not have a moral principle, then, unless he is intending to inhibit some of his desires, namely those which run counter to his principle. In other words, he is a person who is ready to classify some of his desires as legitimate, and others as illegitimate. So much has been evident since the era of Plato and Aristotle, who contended that virtue is the control of the desires by reason.

Now, a desire to inflict harm on another person is the very paradigm of the kind of desire the utilitarian is out to control. What sense would it make to call a person a "utilitarian" (i.e., one who desires the greatest happiness of the greatest number) who went about knocking people on the head just because he felt like doing so? If our aim is to promote utility, then at very least it is to refrain from diminishing it.

Other things being equal, therefore, the utilitarian must classify all desires for the harm of others as intrinsically illegitimate. The only question can be, when are other things equal and when aren't they? The "other things" in question all have to be desires, of course, on the utilitarian view; and thus, it might seem at first glance that the desires of others for gain, at the expense of loss to someone else (known or unknown to them) should count. But this is incorrect also.

At this point, I propose another interpretative "principle" of a sort, though it is stretching the word a bit to call it that. This "principle" is that when applying a principle, we should do so consistently. The aim of the utilitarian is to promote utility, or happiness. It is therefore his aim to inhibit, suppress, or prevent the occurrence of desires which run counter to that aim, whether on his own part or other people's. If it would be illegitimate for him to satisfy his own desires for the harm of others, then it is equally true, for the same reason, that it is illegitimate for him to satisfy the counter-utilitarian desires of anyone else.

Let us put the matter this way. Suppose that killing X would benefit one hundred people, of whom one of them is oneself. Now if one is a utilitarian, then of course, as shown above, one could not count one's own benefit as a reason for killing X. How about person No. 99, then? Ought I not do so for his benefit at any rate? No. For consider the reasoning which No. 99 is to go through, on utilitarian grounds. He of course will discount his own desire as being inconsistent with the utilitarian end. And so will No.'s 98, 97, 96, and so on to the end of the line. Since none of them would be justified, on utilitarian grounds, in killing the man for his own benefit, it follows that *noone's* benefit is a reason for killing him, nor, therefore, the benefit of all of them. It is therefore not just to kill him on utilitarian grounds at all.

It seems to me rather unreasonable that critics should insist on the utilitarian's being inconsistent on this matter. Just how is the goal of the greatest happiness going to be achieved if we tolerate the satisfaction of desires for other people's *un*happiness?

There is a sense, of course, in which the internal character of a desire is irrelevant to the utilitarian. This, indeed, is just what I have been insisting upon in the face of those who want to identify utility with the satisfaction of certain limited desires, such as those which would be called colloquially, desires for "pleasure." But it is one thing to say that the particular character of the desire is irrelevant because all desires should be considered, and quite another to say that no desires of any sort should be rejected, upon consideration. The most obvious consideration there could possibly be for rejecting a desire in any system of ethics is that it is a desire for the exact opposite of the aim of the system.

What this comes to, in brief, is that in calculating utilities, we must not assign positive value to the satisfaction of malevolent desires.

Care must be taken to avoid misinterpretation of this result. It does not mean, for example, that football should be suppressed, or that we should never play jokes on other people. People play football because they *like* to play football, in spite of the fact that they know that they might get hurt. They want the players on the opposing side to do their best. And people are willing to put up with a bit of ribbing or practical jokery if it really entertains them. Principle number one must not be lost sight of as soon as principle number two is invoked!

However, we need to establish more than this, important as this result is. What we need to show is not merely that malevolent desires should be discounted, but that they should actually be given a negative value, such that punishment or other reinforcing action against action on them is desirable. Punishment, the threat of punishment, and the suggestion of the appropriateness of punishment, are intrinsically bad, of course, on the utilitarian view. Therefore, their use needs to be justified. Can we show that their use is justified in the above cases? Yes, we can. In showing that it would be bad to act on a desire to harm someone, in the sense that such action diminishes utility, we have shown *ipso facto* that such desires should be suppressed. Suppose that a person has such a desire, and the fact that it is such a desire, if it occurs to him, doesn't of itself prevent him from acting on it. In this case, either he acts on it, in which case the other party is harmed, or we suppress him forcibly (since we have assumed that he is not amenable to reason at the moment). One or the other has to happen. Which should it be? Obviously, it should be the suppression of his desire to harm the other person (assuming that the other person has done nothing to deserve it). To say that, of two possible outcomes, one is the bad one, is obviously to say that the better should be chosen. In this case, we have shown that the desire to harm the other person is the bad one; it follows, therefore, that that is the one to be suppressed. The innocent party's desire not to be harmed is precisely the kind of desire that the utilitarian system is aimed at satisfying, at a minimum. If there are any desires which should be satisfied, the desire not to be harmed is obviously going to be the first one, on the utilitarian view. Harming one person is just as bad as harming another, of course, other things being equal. But the application of the utilitarian principle is precisely what shows that other things are not equal in the present case.

Thus, we have established that we have reason not only for disregarding malevolent desires in the calculation of utilities, but for suppressing them if their bearers have not suppressed them themselves. From this, the General Principle of Duty follows. Given that a desire to harm someone ought always to be discounted, and to be suppressed whenever its bearer doesn't do so himself, it follows that we are never justified in harming the innocent in order to benefit others. Thus the rug is pulled out from under what is probably the most serious of all objections to the utilitarian view. The objection rests entirely on a failure to permit that principle to be applied consistently. Small wonder that absurd results were obtained. It is still true, as Mill said, that "There is no difficulty in proving any ethical standard whatever to work ill, if we suppose universal idiocy to be conjoined with it."

I want to stress the fact that this result is due to meta-theoretical considerations, and not to any substantive alteration in the utilitarian principle. It is a question of what that principle is being used to do, and not what its internal content is. We are supposing situations in which two or more persons have desires which conflict in the following way: satisfying the wants of A involves no special effects on anyone else's wants, whereas B wants to prevent A from getting what A wants. The question is, are we to count the fact that B wants this very much—he would, we suppose, get a lot of satisfaction from thus decreasing A's utility—as a *prima facie* reason for letting B do it, against which we must reckon the negative utility to A, so that it might turn out that the balance favors B's act? This is what we are asked to suppose by the critics. But this is a travesty. No negative utilities would result from having A satisfy his wants; but, since what B wants is precisely to have a negative utility brought about, such a utility will necessarily result from having B satisfy his wants. Now, in asking whether an act (or a refraining-from-an-act) is morally obligatory or a duty, a requirement of morality, we are, I have suggested, asking whether negative reinforcement would be morally desirable if applied to the act in question. Clearly, it would not in the case of A, for letting him do as he wishes will yield only positive utility anyhow. But clearly it would be desirable in the case of B, for if we do not apply sanctions (which in themselves are always negative utilities, of course) against him, then a negative utility will result anyhow.

Perhaps we can use Baier's terminology to advantage here. Baier has distinguished "*prima facie*" from "presumptive" reasons, as follows:

To say that something is a presumptive reason is merely to say that some fact gives rise to the presumption that it is a *prima-facie* reason. If the former presumption is rebutted, then it is still true that *prima facie*, though not on balance, the agent ought or ought not to enter on this course of action. If the latter presumption is rebutted, then it is not even true that the agent ought or ought not *prima facie* to enter on it.[10]

Baier's own way of distinguishing what does from what does not create a presumption isn't entirely clear to me, though it

---

[10] Baier, *Moral Point of View*, p. 104.

may be similar to the one I want to suggest. At any rate, my suggestion is that if a desire is a desire to harm someone, then this is a desire which does not even create a presumption that it should be satisfied. If one's criterion of evaluation is the principle of utility, desires of this kind cannot, on pain of contradiction, be permitted to get "off the pad" so to speak, let alone "into orbit."

Carrying on the analogy, we might frame another category of desires which, while we permit them off the pad, have to be shot down en route. Such would be the case with desires which, though they are not, as such, desires for the dissatisfaction of others, are nevertheless desires to do things which, under the circumstances, would involve the dissatisfaction of others. Here, certainly, whether we are to suppress the desire in question will depend on the character of the desires whose dissatisfaction is involved. For example, if I want x and Jones wants x and we can't both have it, then the desire which will be dissatisfied by the satisfaction of mine is one whose satisfaction would in its turn have resulted in the dissatisfaction of mine. Here, then, our desires have an equal claim to be satisfied, and some other method would have to be used to resolve them (e.g., we might agree to compete in some way).

To alter the metaphor, we may, in situations of conflict, distinguish some desires as the "aggressors," so to speak; others are initially neutral. Jones is eating a picnic in the park, minding his own business; I want to come roaring through on my motorcycle. Other things being equal, I am in the wrong, since Jones' desires are, under the circumstances, satisfiable without upsetting any existing utilities, while mine are not. The general principle on which we may proceed is that "aggressive" desires are *prima facie* in the wrong. This general principle, it seems to me, is recommended purely by the fact that we are resolved to employ the principle of utility as a moral principle (i.e., as a guide to our actions).

The consequences of the present discussion are drawn easily enough. If we turn back to the various cases in which it is urged that we should punish an innocent man as an example to the community, for instance, or in which the community dislikes him and would be happier if he suffered, or in which they think he is guilty and thus would feel safer if he were punished, the obvious answer is that if we know he is innocent, we ought to step forward and show this. It would, to begin with, be strange if the community felt safer from the knowledge that an innocent man had been punished. But if their reason for being happier if he is punished is not the proper one that criminals should not be allowed to roam loose but the improper one that they don't like his looks, or his ideas, or whatever, then the correct thing to do is to reform or criticize the community, not the innocent man. Real-life examples of this problem abound. For example, in the Southern United States at the present time, it is customary for police officials to imprison, beat, torture, or otherwise suppress people who are trying to draw the attention of the community to injustices from which they are suffering. They do this on the ground that they are protecting "law and order" by preventing the inevitable riots which would follow if the sufferers were allowed to speak. But the riots in question are not avalanches or floods caused by purely natural mechanisms: they are caused by human beings who are supposedly capable of self-control. Obviously it is the rioters who should be imprisoned and suppressed, rather than those who are merely trying to get a hearing for injustices. The appeals of the police to "utilitarian" motives are purely spurious.

The point that people are different from avalanches needs to be emphasized here. So far as I know, all of the examples which have been put forward to expose the supposed absurdity of utilitarianism by pointing to the superior satisfaction which can be achieved by harming the innocent depend for their force on a failure to distinguish "consequences" which are mediated by human thought and will from those which occur through uncontrollable natural forces. If you ignore this difference, you may as well not bother to have an ethical system, since the latter has precisely the purpose of directing and controlling human action by reflection, criticism, and (if need be) punishments. There is no point in criticizing an avalanche, but there is point in criticizing human action. Very well, but if there is, then why should we count it as a positive value to reward the very type of actions which it is the primary purpose of the system to inhibit? Actions such as demanding the heads of people who don't happen to agree with you are plainly of that type.

A corollary previously alluded to in Chapter IV is that positive value is not to be attached to the satisfaction of "moral" desires, that is, of desires or interests of a moral type, as such. Thus, for example, if A thinks that birth control is intrinsically immoral, then the fact that we could satisfy A by prohibiting birth control from being practised by other people has no moral weight whatever. Moral opinions, and hence interests in putting them into practice, are either right or wrong. If utilitarianism is true, then these opinions are correct if in harmony with it, and otherwise incorrect. If incorrect they should be disregarded, except in the sense that they should be corrected. But if they are correct, then the actions sanctioned by them are sanctioned by considerations of the general interest apart from the fact that the opinions in questions are held. Thus, no weight is to be attached to their satisfaction as such.

There is a notion of "tolerance" preached by some people which apparently would consist of agreeing with all opinions opposed to one's own (if one has any). This is an odd kind of tolerance. Ought we to tolerate the South African "Way of Life," for instance? What of the Nazis? Ought we to have "tolerated" them? This is plainly absurd. Surely the only reason for paying attention to the moral views of other people is that there may be something valid about the views in question. We certainly ought to "tolerate" other views in the sense of discussing them and hearing what their proponents have to say, but to act on his principles is to make nonsense of one's moral life in those cases where one thinks his principles are wrong.[11] Why utilitarianism should be singled out for urging the opposite is difficult to say, but it is high time to set the record straight.

Two cautionary points should perhaps be appended here. First

[11] This seems to me to be the net effect of maintaining doctrines recommended by some able philosophers (e.g., H. D. Aiken, *Reason and Conduct*, Essays viii and xiv, especially pp. 142 ff.). He takes Mill to task for not making room for "moral freedom," or "freedom of conscience." This is dark doctrine. Mill, if anyone, is certainly a friend of freedom of thought and discussion, and it seems evident that discussion of questions of value is uppermost in his mind throughout the *Essay on Liberty*. But is this supposed to extend to permitting people to do wrong if they think it right? On what ground is this possible, other than the allowances recommended in Ch. III under "Psychological Hedonism," unless we agree that these actions are permissible? Needless to say, the "existentialists" are the principal purveyors of this peculiar doctrine at present.

is that insofar as contrary moral views may be satisfied without diminishing utility, their satisfaction counts as a positive utility. After all, the only utilitarian reason for dissuading a person from a moral position would be that his acting on the view would lessen utility; If it would not, or to the extent that it would not, its status as a "non-aggressive" desire, in the sense previously established, makes it countable as one whose satisfaction is a good. The other is that there are often reasons of expedience properly so called which force us to take into account views contrary to utility. If Jones' speaking in the public square would cause a riot too large to be controlled by the available forces, what can a responsible police chief do but to try to prevent it? We sometimes know what the right thing to do would be, but simply don't have the resources to do it. Again, the fact that the community will burn me at the stake if I do x, even though my doing x is none of their business, gives me a prudential reason for not doing x. That's just the way it goes. But there is a difference between prudential and moral considerations, and we are interested in the latter at present; the fact that circumstances make it impossible or imprudent to do what is right doesn't keep it from being right.

Punishment and Retribution

By this time, most of the topics generally dealt with under the heading of "the theory of punishment" have been discussed. I have pointed out that the general function of punishment is to control behavior: punishment is what the psychologists call "negative reinforcement." And in the previous section I hope to have deflected the principal bolt in the armory of the critics in the form of the "innocent man" problem. We have seen why there is point in punishment, and why there is evil in punishing those who have done nothing wrong. Two questions remain.

(1) The positive theory of punishment is due primarily to Bentham, whose work in this area remains a classic source.[12] But

---

[12] The essentials of it are found in Ch. XIII of *Principles of Morals and Legislation*. In my opinion, Bentham fell afoul of the "innocent man" fallacy, though.

one notable difficulty has to be met. Bentham has insisted (as I did, in the previous section) that the reason for not punishing persons who are innocent, feeble-minded, drugged, or otherwise not responsible, is that the punishment would then be inefficacious. But Professor Hart has recently accused Bentham of a "spectacular non-sequitur."

He sets out to prove that to *punish* the mad, the infant child or those who break the law unintentionally or under duress or even under 'necessity' must be inefficacious; but all that he proves (at the most) is the quite different proposition that the *threat* of punishment will be ineffective so far as the class of persons who suffer from these conditions is concerned. Plainly it is possible that the actual *infliction* of punishment on those persons . . . may secure a higher measure of conformity to law on the part of normal persons than is secured by the admission of excusing conditions. If this is so and if Utilitarian principles only were at stake, we should, without any sense that we were sacrificing any principle of value or were choosing the lesser of two evils, drop from the law the restriction on punishment entailed by the admission of excuses; unless, of course, we believed that the terror or insecurity or misery produced by the operation of laws so Draconic was worse than the lower measure of obedience to law secured by the law which admits excuses.[13]

Upon some deliberation, Hart decides that none of the "more pragmatic" forms of utilitarianism can deal with this general difficulty either, and so concludes that:

It is therefore impossible to exhibit the principle by which punishment is excluded for those who act under the excusing conditions merely as a corollary of the general Aim—Retributive or Utilitarian—justifying the practice of punishment.[14]

What are we to say to this charge?

I must confess that I find it a very peculiar one. It is admitted that the threat of punishment to the (unwitting) causers of mischief would be pointless. Nevertheless, it is held that the

[13] H. L. A. Hart, "Prolegomenon to Principles of Punishment," reprinted in *Philosophy, Politics, and Society,* ed. Peter Laslett and W. G. Runciman (2d Series; Oxford: Blackwell Publishing Co., Ltd., 1962), p. 174.
[14] *Ibid.,* p. 176.

practice of punishing them might have the effect of increasing the law-abidingness of the community. Now how, we might ask, would this desirable effect come about through the opera tion of this particular cause? For example, suppose that we were to advertise in public places, and also let the word slip out in private, that henceforth anyone physically involved in an act of mischief, whether responsible for it or not, would be punished. What sort of deterrent effect could this possibly have? According to Hart, it would consist in precluding the possibility of deceiving the judge or jury about one's condition at the time of one's act, as when a plea of insanity becomes a "loophole" in the hands of crafty lawyers.

The fallaciousness of this general criticism now becomes apparent. If all and only all persons who were responsible were punished, it is admitted that this situation would be the best, from the utilitarian point of view. The source of the problem is that the system of detection and conviction employed by the public might not actually bring this about. The defects in the system—which, it is admitted, are shown to be defects by the utilitarian standard itself—are such that they permit advantage to be taken by the clever, the unscrupulous, and others who will cause the crime rate to be higher than it would be otherwise. It is admitted that if the system had no defects (i.e., that the clever and unscrupulous would not be able to take advantage of it), this would be better than if the system had the defect of now and again punishing those who are innocent. It is putting it rather weakly, I think, to say that the "terror or insecurity or misery" caused by the more "Draconic" system might happen to outbalance the consideration that the system might be taken advantage of if it were oriented toward punishing only those who are shown (by utilitarian analysis) to need it. The very arguments we have employed to show why those not responsible ought not to be punished so far as the primary effects on the agent are concerned, also show why Hart's argument is, ultimately, untenable. What they really show that we ought to try to do (i.e., ought to succeed in doing, if we can) is to perfect the system so that all and only those who are guilty are convicted. Moral considerations quite obviously have to do with what we can foresee, not what we cannot foresee. We can easily foresee the disutility of punishing those not responsible: namely, that those not responsible are punished (i.e., harmed). We cannot foresee the disutility of succeeding in distinguishing those who are not responsible from those who are, because if we do succeed, then there won't be any such disutilities. (For it is admitted also, I trust, that if the criminal element in the community is in its senses, it will be deterred by the knowledge that it will be caught, and not by the knowledge that it will not be punished if it does it while insane. One cannot plan to do something while insane.) In what way, then, could this conceivably be an argument for not attempting to make the distinction at all? Remember that the issue before us is whether the public might be justified in punishing him, on an occasion when it knows that the accused was not responsible. The issue is not whether it might be justified in punishing him when it does not know that he was not responsible. If the latter were in question, obviously there would be no sense in discussing the whole issue. It would be like the question, ought we to punish an innocent man if we are certain that he is guilty? If we are certain that he is guilty, then of course so far as we know he is not innocent, so we are not punishing an innocent man. The fact that juries and judges are not perfect does not mean that there is a genuine issue here. The same is true of the issue Hart brings up. The question cannot be whether we ought not to punish those whom we know to be not responsible for what they were doing; this is precisely the question answered by Bentham's arguments (and my own) as discussed in Chapter IV. The genuine question is how to find out. The fact that it isn't easy doesn't mean that we shouldn't do it when we can. But the "Draconic" procedures Hart envisages are founded on precisely this premise. Here, everyone might very well know that a person was not responsible, and yet go ahead and punish him. There is no room to argue the merits of this on utilitarian grounds. The question isn't open.

I conclude that this objection to the utilitarian rationale of excuses is unfounded. In fact, it has in common with all of the other objections based on "social effects" that it requires these effects to be the effects of mistakes, errors, accidents, or deceptions. In the case of the "innocent man" problem, the trouble was that the public was told he was guilty, when he was known to be innocent. If he is in fact innocent, then he ought to be released and the public should be told about it, since otherwise an avoidable harm is done. If the public thinks he is guilty, they should be shown that he is innocent, if he is. If the public wants him punished even though it knows he's innocent, then the public ought to be prosecuted instead. Similarly, if the public is somehow deterred from crime by a system of punishing persons not responsible, it must be because the public is either stupid or sick, in which case it ought to be either educated or hospitalized, or because it doesn't realize they are not responsible, in which case it should be told. If no one knows that the accused isn't responsible, then of course we will punish him because we suppose he was responsible. Critics really ought to leave off using these same old arguments which require the assumption that the public or its officers are insane or criminal, or which trade on the assumption that we don't know something that is really so and then accuse us of immorality for acting in ignorance.

(2) The second question concerns the role of "retribution" in punishment. It is generally felt that "the" retributive theory is to be contrasted, in a perfectly general way, with "the" utilitarian theory. According to the latter, it is felt, only the goals of deterrence and reformation of character are legitimate, whereas according to the former, retribution is also legitimate. Actually, as we have seen, the principal aim of punishment is protection: A man cannot very well harm the public while he is behind bars (though his henchmen who are not might, but if they, too, are behind bars? Let us ignore trivial objections). And deterrance is no doubt also an important part of this aim. Moreover, "reform" may be viewed as an extension of deterrance, if it comes to that. Certainly, a system of punishment which had the effect that those punished did not repeat their crimes would be better, other things being equal, than one not having this effect. By this time, I trust, the principle that this is the main aim of punishment is not seriously questioned. What is in question is whether retribution is, in some sense, also a legitimate, if secondary, aim.

This question, as Professor Hart points out,[15] has unhappily been confused with the question whether punishment ought to be directed solely at those who have broken the law. We shall assume that this confusion has been eliminated, and consider only the question whether we are to account it as an intrinsic moral good that an offender be punished, quite apart from the aim of protecting society. This is a difficult question which cannot be brushed off as quickly as some are ready to do. But the reasons why it cannot are, nevertheless, utilitarian.

Let us see why retribution might be thought to be of value. To begin with, few would argue, least of all those "Formalists" who in general are found on the side of the Retributionists, that if the victim forgives the sinner, then there is still value in punishing the latter. Everyone feels, I trust, that the value of retribution (if any) lies peculiarly in the personal relation between the victim and the wrongdoer. Sometimes society at large (especially the more self-righteous—and usually wealthier—members thereof) feels peculiarly affronted or attacked by the wrongdoer. Consequently, it feels itself to be, in effect, the victim, though not perhaps in quite as direct a way as the individual who was robbed, beaten, or whatever. Thus, sometimes society shares in the feeling that retribution is its business. No one would argue that the feelings associated with retribution belong properly (for example) to people in distant countries whose laws have not been infringed upon in the least.

In the second place, it would be admitted on all sides, I think, that the most appropriate form of retribution would be one in which the wrongdoer labors to restore what he has taken from the victim. The case of theft is, of course, most peculiarly amenable to this. Now, we shall see in the next section that reparation has a utilitarian foundation. I submit that retribution is nothing but a special case of reparation, in the following ways.

The feeling of retribution is the feeling of outrage at injustice, a feeling associated with a desire to see the wrongdoer suffer precisely as much as he has made the victim suffer. Therefore,

---

[15] Hart, "Prolegomenon," p. 165: "Failure to distinguish Retribution as a General Justifying Aim from retribution as the simple insistence that only those who have broken the law . . . may be punished may be traced in many writers."

it is the case that, *prima facie*, making the wrongdoer suffer will benefit the victim personally. Retribution satisfies the desire on the part of the victim to "get even" with the wrongdoer: if the victim's loss cannot be restored by bringing him back up to the level enjoyed by the wrongdoer, then at least the wrongdoer can be brought down to the level of the victim, who derives some satisfaction from this state of affairs.

As we have seen, the question must be raised in the case of any given desire whether it is a legitimate one or not. Is the desire for retribution, or vengeance, a legitimate desire or not? Here, I think, is the crux of the problem. Ordinarily, a desire to see another person suffer is, of course, illegitimate, as I have shown in the previous section. In the present case, however, the situation is complicated by the fact that the wrongdoer is in the wrong. He has been the cause of suffering in the first place. Clearly, *he* cannot argue that the desire of the victim to see him suffer is illegitimate, for it is a desire which he himself is responsible for, and could have avoided bringing into existence by not committing the crime in the first place. Thus, we cannot classify the desire of retribution simply and solely with sadistic desires, or desires to aggrandize oneself at the expense of others.

On the other hand, the sort of pleasure gotten from seeing one's torturer tortured himself is not the best kind. It is a pleasure which cannot be had unless one has been tortured. It would be absurd (and immoral) for someone to have a desire for retribution in the same way that he might have a desire for bananas; to go around inducing people to commit crimes against himself so that he could then have the criminal caught and tortured. It is insane in exactly the same way that masochism is insane, except that in this there would be a touch of sadism as well. (Presumably, a person with such a desire would not really mind if the "criminal" weren't responsible, e.g., for the harm done to the "victim.")

Consequently, we have some reason to satisfy desires for retribution, and some reason not to. The best situation, of course, would be not to have any criminals to punish in the first place, so that the subject would never arise. But the next best would be to have the criminals' punishment of such a kind as to repair the damage done (if it is of the reparable kind); and in the case

175

of non-reparable damage, to have a type of punishment which would effectively reform the criminal so that he wouldn't be inclined to perform future crimes of any kind. In that event, we would want him to be able to feel that he had "done his turn," and was entitled to a happy life thereafter, the same as anyone else. Meanwhile, we would want the victim recompensed in some way for his loss, but by means which didn't involve suffering for the criminal, so long as the end of reforming his criminal tendencies were achieved. It is for this reason, I think, that we tend to associate retribution with primitive societies. When one cannot afford prisons, and when the cast of mind of the criminal isn't apt to make him amenable to reformative influences, then it seems to me that the victim might be entitled to see his assailant suffer if that will make him (the victim) happier. There are circumstances, I think, in which the utilitarian viewpoint might justify retribution; it's just that a better state of things is possible, and preferably, we should attempt to forward that better state. In a nutshell, the main trouble with retribution is that there's no future in it.

Besides this, there is a very serious question about the impingement of the considerations giving rise to the controversy about "free will" and "determinism" on this matter. To be conceivably justified in visiting the iniquities of wrongdoers on their future selves, we must suppose in a rather strong sense of 'could have' that they 'could have done otherwise.' Genuine doubts on this subject—genuine, in that they are raised by careful investigation into cases rather than airy speculations—are probably the main source of the contemporary trend away from any kind of retributive theories. Between sociology and psychology, we are coming to see that violent, sadistic, and anti-social acts are very often due to genuine compulsion, thus giving support to the notion that anti-utilitarian behavior (if so we may call it) is a kind of disease. These doubts, happily, need not be incorporated into the theory of utilitarianism, for the net purport of the present section is simply that retribution might be viewed as having utility, under the appropriate conditions. Once again, we do not have to take our choice between supposedly opposed alternatives. Some versions of the retributive theory have the tentative support of utilitarianism, and these are the only versions of it which have any real plausibility to modern minds.

Reparations

Generally, it is felt that we have a special obligation to persons whom we have wronged in the past, the obligation to make "reparations." A corresponding obligation is gratitude, or thankfulness for past kindnesses or services done one. In both cases, the obligation is "retrospective," and on this ground it has been thought to be a stumbling block for utilitarianism. We shall see in the account of promising and related acts of incurring obligations that it is possible to account intelligibly for the relevance of previous actions on utilitarian grounds. The cases of reparation-making and gratitude are somewhat different. In the case of making a promise, the obligation is in a certain sense artificial: the point of making the promise is to create the obligation, and consequently the promiser cannot consistently fend off our efforts to hold him to it by saying, "But what difference does that make?" We have, so to speak, a logical hold on the person who makes a promise, as well as a reason (stemming from the interest and expectation of the promisee) to require him to live up to it. But in the case of reparations and gratitude, this is not the case. No one harms another person in order to incur an obligation of making reparations; nor does he accept services in order to incur an obligation of showing gratitude. Nevertheless, it would be absurd to hold that the person harmed has no special claim on the aggressor, or that the fact that a person has done one a special service should make absolutely no difference to one's future behavior. How, then, do we give an account of these obligations?

To begin with the case of gratitude, it seems to me that unlike the case of making reparations, it is incorrect to class this as an "obligation" in the same sense. Indeed, in the sense in which promise-keeping is a duty, and in which the obligations of citizenship are obligations, I suggest that gratitude is not an obligation at all.[16] We would not be justified in punishing a person for not being grateful, though care must be taken to distinguish failure to be grateful from the kind of behavior which would

[16] It is often classed as a "social obligation." To regard it so is pernicious; this sort of thing can make social life a bore and a chore.

ordinarily be called "ingratitude." An ungrateful person, often, is so called because he treats his benefactor with less respect than would be due to persons having no special relations to him, and not merely because he treats them equally.

To show that gratitude is not a duty, let us consider what can (and does) happen if it is so considered: anyone can put other people in his power by doing supposed kindnesses for them. For example, one gives the "victim" a well-timed present, then reproaches him bitterly and feels very righteous about the whole thing when the recipient does not respond in kind. There is a tribe discussed by anthropologists which carries precisely this kind of behavior to an extreme. Ruth Benedict reports of this culture that a child's father "distributed wealth for him, according to his ability, at a small feast or potlatch, and each gift the receiver was obliged to accept and to return after a short interval with interest that ran to about 100 per cent a year."[17] Even without interest, this makes a mockery of the business of gift-giving. A gift, as the name implies, is not a reward for a special service, nor is it an investment.[18] It is a *gift*: a (more or less) spontaneous token of affection or appreciation. If giving it were to make the giver "one-up" on the receiver, to put a special onus on him to return it, then the way would be clear for people to turn gift-giving into a sort of psychological exploitation. But the status of being obliged to do something is, as we have pointed out, intrinsically of negative value; consequently, if gift-giving could create obligations, the practice would be a bad one.

On the other hand, if the recipient shows no indication that he liked the gift or service, then again the act of gift-giving has miscarried. For the giver goes to the trouble of securing and delivering the gift in order to please, and if it doesn't please, he may as well not have bothered. Consequently, there is a reason for showing gratitude, as well as a reason for not regarding it as a duty. The practice hovers on a sort of delicate tightrope,

[17] Ruth Benedict in "Anthropology and the Abnormal," reprinted in *Philosophic Problems: An Introductory Book of Readings* (New York: Macmillan and Co., Inc., 1961), p. 344.

[18] After writing the above, I was informed that Emerson's essay, "On Gifts," makes this point with much eloquence.

the ideal adherence to which is what we mean by "social grace." It is very easy for this practice to be misused, and the person of sensibility will have a care about being either too liberal or too conservative. One of the chief criticisms of upper-class society is that these niceties are made very much too much of, resulting in neurotic anxiety, on the one hand, and waste of wealth that might be put to better purpose, on the other. All of these considerations are clearly enough of a utilitarian kind.

Making reparation, on the other hand, is (often) a duty. What do we say about this? The critics have, I think, misinterpreted the "prospectiveness" of the utilitarian view. If a wrong has been done a person, then it follows that his life, taken as a whole, will not have as much satisfaction in it as it would otherwise have. What objection is there to calling this a utilitarian consideration just as it stands?

We get into questions of distribution again, of course, and these will be considered later. But at the moment, let us confine ourselves to the single case in which the question is, simply, of whether one owes anything to the victim of one's past acts. This is equivalent, of course, to the question whether one should treat this victim's satisfactions as of merely equal value to one's own. I have tried to establish that harms are punishable on the utilitarian theory, the point being to keep them from happening if possible. If they do happen, however, then this means that the aggressor has subtracted, so to speak, from the sum of human happiness. The aggressor, then, has treated his victim as being not equal to himself so far as the worth of satisfying his desires is concerned, but inferior. We fix this up by over-balancing the victim's future supply of satisfactions, so to speak, until something like the state of satisfaction which the victim would have enjoyed had he not been harmed is restored. Thus, we maximize utilities over the period of time from the onset of disruptions.[19]

Now, many losses are of a type which simply can't be made up at all. Murder is an obvious example, but any permanent damage of a physical or psychological kind is unrestorable. The

---

[19] It seems to me, that this is what lies behind Baier's concept of the "moral equilibrium," with which the above account may be compared. (Cf. *Moral Point of View*, pp. 204–07.)

theory of reparations can therefore be carried too far. Some people regard the commission of crime as a sort of commercial transaction, where you are perfectly free to do harm so long as you make up for it by paying the appropriate penalty. This is nonsense. The point of threatening punishment is to prevent harms from occurring in the first place. Any step that could be foreseen to be necessary in order to prevent it in the individual case would be justified *prima facie*.

Meanwhile, the point remains that if it is possible to do so, reparations are a duty because they constitute the undoing of a harm, and therefore restore the "quantity of happiness" which the victim would have had if he hadn't been harmed. Aristotle's dictum that happiness is a quality of life as a whole is in order here. There is no reason why utilitarians, any more than any other theorists, should be required to ignore the fact that people have memories and that the quality, in their own eyes, of their present and future lives is often a function of their past satisfactions as well.

But Aristotle's remark must not be erected into a dogma. If a person doesn't wish for reparation, or doesn't care for it, then the obligation of making reparations doesn't apply. Society can hold the aggressor responsible for the crime, certainly, because society has a hand in the general functions of punishment. But if it exacts some sort of additions to the stock of the general happiness other than the victim's, then talk of "reparation" is out of place. This would be part of the criminal's punishment.

Here, then, we have a duty the possibility of which would no doubt disappear if people were unable to remember past sufferings, or to derive special satisfactions in the present from services performed in the interests of reparation. But there is this ability, and it is possible to make reparations to whomever has it, or has been wronged. Does this make the duty of reparations a "contingent" one, after all? Not exactly. The point that one's life does not contain as much happiness as it would, had one not suffered at a certain point (all else being equal) is not a contingent one. It is this point of which anyone who can remember what happened in his own past can make use. On the other hand, if we were unable to remember such things, or always miraculously forgot our sufferings but nothing else in our past lives, the point of treating this as a duty would disappear. But of course, if we lacked such abilities, we would not be able to do moral philosophy or much of anything else that is distinctively human, so discussion of this possibility is rather academic.

※

Types of Harms

Our "General Principle of Duty" employs a notion of 'harm' which must now be considered somewhat more carefully. How are we to define this expression for utilitarian purposes?

As a first approximation, we might say that x harms y if x does something to make the subsequent level of interest-satisfactions of y lower than it would have been had x done nothing at all. This is a very inclusive notion, however, which needs some modification. The most important modification is to restrict the interest-satisfactions in question to legitimate ones, where the criterion of legitimacy, as in the first section of this chapter, is provided by the Principle of Utility itself. We must also remember, in the light of the first of the two interpretative principles suggested in the previous section, that so long as the subject knows what he is doing, any effects of our actions on him to which he freely consents will not count as "harms."

The most obvious kind of harm, of course, is physical injury. It is rare that people will consent to be injured, and if a person goes about injuring himself or asking to be injured, it is likely that he is deranged. But an equally important category of harms is that of restrictions on freedom of movement. Those who have their doubts about the connection between liberty and utility very often overlook this point completely. They tend to think that a "utilitarian justification" of freedom is merely an *a posteriori* justification which does not make freedom an intrinsic value.[20] But this is simply incorrect. If a person is absolutely

---

[20] Thus H. D. Aiken on Mill's Defense of Liberty: "From such a point of view neither liberty nor justice or even individual acts of kindness have any intrinsic merit." (*Reason and Conduct*, p. 310). I think that this suffers from the confusion over 'intrinsic' discussed in Ch. IV.

indifferent to what we do to him, then we cannot (logically) restrict his "liberty." The Stoics' philosophy depends upon this point. They saw that if one could just avoid being concerned about what happens, one was to that extent free. The point was perfectly correct, although they carried it entirely too far. (You should be a stoic if you feel like being a stoic; the rest of us, however, will insist on our liberty in a more fullblooded way.) To say that a person's liberty is restricted is not to say that there is something he can't do, but to say that there is something or other which he does or might *want* to do which he can't do. If one of those social engineers about whom certain romantics worry so much these days were to rig things so that, unbeknownst to us, we were "unable" to do anything except what we wanted to do, and then chuckled gleefully about how we all thought ourselves free but weren't "really" free, the joke would be on him. When we can do whatever we want to do, we are free; to say that we are not free when we "can" "only" do what we want to do is absurd. But for that very reason, any restriction on freedom is a harm according to utilitarian principles.

Restrictions on freedom of movement can be self-imposed, and when this is literally true, then of course no harm has been done. Again, it is possible for philosophies starting with this observation to get out of hand and end up saying that we are freest when we have absolutely tied our lives up in knots— so long as we've done it ourselves. Surely we can appreciate this point without getting to the point of absurdity. A person strikes a contract, restricts his own liberty, in order to satisfy other interests for which he cares more. He gets a net gain in what he wants, if he's made a good bargain. Thus it is not a harm if I have struck a bargain with a person which requires him to forego certain types of activity, so long as the bargain has been struck with his full knowledge and consent.

Again, it is necessary to point out that I am not denying the legitimacy of prudential questioning. It is possible for a person to inflict harm on himself in the prudential sense. If a person marries ill-advisedly, goes into the wrong occupation, or joins the Army on impulse, he may end up miserable. The principle is that if a person consents, given that he has knowledge of his circumstances, then it is no longer the public's business to control his actions. For example, it need not imply that no laws may be made to protect a person "from himself." But it does imply that these laws must be of certain kinds. In particular, they ought to be of the "permissive" rather than the "restrictive" kind, in general. They should, for example, make reconsideration possible: marriages should be dissoluble with due regard for the interests of all parties, long-term contracts breakable with penalty clauses, and so forth. The condition that consent must be made in the light of full knowledge must be emphasized. A slave may acquiesce in his present condition because he has been brainwashed, or simply because he doesn't know that it is possible for things to be otherwise. Experience can tell us that people are likely to be happy under some conditions even though they themselves do not presently think so; their present acquiescence, therefore, must be weighed against their present condition of knowledge. None of this seems to me incompatible with the position taken in Chapter III.

Finally, there is the category of psychological harm. This is a difficult one to define, certainly; but it is not necessary to go into the matter deeply here, so long as we recognize the category. Mental cruelty can and does happen, whatever the proper account of it may be. The problem is to strike a balance between those mental agonies and tortures which people go through because they hold beliefs and attitudes which can be changed by a process of argument, and those which can't. Again, the question of "moral freedom" arises here. Some people are in the clutches of their consciences, as Baier points out.[21] They literally can't make themselves do certain things, and they can't participate in a calm discussion of the merits and demerits of those courses of actions. What should we do? To the extent that the courses of action in question are morally neutral, there is only a personal, not a moral problem. But if their moral principles conflict with utility, if we can't get them to discuss the matter rationally and to see who is right, we might have to send them to the psychiatrist. If, for instance, some of Hitler's henchmen really were conscientious in their Nazi activities, then perhaps they ought to have been regarded as criminally insane.

---

[21] Baier, *Moral Point of View*, p. 13.

In any case, the point is that we are not doing them harm, in the morally important sense, if we do what is contrary to their moral principles, so long as those principles are bad ones.

This is perhaps the place at which to take notice of the view that man has a "dignity" that is "above all price and admits of no equivalent." Professor Ladd has asserted that this is the foundation of Kant's view of the rights of men, in emphasizing which "Kant sets himself against every form of utilitarianism."[22] The concept of 'dignity' is, unfortunately, not very clear. It might be said to be a sense of worth, for example, or a sense of one's rights (if the latter, then it could not very well be held to be a "source" of rights), or one's status as a human being. In any of these latter senses, 'dignity' is not something opposed to utility, but simply the sense that one's utilities are to count—which is just what utilitarianism is all about. That is, dignity is not separate from one's other desires, but simply is the sense, or desire, that one's other desires are to be counted.

If it is supposed that dignity is a special and irreducible want or interest, then what? In this case, to begin with, it is not clear that everybody has dignity. Some people think that dancing the frug is undignified; others do not. Again, if you take the owner of a South American plantation who is accustomed to pay several hundred hapless peons to work his holdings at a dime a day, strip him of his wealth and power, and force him to labor in the coffee fields along with the rest, his dignity would most likely suffer very much more than his muscles. I suppose that this is not the concept of 'dignity' Kant has in mind when he announces it to be "beyond all price"; but whether he would or would not, it seems rather likely to me that the situation described above would be conducive to justice rather than the reverse.

I conclude that the notion of dignity has no special moral status. Either it is equivalent to what is already the main concern of utilitarianism (i.e., the equal claim of all persons' desires to be satisfied, regardless of who the person happens to be); or, if it is not, then it is simply one more desire among others, to be

[22] Found in the Translator's Introduction to Kant's *Metaphysical Elements of Justice* (New York: Bobbs-Merrill, Co., Inc., 1965), p. ix. This quotation is found near the end of Part II of the *Fundamental Principles of the Metaphysics of Morals*.

taken into account but certainly not to be given special weight. Indeed, it seems clear that our account of utility implies that a person's dignity, in the irreducible sense, should count for roughly as much as the person having it wants it to count for, relative to his other desires. That a person's dignity would be offended is *prima facie* a reason for not doing what would offend it; but which of his other desires is to count as outweighing his sense of dignity is up to him.

While we are on this subject, it is worth pointing out that many of the examples raised in criticism of utilitarianism involve acts the harms of which are conditioned by social institutions. These can be changed. Stealing is an example. If a poor person steals from a millionaire, is it wrong?[23] This depends, in part, on whether the system by which the poor person is poor and the millionaire is a millionaire is justified. If it is not, then stealing from him may not be wrong at all. On the contrary, the millionaire may be the one who is the thief. The general point here is that we mustn't be too hasty in discussing such cases. Until the interest which has been infringed upon has been shown to be legitimate, the act of infringing on it has not been conclusively shown to be wrong. This is perhaps the principal source of difficulty in social philosophy, in which we must weigh the justice of institutions against the acts of individuals carried out against the background of those institutions. We will consider examples of this in the following sections.

Incurred Obligations and Duties: Promising as a Paradigm

We have seen that while some types of harm are specifiable without reference to any artificial institutions, some are not. In

---

[23] Some have questioned even that it is a "harm" at all. These people are surely using the word 'harm' in a narrow sense. There is some justice in this, on the basis of ordinary usage. But the same cautions applied regarding Mill's sense of 'pleasure' in Ch. III surely apply here about his, and our, sense of 'harms.' If I filch the diamonds of an old lady who "won't miss them," the question whether she has been harmed is surely to be settled by seeing whether she, in fact, *will* miss them. It might be replied that if she complains, it's just because she has a right over them by law; our account in the next section will deal with this question. But it is surely disingenuous, in general, to argue that theft does the victim "no harm."

the present section, I shall advance the thesis that most of the "retrospective" obligations and duties, those which are incurred by (past) acts of the agent, may be brought under our general principle of duty by establishing that the content of these obligations is due to the harm which would be done if they were not carried out, where the conditions making for the harm in question are created by the agent. While promising is the outstanding example of this kind of institution, all types of "practice" rules are also amenable to this analysis.

In Chapter V, I alluded to a "third view" of rules which was not discussed there. Our point of departure here will be John Rawls' celebrated paper, "Two Concepts of Rules,"[24] in which a fundamental distinction between the sort of rules exemplified by "When in doubt, don't do it" and that exemplified by 'Keep your promises,' is argued for. He calls these two "conceptions" of rules, the "summary concept" and the "practice concept." The "summary" type of rules are "reports that cases of a certain sort have been found on other grounds to be properly decided in a certain way."[25] By 'other grounds,' he means here that the grounds on which they are decided can be understood in the absence of knowledge about the rule: the particular cases are logically prior to the rule. Thus, one might have discovered that cats can be most efficiently skinned by starting at a certain place; and one might then pass this knowledge on to a learner of the trade by saying, "When skinning cats, starts here and then . . ." The learner might, of course, discover some other equally efficient or more efficient way to do it ("there's more than one way to skin a cat"). If so, then he will be quite justified in doing it this other way. The rule is sound only to the extent that its point is best achieved in the way it says to achieve it.

If we contrast this, however, with the rules of chess or baseball, we get a much different picture. Thus, to use Rawls' example:

In a game of baseball, if a batter were to ask, "Can I have four strikes?" it would be assumed that he was asking what the rule was; and if, when told what the rule was, he were to say that he meant that

---

[24] *Philosophical Review* (New York: AMS Press, Inc., 1955).
[25] *Ibid.,* p. 19.

on this occasion he thought it would be best on the whole for him to have four strikes rather than three, this would be kindly taken as a joke.[26]

The point may be put more generally by saying that the rules (roughly speaking) *define* the game, so that it makes no sense to bring up some completely different set of activities and ask, "Why can't I play baseball (chess, polo. . . .) this way?" Of course, you might find one game preferable to another, as a game, or as exercise, or what have you, but that is another matter. Criticism both within the framework of the game, and of the game as a whole, is always possible. As Rawls says:

One might contend that baseball would be a better game if four strikes were allowed instead of three; but one cannot picture the rules as guides to what is best on the whole in particular cases, and question their applicability to particular cases.[27]

The point remains, then, that "To engage in a practice, to perform those actions specified by the practice, means to follow the appropriate rule."

But how do we apply this to ethics? Here, things become a bit more complicated, I think, than has been made out. Rawls says, for example:

If one wants to do an action which a certain practice specifies then there is no way to do it except to follow the rules which define it. Therefore, it doesn't make sense for a person to raise the question whether or not a rule of a practice correctly applies to *his* case where the action he contemplated is a form of action defined by a practice. If someone were to perform an action specified by a practice, the only legitimate question concerns the nature of the practice itself.[28]

He applies this reasoning to the business of promise-keeping, as follows:

[26] "Two Concepts of Rules," p. 26. I can't resist mentioning that in my day, we customarily gave four strikes to girls and certain other personages; and certainly our principle was that this would make for a better game "on the whole."

[27] *Ibid.*

[28] *Ibid.*, p. 25.

What would one say of someone who when asked why he broke his promise, replied simply that breaking it was best on the whole? Assuming that his reply is sincere, and that his belief was reasonable, . . . I think that one would question whether or not he knows what it means to say, "I promise" (in the appropriate circumstances). It would be said of someone who used the excuse without further explanation that he didn't understand what defenses the practice, which defines a promise, allows to him.[29]

What are we to say to all of this?

Certainly Rawls has an important point by the tail here. But we must be careful to see who is wagging, and who is being wagged, in this matter. It is all too easy to lapse into a kind of pseudo-Wittgensteinian mysticism at this point and declare that promises "just are" this sort of thing and that "we would say that he just didn't have the concept of . . . ," when it seems to a lot of people that maybe they aren't that sort of thing after all, and that so far as we know, we have the concept but still don't "see" it. Rawls himself, for instance, has certainly gone too far when he says that the excuse, "I thought breaking it would be best on the whole," would be rejected as merely revealing ignorance of the nature of the promise-keeping institution. In fact, that very excuse, if well supported, would be perfectly legitimate so far as I can see. If the promisee agrees that it was best on the whole for the promiser to break his promise, he puts himself in a pretty bad light if he goes on to say, "But you still should have kept it." What sense would it make, one can counter Rawls, for *him* to say that it was best on the whole for the promiser to break it, and yet continue to insist that he should have kept it? I suggest that the promisee could be accused here of failing to understand the sense of the expression 'best on the whole' if he were to follow through in that way. Clearly, if he is to support his view that the promise should have been kept, he has to show that it was *not* best on the whole for it to be broken.[30]

What Rawls must surely have meant, I believe, is just that

[29] *Ibid.*, p. 17.

[30] Baier, for example, argues that the question, "What shall I do?" *is* the question "What is *the best* thing I can do?", *Moral Point of View*, p. 85. Surely he is correct.

part of the support for the promisee's contention that the promise should have been kept must lie in the fact that the promise was (appropriately or properly) made. The promiser would indeed lack the concept of promise-keeping, if he thought that the fact that he made the promise made *no difference at all*. And critics of utilitarianism have accused it of just that. Thus, W. D. Ross, for example, says:

Suppose, to simplify the case by abstraction, that the fulfilment of a promise to A would produce 1,000 units of good for him, but that by doing some other act I could produce 1,001 units of good for B, to whom I have made no promise, the other consequences of the two acts being of equal value; should we really think it self-evident that it was our duty to do the second act and not the first? I think not. We should, I fancy, hold that only a much greater disparity of value between the total consequences would justify us in failing to discharge our *prima facie* duty to do A. After all, a promise is a promise, and is not to be treated so lightly as the theory we are examining would imply.[31]

Obviously, Ross thinks of the utilitarian view as giving no weight whatever to the fact of having made the promise, as such. The difference between Ross and the recent proponents of the "Rawlsian" analysis lies in the question, how to account for this *prima facie* obligation which we all know is there, and which utilitarianism (supposedly) cannot account for. As we know, Ross apparently held that the *prima facie* obligatoriness of promising was synthetic and *a priori*. "In fact it seems, on reflection, self-evident that a promise, simply as such, is something that *prima facie* ought to be kept."[32]

The recent analysts, on the other hand, want to make the obligatoriness of keeping promises in some sense a matter of logic. In fact, it has been argued that this analysis of promising shows that we can logically derive an 'ought' statement from an 'is.' In "How to Derive 'Ought' from 'Is,'"[33] John Searle lists a sequence of sentences which, he claims, are so related that each later member follows logically from each earlier member,

[31] Ross, *The Right and the Good*, p. 34, 35.
[32] *Ibid.*, p. 40.
[33] *Philosophical Review, 1964.*

the first being clearly factual and the last clearly evaluative. Or at any rate, the relation is "not just a contingent relation; and the additional statements necessary to make the relationship one of entailment do not need to involve any evaluative statements, moral principles, or anything of the sort."[34] The sequence is as follows:

(1) Jones uttered the words, "I hereby promise to pay you, Smith, five dollars."
(2) Jones promised to pay Smith five dollars.
(3) Jones placed himself under (undertook) an obligation to pay Smith five dollars.
(4) Jones is under an obligation to pay Smith five dollars.
(5) Jones ought to pay Smith five dollars.

The key step here is that from (2) to (4). We can all accept that from (1) to (2), provided that Jones knows what he is doing when he says this, and Smith understands him to be doing this (see qualifications below). The step from (4) to (5) is perhaps all right too, provided that 'obligation' does not merely mean ' "obligation" ' (i.e., 'is thought to be under an obligation'). But what of the steps from (2) to (4)? Searle admits that (3) only follows from (2) "other things being equal," and that a similar reservation is needed for the step from (3) to (4). But even so, (4) does not follow from (3) *at all*.[35] What follows from (2) is that Jones *regards* himself as being under an obligation to pay Smith the five dollars. But it doesn't even follow "other things being equal" that he therefore *is* under the obligation. The statement, "people are under obligations when they regard themselves as being under obligations, other things being equal," is scarcely meaningful, let alone true. Obligations cannot be created out of thin air, and they cannot be created by the waving of any magic wands, including verbal ones. Suppose Jones comes dashing into the room and says, "I acknowledge an obligation to shoot myself at dawn!" The proper thing to reply is, "Oh, really? Why?" And if he doesn't give some good reason, then we will simply reply, "Oh, come off it, Jones; see your psychiatrist!"

[34] *Ibid.*, p. 44.
[35] There is always the dithering between "He promised, but had no right to," and "He didn't really promise," to which we alluded in Ch. IV by reference to Austin, however.

Searle talks as if the verbal act *creates* the obligation, in some way, though with the assistance of "institutions" created, evidently, by the rest of us. He characterizes such "facts" as that Jones promised to pay Smith five dollars as "institutional" rather than "brute" facts.[36] Those of us untrained in the new occult art of changing facts into values will recognize this as simply a slippery way of saying that these institutions are thought to incorporate values. But there can be good and bad institutions, just as there can be good and bad games (Russian roulette and dueling, for example); and the question is, what makes the institution of promising worth practising? Rawls' insistence that we just can't raise this question on individual occasions of promising is false. If I promise to blow up a bridge, and then reflect that I ought not to have done so, I am perfectly justified in defaulting, despite the fact that I regarded myself as bound at the time. Well, why aren't all promises like that? That is what we must answer. Only an evaluative principle can answer this question.

The truth about promise-keeping, I think, is as follows. To begin with, a person *cannot* put himself under an obligation just by saying, "I promise. . . ." There are many conditions necessary before we can regard a promise as creating an obligation. Let us look at some of these conditions. (1) The promise has to be to somebody else. Promises can, of course, be made "to oneself," but they are not the public's business. We cannot morally hold a person to such "promises." Nor can we make morally obligating promises to a mountain or a sheep. One person must promise another person, before the promise is binding. (2) The promise must be a promise to do something which is morally permissible: promises to do evil are not valid. (3) The promiser must be under no more stringent obligations at the time of carrying out the promise. This is why one would need to add "other things being equal" in Searle's fifth sentence,[37] and everyone realizes its importance. But they often have failed to reflect on its import. Clearly, there has to be some way of

---

[36] Searle, *Philosophical Review* (1964), pp. 54–56.

[37] Cf., the criticisms of Searle's article by James and Judith Jarvis Thomson in *Philosophical Review* (Oct., 1964), "How Not to Derive 'Ought' from 'Is,'" and by Evan K. Jobe, "On Deriving 'Ought' from 'Is'" in *Aanalysis* (April, 1965), p. 174.

MORALITY AND UTILITY

determining relative stringency of obligations here, and it is
plausible to claim that utilitarian considerations must be employed to do it. If I have promised to eat lunch with you, but
can save a life by missing it, then I am right to break the promise. But if I have promised to do something that will save your
life, then if I can have lunch with someone by defaulting, I am
wrong to break the promise. Plainly, the amount of good I can
do, or evil I can avoid, by breaking the promise is the determining factor, apart from other obligations of the same sort as
promise-making such as duties of office. If we can give a utilitarian account of these as well, then utility will be the sole
determining factor at bottom. (4) Certain circumstances, un-
foreseen at the time of making the promise, can arise which
invalidate it. Which circumstances? Apart from those of the
type discussed in (3), they are those which affect importantly
the way in which the carrying out of the promise will achieve
the purposes which the parties had in making it. How serious
the change in circumstances has to be is measured by the degree
of importance of the interests affected, plus the amount of
trouble it takes to perform the promise. If the promiser can
easily keep it, and his own reason for making it was not seriously
affected, then he should keep it; but if it is very difficult for him
to do so, then it should be re-negotiated and the other party
ought to release him. Note that these are all utilitarian considerations. (5) Finally, if the promisee simply loses interest, then
the promiser has no obligation; and similarly if the promisee
doesn't accept the promise, or releases the promiser for reasons
of his own. This is the crux of the whole matter.[38]

If we ask, now, "Why do we have a *prima facie* obligation to
keep promises?" the answer is evident. When I promise you to
do something, I do so because you are interested in the performance of it, and by promising you that I'll do it, I have led you
to expect that I will do it in a way that you would not have
expected me to do it if I hadn't promised. Consequently, if I

[38] This view was substantially advocated by Pall S. Ardahl, University
of Edinburgh, in a paper read before the meeting of the Central Ontario
Philosophical Group, Toronto, Canada, April 23, 1966. Professor Ardahl,
however, disapproves of my claim that promise-keeping is a *prima facie*
duty.

default, it is more serious than if I hadn't promised, because this expectation is then disappointed.

Why, then, is keeping promises a duty if made under the above conditions (and perhaps saying "I promise" when not under those conditions doesn't really count as "promising," though this is not an important question by now)? It is because in defaulting I do you a harm, and we have a general duty not to inflict harms. Not all disappointments of expectations count, of course; if your expectation is illegitimate, then I am not obliged to avoid disappointing it. But it would make no sense for me to argue that your expectation is illegitimate when it is created by my promising you something, for the whole point of my promising was to create just that expectation. This is what makes promising a useful institution in human affairs.

Thus, the excuse "because it was best on the whole for me to break it" is a perfectly proper one, though one which cannot be offered if I do not take into account the disappointment which you will feel if I default, and the extent of your interests which will be unsatisfied by this failure. And this is all there is to it.

That it is all there is to it is amply borne out by any considerable observation of the way people actually behave about promisings. From the way some philosophers talk, you would think that the "ordinary moral consciousness" regards promise-keeping —*any* promise, made under any circumstances—as utterly sacred and to be kept though the heavens fall. This is simply untrue. Of course, the ordinary moral consciousness itself is not sacred, either. But more people behave in a sensible way about promising than in the neurotic way recommended by Kantian philosophers. In fact, people break promises without qualms when they are of very minor importance and when there is reasonable certainty that the other parties won't mind or "will understand"; and they do not regard other people's promises made to them as world-shattering occurrences either. None of these facts make sense on any view other than the utilitarian.

Thus, on the utilitarian account, there is a *prima facie* obligation to keep promises; moreover, this is true in virtue of the logic of the expressions employed. It is, indeed, considerations of interest which make the logic of these expressions what it is.

Certain contentions of both Ross and Rawls may be appreciated in this light. Ross' claim that there has to be a good bit of difference between the expectable utility of breaking the promise and that of keeping it before we are justified in breaking it, is perfectly correct. It is correct because, of course, the function of making the promise is to single out the promisee's interests, to elevate them above the surrounding background of interests which we conceivably might be able to satisfy. The mechanism of the elevation consists in causing the promisee to alter his behavior by making the promise, and by creating expectations which would otherwise not have existed and which will be disappointed if we default. Had Ross gone to the trouble of examining genuinely specific cases of promising, as opposed to his artificial schemes of "1000 units of goodness" and "1001 units of goodness," etc., he would have seen this. If Jones promises to meet Miss Smith at Maxim's at six, think of all the things she does which she wouldn't otherwise have done: she rushes home from work instead of enjoying a leisurely drink with the gang, spends an hour washing and making up, looks forward keenly to the appointment and the dinner, perhaps pays cab fare. After all this, if Jones doesn't show up, he had better provide a pretty good excuse.

On the other hand, suppose that it's really no bother at all, she would have eaten at Maxim's anyhow (does it all the time) and doesn't much care whether he shows up or not. In that case, his excuse doesn't need to be nearly as strong. In the former case, just happening to run across an old friend won't do the trick, but in the latter, it might very well. It all depends, and quite transparently depends, on the amount of trouble the promisee goes to, and the degree of his expectation created by the promise. These are plain facts with which anybody is familiar from daily life, as well as from novels, movies, and history books, and they are facts which could hardly have been overlooked if theorists had taken the trouble to go into specifics on the matter.

Rawls, too, may be accused of overlooking this range of facts. He talks as though all promises were terribly solemn, and as though all were of more or less the same (high) degree of seriousness. This is patently false, but is surely what he is assuming when he says that the excuse, "I thought it best on the whole" is unacceptable. As with Ross, we need only point out that this excuse (justification, more accurately, but one which calls for an excusing sentence from the promisee) is perfectly correct in form, but needs to take into account the trouble and disappointment of the promisee as well as the happiness of everyone else. Why anyone should ever have thought that the utilitarian view, of all views, requires us to ignore the promisee's interests for the sake of everyone else, is difficult to see. The cause, I suspect, is traceable to the confusions about the "intrinsic nature" of acts versus their "consequences" discussed in Chapter IV. The account I have given above shows that certain utilities are involved in the "very nature" of promising, since promising, in standard circumstances, creates expectations and alters behavior by a specific act of the promiser, while in those unusual conditions in which it does not, we regard the "promise" as invalid or otherwise lacking in moral force.

Thus far, we may sum up our results as follows. In so far as promising, and other institutions wherein parties "bind" themselves in any way are concerned with utilities, we must divide the relevant utilities into two classes. We might call these "antecedent" or "natural" ones, and "consequential" or "artificial" ones. By the former, we mean those utilities which would have existed apart from the act of promising; among these, as everyone agrees, are to be found the reasons for making promises in the first place. As everyone also agrees, these utilities are not, in general, such as to bind one. We are rarely obligated to make promises; obligation comes in when it's a matter of keeping those already made. Now, what I have called "consequential" utilities are those utilities which exist in consequence of making the promise, which wouldn't exist without the "institution," and hence "artificial." These, I am arguing, are such as to create obligations. It is true that they are such because they are intended to be such, and that they involve getting, as I put it, a dialectical grip on the promiser, who is in the position of contradicting himself, if he denies that he is obligated once he has made a promise. It is, nevertheless, the relevant utilities which create whatever obligation there is. All that is necessary is to see that the situation vis-à-vis utilities is not the same after the promise as before. That this should be owing to the "logic" of the institution is true, but compatible with the general utilitarian view.

Some brief attention to special cases. Promising figures prominently in those "desert island" cases of which critics are so fond. You make a solemn promise to a friend who is about to die that you will tend his roses on the desert island you've been sharing for so long; he dies; a boat comes by. Should you take the boat or keep the promise? Perhaps it is too obvious that one should take the boat in any case, so let us instead simply ask whether you should keep the promise other things being equal, supposing that you don't much like gardening. In this case,[39] the main question is why you made the promise in the first place. Presumably it was to satisfy your friend's concern for his roses. But is this a legitimate concern? If you don't think it is, then you shouldn't make the promise. If you do think it is, then you have a reason to keep it if you make it.

We sometimes have desires which can only be satisfied by the creation of conditions we will never know about, e.g., for our manuscripts to be published posthumously, our roses to be tended, etc. The satisfaction of these desires cannot, of course, produce feelings of satisfaction in us; and this might be a reason for thinking these desires unreasonable. Nevertheless, it is worth pointing out that if you tend your friend's roses in the above case, you are doing it in order to satisfy his desires, and if you default, you will have left this desire unsatisfied. Such "satisfactions" come within the purview of utility as I have specified it, but surely we all feel that these are pale ghosts of satisfactions, and not to be counted for very much.[40]

Finally, death-bed promises and the like are made under emotional duress, and all contracts made under duress must be

---

[39] The present discussion derives from my article, "The Desert Island Problem," *Analysis*, 1963. My example is due to Roderick Firth.

[40] Aristotle, in *Nichomachean Ethics*, Book I, Ch. 10, 1100a27, appears to take much the same view here as I do, saying that "It would be odd, then, if the dead man were to share in these changes and become at one time happy at another wretched; while it would also be odd if the fortunes of the descendants did not for *some* time have *some* effect on the happiness of their ancestors." Ross' translation, in *The Basic Works of Aristotle*, ed. R. McKeon (New York: Random House, Inc., 1941), p. 947.

viewed with suspicion. Ought we to hold someone responsible for performing acts which he promised to perform under such circumstances?[41] Certainly there are better things for him to do, and there's much to be said for leaving it entirely up to him.

Why do we raise monuments to the dead? Is it for their sakes, or for ours, by way of setting examples and reminders? Surely the latter. So if no one, including oneself, derives any spiritual benefit from such examples, then I suggest that there isn't any reason to erect them. Many people do have sentimental reasons for such activities, and a sentimental reason is still a reason. Moreover, the fact that sentimental reasons are reasons is not in itself a sentimental matter at all. Utility consists in the satisfactions of any interests, sentimental or otherwise.

The upshot, then, is that there are even reasons for making promises to those who are about to die, and for keeping them once made. But there are also reasons for viewing them with suspicion, and very good reason for not regarding them as matters of general public interest. Whether you should do anything for the sake of people now dead is entirely your concern, and not the general public's.

Now we may turn briefly to some related areas in which the general type of analysis I have applied to promising is relevant. One example is the weight given to the "status quo." When a person has been in a habit of doing a certain thing, and other people come to rely on his performance of it, to have a stake in it, then we feel in general that it would be to the man's credit if he served notice of substantial changes, if he has a good opportunity of doing so. This is doubly true of institutions of all kinds. Whenever an activity creates an expectation, there is

[41] Hare, in considering this question, proposes that we apply his test of "universal prescribing": if the person contemplating breaking such a promise were himself on the deathbed, would he be "prepared to accept the singular prescription . . . that, in such a situation, the man at his bedside should, just to keep him 'happy,' make a promise which he is not going to fulfill?" *Freedom and Reason*, p. 134. But the ultimate relevance of questions of the form, what would I do if I were you, is not clear. (Some discussion of this will appear in Ch. IX, below.) Hare goes on to say that "Most of us would be extremely averse to being deceived in this way," which may or may not be true. But it isn't clear why we should put the thing this way, since *ex hypothesi* the man on the death-bed doesn't *know* he's being deceived; so the fact that he wouldn't like it if he knew he were may not be in point.

moral value in letting people know of changes in it; and when our activity is intended to create just this expectation, we have an obligation to serve notice.

A somewhat different example is that of truth-telling, which is another favorite obligation of the deontological camp—one of the special trumps in the anti-utilitarian's hand. It can be shown readily that here, too, the deck was stacked.

Let us consider what lying is. It is not, of course, simply making false statements. It is, at least, making false statements when one knows they are false. But this isn't enough either. They must be made to certain other people and not just to oneself, of course; but this is still only a necessary, and not a sufficient, condition. To see this, consider the following. Suppose that I walk into the faculty lounge and, in plain hearing of all present, solemnly announce, in a perfectly sincere tone of voice, knowing just what I'm saying, and knowing perfectly well that it's false, "Snow is green." Have I told a lie? Of course not. In fact, everyone present would assume that I was playing some sort of joke, or had gone off my head. In order to lie, there has to be some reason to suppose that the victim will be misled.[42] So suppose that you pick a subject where the victim will be misled. Now have we told a lie? Well, certainly we are getting warm. Even then, however, there is another condition that we seem to have to add. Suppose, for example, that I mislead people about entirely trivial facts which they do not put to much use, or which, upon discovering that they have been misled, turn out to be rather amusing. Well, these aren't exactly lies, yet. Here we have to say that I am just "kidding."

Then there are "white lies." Are white lies really lies? Only in an attenuated sense. Suppose I have been to a party and I thought it pretty dull. Does the hostess really expect me to say so? On the other hand, it's difficult to avoid saying something as I go out the door. So I say, "Thanks for the nice party," or something of the like. This is "keeping up appearances," and a

---

[42] This is what makes for difficulty in the notion of self-deception. For an interesting analysis, see F. Siegler's article of that title, in *The Australasian Journal of Philosophy* (1964). Since writing this, Mr. Siegler's views on "Lying" have appeared also in *American Philosophical Quarterly* (1966). His subtle analysis seems to support my account, so far as the morality of it goes.

very useful thing it is. We don't quite want to call it lying, because it isn't quite the sort of thing we have in mind when we say that lying is wrong.

Now this does not mean, as some have said, that the statement "lying is wrong," is analytic (" 'lying' being defined as: 'telling falsehoods when it's wrong to do so' "). For it is not analytic at all. It's just that a falsehood is only a lie, in an unqualified sense, when the victim has been misled about something of some importance or interest to him. But the teller of the lie cannot assume, without evidence, that what he has to say is of absolutely no interest to the victim. And this is not all. It is important to see that the interest in question need not be an interest of any specialized kind. It may simply be an interest in knowing the truth.

The fact is that people in general do not say things to other people, unless the other people are interested. If they are interested, then what they are interested in is the facts about whatever the subject of conversation may be. For example, if I am interested in trains, then it analytically follows that I am interested in the facts about trains, and not in falsehoods about them (except in the sense of knowing that certain statements about trains are false). The facts about trains are those reported by true statements about them, not false ones. It follows generally, therefore, that in any standard communicatory situation, the hearer has an interest which will be disappointed if he is told a falsehood. It is therefore true that we ought, *prima facie*, to tell the truth. This again is an interest we could not formulate (nor disappoint, therefore) apart from artificial institutions—viz., language, in this case. Just as in the case of promising, the artificial institutions do not "create" obligations by a mystic wave of some verbal wand. The obligations exist only because the interests exist.

It is important also to point out that this does not mean that the truth is "intrinsically valuable." If that were so, no jokes would be morally permissible; moreover, we would all presumably have to regard it as morally valuable to absorb facts ad infinitum, which is clearly absurd. The truth is, of course, that the truth is valuable because we are interested in what it's about, and to the extent that we just don't care, the truth as such is absolutely indifferent. (But how do we know that we won't be interested some day? Well, we don't; and if we aren't, somebody else might be. It is therefore always reasonable to get at the truth rather than the reverse, while one is about it.)

The account of promising is, of course, extendable to a great variety of other "institutions" with similar logical properties. Precisely the same considerations show that we ought to keep agreements of any kind: contracts, duties of office (which are assumed upon entry), oaths, etc. In all of these cases, the conditions of incurring the obligation are conditions in which interests are involved. The interesting questions arise here when the outlines of the institution are unclear. An example of this is living in a certain country. Do we incur the obligations of citizenship? And just what are they? How about marriages? To exactly what does one commit oneself when one says, "I do"? We do not have space to treat each institution by turns. But it is worth pointing out that these institutions are alterable. If it can be shown that there is a better way of doing something— for instance, if we would gain by regarding different things as the "obligations of citizens," then a good state will make the appropriate changes. We always should be on the lookout for ways to improve these institutions, for just because we are putting them in the category of obligations, they are onerous to at least some people.

I submit that the thesis of "Act utilitarianism" remains sound here. As the outlines of an institution become vaguer, it becomes less clear whose interests are disappointed by default of supposed duties. When it is clear that nobody's would, then the *moral* obligation ceases. Thus, for example, with defunct laws, such as those against the sale of birth-control devices in some places, we are clearly justified in disregarding these altogether. If the state enforces them, then that gives us a purely prudential reason for obeying, and a moral reason for speaking out against them. But the moral reason for obeying them is absent. Only where it is reasonably clear that one is doing someone harm by defaulting, and where the interest harmed is a legitimate one, is there an obligation to conform. Fortunately, in societies that are not completely moribund, the vast majority of our public obligations are of this kind.

CHAPTER VII

Distributive Justice

Next, perhaps, to the "Innocent Man" problem reviewed in the preceding chapter, it is safe to say that the problem of distributive justice or fairness is the most influential of the popularly-regarded stumbling blocks to utilitarian theory. It is alleged that there is a conflict between the goals of maximizing happiness and of distributing it equally or, if this is different, equitably, where equitability involves proportioning to merit in some sense. It is held that there is a fundamental obligation to distribute things in accordance with one or both of these principles. Thus, for example, we find E. F. Carritt commenting as follows:

> Most of them (utilitarians) really admitted this when they found it hard on their principle to allow for the admitted obligation to distribute happiness 'fairly,' that is, either equally or in proportion to desert. This led them to qualify their definition of duty as 'promoting the greatest amount of happiness' by adding 'of the greatest number,' and to emphasize this by the proviso 'everyone to count for one and no more.'[1]

Latterly, we find Frankena maintaining this as the only really serious objection to utilitarianism (at least, a broadly construed utilitarianism). According to Frankena:

> To my mind, there is a decisive objection even to rule-utilitarianism. . . . Suppose we have two rules, R_1 and R_2, which cannot both be made a part of our morality. Suppose further that in the case of each rule we know the results of everyone's always acting in appropriate situations on that rule . . . and that even when we compute, as best we can, the values of those results we find that the score is even—in

[1] Carritt, *Ethical and Political Thinking*, pp. 63–64.

both cases we obtain the same balance of good over evil in the long run for the universe as a whole. Then, the rule-utilitarian must say that R_1 and R_2 will serve equally well as principles of right and wrong and there is no basis for choosing between them. But it still may be that they distribute the amount of good realized in different ways: acting on R_1 may give all of the good to a relatively small group of people without any merit on their part (to let merit count at this point is already to give up utilitarianism), while acting on R_2 may spread the good more equally over a larger part of the population. In this case, it seems to me that we must and would say that R_1 is an unjust rule and that R_2 is morally preferable.[2]

Mill, as we know, had delivered himself on this point as follows:

That principle is a mere form of words . . . unless one person's happiness, supposed equal in degree . . . is counted for exactly as much as another's. Those conditions being supplied, Bentham's dictum, "everybody to count for one and nobody for more than one," might be written under the principle of utility as an explanatory commentary.[3]

But Frankena agrees with Carritt that this statement of the matter involves an alteration of the principle:

Mill might reply that we should understand the principle of utility as enjoining us to promote the greatest good *of the greatest number*, which is, in fact, how it is often formulated. If we understand it thus, the principle does tell us that we are to distribute a given quantity of good to more people rather than fewer, when we have a choice. The principle of utility thus becomes a double principle . . . it has become a combination of the principle of utility with a principle of justice, and to read it thus is to give up pure utilitarianism for the view that . . . there are at least two basic and independent principles of morality, that of beneficence or utility which tells us to maximize the total amount of good in the world . . . and that of justice.[4]

---

[2] Frankena, *Ethics*, p. 33.
[3] Mill, *Utilitarianism*, p. 58.
[4] Frankena, *Ethics*, pp. 34 and 35. I cannot forbear to ask what in the world it means to say that the standard formulation of the principle of utility by Bentham and Mill, in terms of the "greatest happiness of the greatest number," represents an "abandonment" of "pure utilitarianism!" Isn't this rather like criticizing Christ for deviating from "pure" Christianity?

Perhaps the great majority of ethical thinkers would accept these criticisms. They raise a number of difficult and important questions, and in my opinion, trade on a number of confusions. In view of the seriousness of the charge, and the weight it is so generally regarded as having, there is nothing to do but to go into all of the concepts involved, with some care. I believe that we shall see, in the course of this examination, that the picture Frankena and Carritt present is seriously misleading.

Since a general review is needed, I will try to take up the relevant topics in suitable order, leading to a sketch of a general theory at the end. The first subject, certainly, is that of distribution and in particular, what it is to "distribute happiness" (or "good," in the relevant sense). Then we shall have to consider when and how one can (or does) have "obligations" to distribute happiness. Third, I will consider how fairness is based on utility, and will offer additional remarks on "fairness." Finally, some considerations about the moral foundations of political economy will round out the subject, insofar as there is space to do so within the confines of this book.

Distribution and Happiness

Distribution. To "distribute" is, generally, to give or to bestow; in particular, to do so when there are at least several persons who are in some sense the relevant class of potential receivers. What might make a person a member of this relevant class is a question which we will pursue in the section below. Meanwhile, we may remind ourselves of the conditions under which one can distribute. In particular, what is being given or bestowed or distributed must be (1) transferable, and (2) divisible, where several recipients are involved; in order to be transferable, what is being transferred must be initially, in some sense, the giver's; and in the end, must be in some sense the recipient's. Now, moral philosophers talk about the distribution of various things which do not quite meet these conditions as these terms associated with distribution are normally used. They talk, for example, of distributing praise and blame, punishment and even rights, as well as more ordinary things such as legal property. (And even 'legal property' takes in quite a bit.) Bestowing praise, however, doesn't exactly involve transferring something of mine to various recipients who then have something which I had before and now no longer have. But there are analogies. For example, we talk of praising when praising was "not mine to give," and certainly so of punishing. At any rate, we are brought quickly to the general subject of property, ownership or possession.

Property. In the most developed sense, to say of something that it belongs to Jones, is his property, is to say that he has certain rights as to its disposition and/or use. Rights to the disposition or use of something are, in the legal sense, matters of law, which are therefore subject to legislation and so alteration; while in the moral sense, if we may speak confidently of "the" moral sense here, to own, i.e., to have a right to something must be in some way a matter of its being a morally good thing that the person said to own the thing should be thought of as having the status to which a right to a thing consists. Again, as we move away from legal property and get into thoughts, ideas, praise, etc., we get only analogies to this. (All of this will be developed below.) At any rate, this takes us to rights of ownership.

Rights. Wanting a notion of rights of ownership (i.e., rights "to a thing"), we must move to rights in general, of which property rights are a subset. Following the general trend of social philosophers, it seems to me that the basic notion of a right applies to a person's actions. Now, for A to have a right to *do* x is, surely, for it to be the case that other persons have a duty or obligation not to prevent A from doing x, i.e., not to interfere with his doing x, if A pleases. This means, of course, that they may neither force him to do it nor force him not to do it. (This is the "liberty" sense of 'right.' If I am obliged to do x, then I have a right to do x in half of this sense, namely, that it would be wrong for others to prevent me from doing x, but not in the other half, since it would then be right for them to require, insist on, or force my doing of it. But we can neglect this.) There are other irrelevant complications here. For example, sometimes a person has a right "over" or "against" another specific person: if A "owes" B five dollars, then B has a right to five of A's dollars, transferred in a fairly specific way. Other persons then have (1) an obligation not to interfere with A's giving B the five dollars, or with B's receiving it, but also (2) an obligation to apply certain pressures to A if he doesn't come across, perhaps consisting in (3) an obligation to assist B in getting the five out of A, e.g., by giving information to the police if required; and in the sense in which law is involved, it will be the case that (4) there exists a specific group of law-enforcing agents whose special duty it is to apply force, if necessary, or otherwise take steps to ensure A's payment to B. All of these complications are not to the point here, since they are just variations on, and specifications of, the general theme that a right of A is an obligation on the part of others not to do various things (and sometimes to do various things), the general effect of which is to let A do as he pleases in respect of a certain act or activity or range of them.

Property rights, in particular, are thus a sub-class of rights in general, namely the rights to perform various actions involving the item which is said to be A's. Generally, these actions consist in "using" the item; again, there will be various things that the use of an item consists in, varying with the item, and sometimes the range of acts protected as rights will be limited to a certain stretch of those which it is logically possible to perform involving the item in question.

Now, the point of all this so far is that talk of distribution must in general proceed against a background of established institutions, either moral or legal, and generally a mixture of both. Lacking any specification of what "belongs" to whom, we are rather at sea, since it follows that we won't know what will constitute a "distribution" for the purposes at hand. And especially so when we talk of distributing "good" or happiness.

"Distributing Happiness." Clearly, what we can distribute, in the ordinary sense, are various items of use; likewise, we can

distribute various psychological effects, so to speak, though in a somewhat different sense. All of these may be distributed in the hope or on the assumption that they will make the recipients happier. In fact, this would normally be the case, since giving something to someone is to be distinguished from forcing it down his throat, for example, and thus we can assume that the recipients want the item in question. In turn, this normally implies that they like, enjoy, are pleased with, or otherwise have a pro-attitude toward the (use of the) thing in question. But to talk of distributing happiness is, clearly, necessarily elliptical for doing this sort of thing. Consequently, there is always the danger of oscillating back and forth between distributing certain material objects (say) equally, which of course might result in unequal satisfactions, *versus* distributing them in some "unequal" way which might, however, result in more nearly equal satisfactions. Added to this is the difficulty of being quite sure about any of these effects' being produced by any given distribution. All of this will have to be taken into account.

"Obligations to Distribute Happiness Equally"

Obligations to Distribute. That I have an obligation to give something to Jones entails that Jones has a right to the thing in question, and if the emphasis is on 'I,' then it entails that he has the right "against" me in particular. At this point, a few reminders from our previous dealings with justice, and a few more from common sense, are in order. What common sense tells us, surely, is that we do not in general have an obligation to distribute things: What we own is *ipso facto*, what we have a right to use and hence, normally, to dispose of, as we see fit. Being what it is for us to have these rights, and obligations being what we have said in Chapter V, it quickly becomes evident both that we do not normally suppose that we have obligations, in general, to distribute anything, and that there is good utilitarian reason for this belief. *A fortiori*, we would have no obligations in general to distribute equally.

To illustrate: if, for example, it is conceived that Jones, who is a millionaire, has justly acquired it, then certainly if he takes it into his head to give a hundred thousand dollars to some poor beggar he meets on the street one day, but not a single dime to the next one, is he doing somebody an injustice? Bear in mind that we are supposing that he has a right to his money, and that the beggars do not have a right to more than they have (viz., nothing). This may well be far from the case, and certainly considerations of distribution may determine this as well. But after all, the critics who have brought up this matter have not in general been communist radicals who believe that our present system of distribution is unjust,[5] and if they did, they might have done well to make this clear at the start. Obviously there is no sense in discussing how a particular lot of goods ought to be distributed if the person doing the distributing had no right to it in the first place.

In fact, there is no sense in discussing the justice of distribution in a pure vacuum (as is usually done) at all. It is time to consider some reasonably genuine situations, of which I submit the above as a good example. And the lesson thus far is simply that in the absence of any special obligation, we have no general obligations to distribute anything at all, and thus no obligation to distribute it equally.

Obligations to Distribute Happiness. It is even less obvious that we have an obligation "to distribute happiness." For one thing, this is not in general within our power, and the power to distribute it "equally" among all sorts of random persons, which presumably is what critics would want the utilitarian to do (?), is even less so. Making people happy is the kind of thing which, certainly, is *good*, and according to utilitarianism more obviously so than on any other view; but an obligation? Surely not. Obligations or duties are to avoid harming others, either in general ways or in specific ways made possible by institutional devices.

[5] Far from it, judging by their usual tone!

Thus, there are two strong reasons to deny that there is any general obligation or duty to distribute happiness: it is not within our power, and it is not the right sort of thing to be an obligation or duty.

Obligations to distribute equally. When we have no pre-existing obligations to give something to anyone, there can be no obligation to distribute equally, as we have seen. On the other hand, suppose that you do have an obligation to distribute something in a certain way. Suppose, for example, that you are a trustee for some philanthropy or for a will, and that the terms of the will call for you to distribute the money equally among a certain number of people. In that case, you should distribute equally; but by the same token, if the terms call for an unequal distribution, then you should distribute unequally. Again, the terms might simply say to distribute it among *n* people, e.g., among "all my sons." In that case, it would surely be presumed that it was to be distributed equally among them, since the mode is unspecified.

Now why make this presumption? The reason is certainly not far to seek. If, for example, I have a lot of money which I want to distribute among a certain group of people who all have a certain reason for coming into my favor so that I take the trouble to include them in the will at all, and I then do not bother to say how much each should get, I am obviously implying that they should get the same amount. For why do I bother to mention them at all? Suppose my executor gives Harry $10, Tom $50, and Dick $50,000. How could he possibly suppose that this is what I meant, in the absence of special information? What would be the point of including Harry at all? It's simply irrational to proceed in this way without some special authorization.

It might be thought that this account "presupposes" the very point at issue. But this is not true. The point at issue is, I take it, an evaluative one. But the preceding paragraph has no special concern with matters of value. Suppose that I say that I have a dozen fir trees in my back yard. You come and inspect, and discover that indeed, I have one fine tall stately one, and eleven month-old seedlings. What would you think? Or that I have a "family" of nine, seven of whom turn out to be cats? The fact is, that in using unqualified group-terms, we imply that the members of the group are all reasonably similar in the respect implied by the term. It's a simple matter of communication. Terms connote similarities; if the dissimilarities are extreme or substantial, it will be misleading to cover them all by a term which has to be stretched considerably to take them all in.

Numerous authors have commented on the apparent triviality of axioms of justice. Sidgwick, for example, observes that:

Some have said that the only sense in which justice requires a law to be equal is that its execution must affect equally all the individuals belonging to any of the classes specified in the law. And no doubt this rule excludes a very real kind of injustice: it is of the highest importance that judges and administrators should never be persuaded by money or otherwise to show 'respect of persons.' So much equality, however, is involved in the very notion of a law, if it be couched in general terms; and it is plain that laws may be equally executed and yet unjust.[6]

The prominent element in Justice as ordinarily conceived is a kind of Equality: that is, Impartiality in the observance or enforcement of certain general rules allotting good or evil to individuals. But when we have clearly distinguished this element, we see that the definition of the virtue required for practical guidance is left obviously incomplete.[7]

This is certainly correct. 'Equal,' is a notion the application of which requires other notions. To say that x is "equal" to y is to say, short of the case in which x is absolutely identical with y, that there is some respect in which x is sufficiently similar to y, preferably in some quantitatively variable respect, to account them of the same sort. What the "sort" is depends on what the respect is, which depends on what you happen to be talking about; and similarly for equality in ethical contexts. If you have a rule, then you can talk about inequalities in its application.

[6] Sidgwick, *Methods of Ethics*, p. 267.
[7] *Ibid.*, p. 293.

But where does the rule come from? Clearly we would need some independent standard for this; and utility provides one such standard.

Utilitarian Theory of Distributive Justice

We are now in a position to begin to formulate the utilitarian view on these matters. In the first place, we have seen that there is no general obligation on the part of an individual to distribute anything nor to distribute it in any one way rather than any other. In the second place, if an individual, or a corporation, or any group, does have an obligation created by some contract or other arrangement, to distribute something, then they ought to distribute it in the way called for by the terms. If the terms specify that it is to be distributed "in the way the executors see fit," then the executors do *not* have an obligation to distribute equally, unless they see fit to do so.

Moral Preferability of Equal "Distribution of Happiness." All of this presupposes, as we have seen, some method for appraising proposed rules or secondary principles; and the question is whether, at this level, utilitarianism calls for equal distribution of happiness in any sense. To be more precise, our question is whether an equal distribution is better than an unequal one, other things being equal. Now, this is still a very abstract question, and as such, should be treated with grave suspicion. What do we mean exactly? The question of measurement, especially, becomes paramount. Still, we must begin in the abstract. We shall suppose, what is plainly false, that it makes perfectly good sense to speak of "units" of happiness, units which, moreover, I can in some way bestow or supply, i.e., distribute. What can we say, under these circumstances? I think that there is an abstract argument for preferring equal distribution, quite apart from considerations of "marginal utility," etc., although these will be considered shortly.

To understand this, then, let us begin by recalling Frankena's admission that

It is true that the principle of utility requires us, when we are determining what to do, to count the effects of each action or rule on everyone and to weight equal effects equally in the computation of the score for each action or rule no matter who is concerned.[8]

This, he claims, must be distinguished from Mill's "confusion" in failing to see that nevertheless this is compatible with distributing the "same amount of good in different ways." According to Frankena, in other words, the considerations of equality all come in in reckoning up the amounts, and not in distributing it once reckoned. But this is not so. Imagine that I have it within my power to distribute twenty-five "units of happiness" among five different people, one of whom is myself. Now, imagine my confronting the other four people and saying, with a perfectly straight face, "Utilitarianism asks us to maximize happiness without regard to whose happiness it is; but this is compatible with any kind of distribution. Therefore, I have decided to take all twenty-five myself!" This is ludicrous. Is this compatible with the supposition that I have, as a basic moral principle, the belief that "equal effects are to be weighed equally in the computation, no matter who is concerned?" The other four chaps aren't going to believe it! And neither do we. A person who behaved in the above manner could not seriously be maintained to be a utilitarian. In believing that whose happiness it is is literally indifferent, he is *ipso facto* adopting the position that I am no more deserving of happiness than you: that is, that our desires have an equal claim to be satisfied. Having an equal claim to be satisfied is what it *means* to "count them equally."

Now the fact that I put the above problem in terms of distributing to persons, one of whom is myself, is merely a graphic way of establishing the general point that difference of person is not to be "respected." For if it would be absurd for me to claim that I was acting in accordance with the principle that whose satisfactions are in question is indifferent if I load the dis-

[8] Frankena, *Ethics,* p. 34.

tribution in my own favor, it would be equally absurd to load it in anyone else's favor.

The net effect of this argument, I think, is to deny that we can first make the computation, accounting everyone equal, and *then* do the distributing, in just any old way whatever. Which brings us to the subject of measurement.

Measurement. When we reckon utilities, it is admitted, equal desires should count as equal in utility. But this is already to admit that it makes no sense to say that we can, after making our calculations, distribute in just any way we wish. For this means that if, for instance, you desire something as much as I do, and we cannot both have it, and we can split it so that each of us will get some of the satisfactions we want, then it is *prima facie* preferable to split it. This is what it *is* to say that your desire is no better or worse than mine, i.e., that whose desire it is is indifferent. Regarding people's satisfactions as of equal value means attaching the higher value to the situation in which they are satisfied equally, or as nearly so as possible.

Now, it can of course happen that various deviations from this model develop. The item in question might not be splittable (consider the case of Solomon, the two ladies and the one baby). Or, one might want more than the other, and enough be available to satisfy both. If there are twelve, and you want seven and I only want five, then "equal distribution" is not called for. But what if we both want more than there are, only you want it more than I? What does this mean?

It is at this point that we are confronted with bogeymen. Critics, with their talk of "units of happiness" and "two million people half as happy as one million," suppose that we might have some method of measuring happiness in the abstract, as though we could attach some sort of meter to people to see how their hedonic states are doing. When they are criticizing utilitarians, they hide our actual methods of determining these matters in a convenient hallway, to be pulled out later under the guise of a rival theory. But happiness is not a quantity like water or sand, which might be found lying about in puddles or piles quite irrespective of what people want, demand, ask for, work for, or worry about. The reason why utilitarianism has always been formulated—in its "pure" form—in terms of the "greatest happiness of the greatest number" is precisely that happiness is necessarily found in persons, and that we can detect its presence or absence in them, in those cases in which they are not identical with ourselves, only by observing them, talking with them, acting with them. We *have* no other methods of "measuring" happiness than these.

To help focus matters, consider the question put by Hare, as follows:

Are we, in any case, to treat each *person* as one, or each *desire* of a person as of equal weight to the same desire, of the same intensity, had by some other person? The two methods might lead to different results; for there might be two people, one of whom, A, had altogether very moderate desires, whereas the other, B, had many and very intense desires. As a result, it might be the case that, where there was a choice of giving something to A or giving it to B, the desire for this thing came right at the top of A's desires, as ranged in order of intensity, but only in the middle of B's order, and yet that, all the same, B wanted it more than A did. If a sense can be given to this description, we should, if we were treating each *person* as one, presumably give the thing to A; but if we were comparing *desires* one with another, simply on the basis of their intensity without regard to who has them, we should have to give the thing to B.[9]

In the first place, why shoud Hare associate the supposed concept of "treating each person as one" as opposed to treating "each desire as one," with the preferring of B's satisfaction to A's in this case? I submit that this is arbitrary. If B literally wanted it more than A, it would be to A's credit to yield it to B, supposing that A had some kind of claim on it. He would not be denying thereby that he, A, was as much of a "person" as B. It seems that Hare is unconsciously slipping back into the pernicious habit of some schools of metaphysics, in which words continued being used in a certain way when the logical conditions of their application no longer obtain. The metaphysician talks about "reality," "the One," or "the Absolute" without supplying the needed answers to the questions, "real what?"

[9] Hare, *Freedom and Reason,* p. 120.

213

"One of what?" "thing that is non-relatively what?" Similarly, to talk about "equality of persons" is meaningless, as Sidgwick pointed out, in the absence of some rule or other whose application is in question. "Give each person one banana" supplies a meaning for equality of treatment. But "treat each person as one" does not; and therefore it no more implies the method which would prefer B to A than that which would prefer A to B in Hare's example.

Hare also clouds the picture by talking exclusively in terms of obligation and duty, and never simply in terms of good and bad. But it will not do to say that people have a right, simply in the abstract, to happiness, unless perhaps from God. If we suppose that A had a right to the item in question and B did not, that of course would alter the picture. Then A would be cheated if it were given to B instead. But we are not supposed to be presupposing any particular structure of rights here. I submit that under these circumstances, and if we focus on this one case, without regard to past or future satisfactions of A versus B, that there is more value in giving the item to B, if the case is specified. The truth is, it is meaningless to say that a desire could be at the top of A's list (if A is a human being at any rate), and still weaker than a desire in the middle of B's list. Such would be the purport of our remarks on measurement in Chapter III.

But we are not to look at cases only from the perspective of the immediate moment. Suppose that A has yielded a share, so to speak, to B in the past. In that case, we might want to prefer A to B next time around, even if B's desire is the more intense on that occasion as well. For we are to maximize everyone's satisfaction, all around, and "maximization" has time as one of its dimensions. A has, in effect, put off a possible satisfaction in favor of B at one time, so that the second time around he will have, so to speak, a credit on his hedonic account. We can describe this either as constituting a factor in the weight of A's future desire (so that we reckon his desire the second time as more intense than it was the first time), or else as a factor independent of intensity. In either case, the policy of not respecting persons when we satisfy desires would countenance giving A some preference to B if B has had preference in the past.

Some further points of moderate importance should be considered before we conclude. These are marginal utility, envy, "merit," and trades.

Marginal utility and envy. It remains true that circumstances enable us sometimes to maximize utility at the expense of equality of distribution. If a desired thing is such that dividing it beyond a certain point will destroy its utility altogether, then one cannot maximize extent. In a very common range of cases, including by far the most important for considerations of distribution, namely money, the phenomenon of diminishing marginal utility is in evidence. All experience indicates that a unit increase in income does not produce, in general, a "unit increase" in well-being, happiness, or satisfaction. Generally speaking, it seems more likely that an increase of a certain percentage of one's present income is what will produce a "unit increase" in happiness. Thus utility will ordinarily be maximized by increasing the income of a large number of poor people by a small amount each, than a small number of rich people by a large amount each. That wealth is not at all correlated with satisfaction may be dismissed as romanticism; but that twenty dollars mean as much to J. Paul Getty as to a man on relief just isn't true.[10] However, this is an empirical matter, and deviations can and do occur.[11]

There is also the fact of envy to consider. It might be argued that a reason for distributing equally is that inequitable distribution will cause envy among the shorted parties. As every parent knows there is a sense in which this is perfectly true. But as a theoretical factor for moral purposes, it must be discounted. As usual, we must ask whether envious desires are legitimate or not.

[10] It doesn't follow that the theft of his money is therefore of no account. Theft constitutes a harm, to be considered as long as what is stolen was rightly the purported owner's. But it may well be questioned whether a fortune the size of Getty's ought to be permitted to accumulate.

[11] John Rawls, in "Justice as Fairness," reprinted by Peter Laslett and W. G. Runciman (eds.), *Philosophy, Politics, and Society* (2d Series; Oxford: Blackwell Publishing Co., Ltd., 1962). He appears to take it as axiomatic that considerations of marginal utility provide the only *prima facie* case for equality of distribution on utilitarian theory. Cf., pp. 149, 150. (Of course, I am denying this view.)

If they are, it must be because there is some pre-existent reason for distributing equally; and if they are not, then they shouldn't be taken into account, in principle.[12]

However, we mustn't be too short with this argument. It could, certainly, just be a psychological fact about people, or at any rate about people in our culture (and clearly not true even of all of them) that they are pained at the knowledge that others are getting more than they.[13] Whatever the source of such desires, most of us know that they are difficult to suppress when they exist. This, then, constitutes a supplementary consideration.

Merit. Critics have also complained of the inability of utilitarianism to account for the principle of distribution in accordance with "merit." Here, too, confusion and muddle have obstructed progress. To begin with, the objection is usually voiced in such a way as to imply that there is some sort of general quality called "merit," assessable independently of any considerations of special purposes or activities. Incidentally, this idea is the sort of thing you would expect to find circulated by a decadent and unscrupulous aristocracy with an eye to justifying its dominant position by ideological means; but the briefest inspection shows that such a notion is nonsense. There is no such thing as "general human merit." There is moral merit, athletic merit, pianistic merit, ditch-digging merit, and what-have-you, and the reasons for "rewarding" each of these things are specifically different. To take an example, suppose that a group of people get together to form an athletic organization, for the purpose of holding contests to see who can run fastest, jump highest or farthest, or whatever. The rules for each such contest determine what "merit" is for the particular case. In a foot race,

[12] Here again, I find the remarks of Richard Robinson useful. He properly emphasizes the dangers of confusing the sense of justice with simple envy. See *An Atheist's Values*, pp. 178–81.

[13] Hospers, in *Human Conduct*, seems to regard the fact that the other parties might not know, or that even if they do know, the total quantity of good in an inequitable distribution might nevertheless be greater, as the fundamental points here. But the question of the legitimacy of envy when it occurs is clearly more fundamental still.

merit is proportional to speed; in a jumping contest, the height attained by the method specified; and so forth. To classify these abilities as "merits" is to say that these are the abilities which the participants and supporters of the activity are interested in, and which therefore they will be disposed to praise or otherwise reward. The proposition that "merit should be rewarded" is, in other words, simply analytic. Imagine holding a foot race, specifying that the prize will be so-and-so, urging each contestant to run his fastest—and then giving the prize to the man who came in third! (On grounds of his "general human merit," perhaps?) The person who came in first has, obviously, been duped. One might be inclined to call this "unfair," except that it is really too bizarre: it smacks of lunacy. One could, of course, hold a quite different kind of contest, the point of which was to cross a line precisely third. That would be a bore, perhaps, but not a contradiction.

Next, let us point out that people who are uninterested in athletics need not bother to come, and of course will not cheer the winners, nor participate in the other rewarding activities for these particular endeavors. All of this is obviously sanctioned by utilitarianism: The rewarders are doing what *they* want to, the contestants are doing what *they* want to, and those who stay home for lack of interest are doing what *they* want to. Where is the difficulty?

Trade. Another factor of importance in distribution theory is trade. Supposing that two people, no prior obligations assumed, should agree to exchange certain goods. In an unforced trade, it may be presumed that they do this for mutual advantage, and if the goods are "as advertised," and their desires do not change in the meantime (both of which can happen, but ordinarily does not), then the trade will be successful. This is as much as to say that their mutual utility will be increased. Consequently, we have a *prima facie* argument in favor of trade as an institution, so long as the above conditions are met.

It is clear that this concept is important in both economic and political theory. "Log-rolling," for example, is a type of trade, in which the participants are agents for other people's utilities. It has its dangers, but there is virtue in the practice if exercised with caution.[14]

Summary. I shall now try to sum up the results of this rather complicated discussion. My main concern has been, in effect, to complain that what Frankena, Carritt, and other critics regard as two independent factors, i.e., "quantity" and "equality of distribution" of utility, are not independent in the way supposed. I have argued that this is a completely misleading picture of the theory. The move from consideration of my own happiness to consideration of the general happiness (my own satisfaction to the general satisfaction, my own good to the general good) is the essence of utilitarianism. This means that it involves making "extent" one of the measures of quantity which, of course, is Bentham's view. According to him, "extent" is one of the factors to be taken into account in determining the "value of a lot of pleasure or pain." To suppose that the "quantity" of pleasure or happiness is one thing, and, quite independently, its "extent" another is simply incoherent. We are not, of course, given directions as to what to do when we have to choose between satisfying more people less and less people more; indeed, we could not very well have done so, in view of the fact that no method for attaching numbers to the "quantities" is question is available or even, perhaps, possible. The only thing that is clear is that it isn't clear precisely what to say here: but critics talk as if it were.

It might help to take an analogy, which will have at least some of the complexity of the present question. Suppose that we are arguing the question whether the Ferrari is faster than the Ford. The Ford, we find, will go faster in a straight line or around a banked oval than the Ferrari; but the Ferrari will come up with shorter lap times around a twisty road-racing circuit. Which is the "faster"? Well, it depends upon how the factors are to be weighted. But how do we decide this? It isn't clear. What's clear

[14] Cf., the article, "Philosophical Problems in Majority Rule and the Logrolling Solution" by Hardy Lee Wieting, Jr., *Ethics*, 1965.

is that if the Ford would beat the Ferrari under *any* conditions, than it's "faster," unqualifiedly. Again suppose that we want to know whether Minnesota is "lakier" than Florida. Florida, it turns out, has three times as many lakes as Minnesota, but Minnesota has more square miles of lake. On the other hand, Minnesota is half again as big as Florida, so that Florida has a higher ratio of area of lake to area of land. Then again, most of Florida's lakes are really swamps. What now? It isn't clear; it depends on what we're after.

Similarly with utility. What we want to do is to satisfy as many people as much as possible. Other things equal, the more people satisfied, the better; and other things equal, the more satisfaction for any given person, the better. But what is it to satisfy two people equally? A larger proportion of their desires satisfied, or the one most intense desire of one versus many of the less intense desires of the other? Lacking precise measures, we can only ask, guess, and experiment.

A distribution which satisfies everybody is best, and a distribution which everybody agrees to may be presumed to be best, assuming everyone is well informed, that envy is carefully discounted, that no one antecedently had an advantage to which he had no right, etc. My contention is that this result is what one arrives at on the basis of considerations of "pure" utilitarianism, and that it is, probably, identical with what would be recommended by Frankena and the others who have considered this question. If it is said that there is a "bias" toward equal distribution here, then we shall just have to reply that this is what utilitarianism is all about.

"*Justice as Fairness.*"   Before turning to the project of sketching the outlines of a theory of economic distribution, I want to consider the view of Professor Rawls, found in "Justice as Fairness" which has received considerable attention in recent years. He believes that the principles he advances are fundamentally different from, and incompatible with, those of utilitarianism; I shall try to show that this is not true.

Most of his criticisms, to begin with, are couched in rather tendentious terms. Consider, for example, the following:

[Utilitarianism] regards persons as so many *separate* directions in which benefits and burdens may be assigned; and the value of the satisfaction or dissatisfaction of desire is not thought to depend in any way on the moral relations in which individuals stand, or on the kinds of claims which they are willing, in pursuit of their interests, to press on each other.[15]

Both of these last assertions, which apparently are thought to be corollaries of the opening sentence, are surely unfair. It is self-contradictory to say that utilitarianism, which is a moral theory, tells us to *neglect* the "moral relations in which individuals stand." A moral theory determines these relations, and if they exist, according to the theory, then of course the theory does not hold that they should be neglected. Nor could the utilitarian allow that the "kinds of claims which individuals are willing to press on each other" may be "neglected." It is, as I have urged, impossible to measure utilitarian values irrespectively of what individuals are "willing to press on each other"; indeed, it is precisely in the context of conflicts of interest that moral problems arise at all. If in the light of all relevant information, a particular individual does not wish to "press a claim" for x, then one must assume that he is not interested in x, unless his ability to press a claim has been artificially restricted; but if he does, then that is precisely the kind of information on the basis of which we can assign a positive utility to giving him x. And if other individuals press the same claims, in the light of what is known about x, then they too must be considered.

To take an example of what Rawls considers to be an application of these general criticisms, consider his contentions about slavery:

But as an interpretation of the basis of the principles of justice, classical utilitarianism is mistaken. It *permits* one to argue, for example, that slavery is unjust on the grounds that the advantages to the slaveholder as slaveholder do not counterbalance the disadvantages to the slave and to society at large burdened by a comparatively inefficient system of labour. Now the conception of justice as fairness, when applied to the practice of slavery with its offices of slaveholder

---

[15] Rawls, "Justice as Fairness" (see *supra* n. 11), p. 151.

and slave, would not allow one to consider the advantages of the slaveholder in the first place.[16]

But this confuses questions of distribution with the kind of questions discussed in Chapter VI. The principles of interpretation there developed are intended to show that the utilitarian cannot consider the "advantages to the slaveholder in the first place" either, since slavery, by definition, involves forcing people to work for one's benefit against their will. Thus, the desire to be benefitted in that particular way is ruled out of court from the start. I suspect that this confusion lies behind much of the readiness both to criticize the supposed utilitarian theory of distribution, and to suppose that there is more of an obligation to distribute equitably than there is. Once we have seen this, the question resolves itself into that of assigning values to different distributions when the question of obligations *has not yet arisen*, i.e., when we are formulating the kinds of social practices, or the criteria for judging such practices, that we are to regard it as morally desirable to put into effect in a community. In the light of this, it seems to me that both of Rawl's two "axioms" of justice are derivable from the position I have been developing throughout this book. The first is as follows:

First, each person participating in a practice, or affected by it, has an equal right to the most extensive liberty compatible with a like liberty for all.[17]

Note that the word 'equal' can be deleted here without altering the meaning of the principle. According to our view, everyone should always have maximum possible liberty. Everyone has a right not to be harmed in any way, and any infringements on his liberty are harms (as was argued in Chapter VI, above.) It follows that no one may be required to do anything, including (therefore) participating in a "practice" as determined by legal arrangements, without his consent, unless the failure to consent is itself based on antiutilitarian grounds. But all "practice rules" are of this type, as we have seen in Chapter VI, since participants

---

[16] *Ibid.*, p. 152.
[17] Rawls, "Justice as Fairness," p. 133.

to them are bound by them only if they know the rules. It will be argued in Chapter VIII that in the case of other social institutions, their justification will require that each has a reason to participate, in the absence of which we would be justified in excluding him from the benefits of the practice altogether (by excluding him from society).

The second principle follows from the preceding:

Inequalities are arbitrary unless it is reasonable to expect that they will work out for everyone's advantage, and provided the positions and offices to which they attach, or from which they may be gained, are open to all.[18]

Here 'inequalities' refers to inequalities of treatment. This means that the person elevated is, in some way, elevated at the expense of the others. Rawls plainly does not mean inequalities of just any kind, or as such, since many or most inequalities are plainly irrelevant to contexts of justice, at least of the social kind. ("Poetic" or "Cosmic" justice is another matter.) But if an inequality is created at the expense, *prima facie*, of those who are not elevated, then it must be compensated for by a corresponding gain of some other kind in order to be justified;[19] this much is evident from Chapter VI. The word 'arbitrary' is in order here, so long as it is understood in its evaluative sense; but plainly the evaluative sense is justified by the point just made.

Where the inequality created does not actually work to anyone's disadvantage, however, such a restriction is too strong.

---

[18] *Ibid.*

[19] My colleague, Lawrence Haworth, has suggested an important amendment here. He points out that some of the "offices" which will be assigned, e.g., in wartime, will work to the total disadvantage of their bearers (e.g., some soldiers will be killed). He goes on to say that "If one knew in advance that he would be the one disadvantaged by an inequality he would not be swayed by the consideration that a net advantage would be gained at his expense." Rawls' principle would condemn it, then, as it stands. However, Haworth points out that we can plausibly adjust the principle by observing that "in advance of the relevant information concerning who will benefit from and who will suffer from an inequality, each must regard a proposed inequality that would result in a net disadvantage . . . . as a *gamble*, and must decide whether accepting the inequality would be a good gamble for him by taking into account the chances of his losing." This is a well-taken point from "Utility, Equal Freedom, and Equal Shares," to appear in *American Philosophical Quarterly*.

What should surely be said is merely that inequalities are arbitrary, so long as they don't actually work out to anyone's disadvantage.[20] Finally, the provision that the offices created by the inequality be open to all is evident enough. If someone wants to apply for one of the offices in question, then to exclude him is to dissatisfy one of his wants. Thus, the only relevant reason for rejecting him is that someone else is better qualified; this is a relevant consideration because a public office exists to serve the public. To say that it wants a certain job done is to say that it wants it done as well as possible, and the ground for selection is therefore inherent in the position. But it follows equally that the interest of the public will best be served by the best applicant.

Thus, it seems to me that we may accept these important principles without thereby altering the utilitarian position.

Summary on Justice and Fairness. There is a tendency to broaden the sense of the word 'justice' to take in essentially the whole of morality, and the present reflections and considerations show why this is so. The fundamental idea of justice is doubtless equality of treatment of various kinds, and the essence of the utilitarian position is that we are to regard others as equal to ourselves in point of the value of satisfying their interests. Justice, in the narrower sense, does not take in such things as benevolence, love, generosity, and the like, because as Rawls properly emphasizes, it is reserved for cases of conflict of interests, cases in which we must tread a narrow line because important interests are at stake, of which not all can be satisfied. This in no way conflicts with the general utilitarian scheme. On the contrary, I contend that the notion of justice makes sense only because of the principle that moral value is measured by the satisfaction of everyone's interests. (To add 'alike' here is otiose, for as we have seen, it follows from the statement that the interests of everyone are to be satisfied, rather than some special few, that no one is to be preferred to anyone else.)

The sense that there is some fundamental difference between

[20] This point is also made in Haworth's paper, "Utility, Equal Freedom, and Equal Shares."

considerations of utility and considerations of justice is due, I think, to the previously noted tendency to speak of "equality of persons" without attaching any clear sense to it. When we inspect such expressions more closely, we see that the interpersonal "equality" in question is no more and no less than that postulated by the utilitarian position, once we realize what is involved in interpersonal utility-comparisons. Finally, we must not expect every practice presently recognized to come out just. Who supposes that this is the case? The question comes down to whether the principle of utility provides a plausible or adequate basis for the appraisal and revamping of the prevailing institutions.

Since economic institutions are, surely, the most prominent of those concerned with distribution, I propose to close with a sketch of a theory of economic justice. This sketch is admitted to be speculative; I propose it only by way of showing the way in which, it seems to me, utilitarian considerations should be brought to bear.

Economic Justice

The question of how money is to be distributed is the question of how exchangeable goods and services are to be distributed. Few questions in applied moral theory could be more important than this one, at least in our present stage of advancement; for exchangeable goods and services constitute, surely, the great bulk of everything of interest to people. The tendency to brush this aside as "materialistic" is misguided, both because it is made from a parochial point of view, and because even from such a point of view, the point remains valid. "Spiritual" values are as expensive in their realization as any other, and more so than most. Even saints must eat.

In a sense, money is an abstraction: it represents anything that can be exchanged (i.e., ownership of which [or use of which] can be transferred, and which is scarce enough so that effort must be invested to acquire it). We can therefore assume that everybody wants an indefinite amount of it. Thus the general condition under which questions of distribution involve questions of justice may be presumed to hold: namely, that there is (at any given time) a limited amount of something that everyone wants an unlimited amount of. (Exceptions to this are essentially irrelevant here. A few will want to put themselves out of the money economy altogether, but we may reasonably limit the discussion to the rest, who constitute the vast majority.) Our general principle is that everyone should have as many satisfactions as possible. *Prima facie*, therefore, our initial position will be that an even division is best.

However, money isn't found in a "natural state," just waiting to be mined, so to speak (although one way to make money is, sometimes, to mine something else). For all practical purposes, the things we are concerned with here are at least partly the creations of human effort. Thus, two extremely important conditions, so important that they might be thought to nullify altogether the force of our derived presumption of the initial desirability of equal distribution, must accordingly be taken into account. These are that (1) the conditions—partly natural, partly the product of previous applications of effort by either the agent or other parties—under which effort is applied have a radical effect on output; and (2) people engage in these efforts, in the first instance, to satisfy their own wants (whatever wants they have, which might, of course, include the desire to satisfy the desires of certain other people).

Now, in regard to (1) above, let us remember that we are ignoring any present arrangements and working from scratch. Assume, then, that nobody presently "owns" anything. Bear in mind also that 'own' is an evaluative concept, and that we can alter any existing arrangement. Thus, the question is who should own what. For the present purpose, the question is, how do we apportion the natural resources of the world, which are of an immensely varied kind, among the population, which in its turn is immensely varied in ability and stature? This is a problem of great difficulty in practice; it is hard enough to know what to say in theory. But we can make a start. For one thing, if two persons of equal ability work on land of very unequal fertility, then one will end up with much more than the other. This is unsatisfactory, for in view of our *prima facie* requirement of equality, and in view of the fact that no prior claims of owner-ship exist to be taken account of, the man with the worse land will be effectively shortchanged. On the other hand, if persons of unequal ability work on the same type of land, then what? Is this also unfair? Well, not exactly. It is unfair from the "cosmic" point of view, no doubt. One might argue that everyone ought to have had equal abilities. But the fact is, they do not. If our human arrangements enable both to produce as much as they possibly can, then no charge of unfairness could be levelled against them from the moral point of view. So, the initial result is that each person should be given resources from which he is able to produce as much as he possibly can (if he applies him-self). If resources are not available to this extent, they should be scaled down proportionately, *prima facie*.

Thus, we have a scheme for maximally utilitarian initial con-ditions. But there is one qualification to be observed. If a person's abilities can be improved by effort of ours, then of course we shall have a reason to improve them. Under what conditions should we expend effort in this direction? Whenever there is a net gain in total utility, of course. But the ratio between ex-pected output and required input will depend on the level of the ability in question. If, for example, a person is handicapped in some serious way, the utility of relieving him, if it can be done at all, is extremely high. It is reasonable to "charge" nothing at all for such services, as we are only helping him up to the point where he has a chance of getting along in the world at all. But for increasing the abilities of already able people, we shall want to "charge" a good bit more.

Two principles have been historically influential in the thought of theorists on distribution: "A man is entitled to the fruits of his own labor," and "From each according to his abilities, to each according to his needs." There is an element of truth in both, but each may be misused. Let us consider each in turn.

That a person is, *prima facie*, entitled to the "fruits" of his own labor follows from consideration of (2) above, together with the principles advanced in Chapter VI. If, for example, a person is gathering wood, and the woodlot is "his," then if I com-mandeer a few pieces without leave, I am inflicting a harm. Any such action would be contrary to the interest of the laborer in question, just because what he's doing is interfered with. The fact that what's he's doing is increasing his wealth is beside the point, so long as the resource allotment from which he derives it is just, in the sense already outlined. But what if it isn't? And what, in particular, if he is laboring with public resources? After all, initially all resources are "public." They are allotted in a particular way only on the assumption that that allotment will maximally promote the general utility. (We could as well have envisaged "free rental" of a sort, up to a certain point, rather than an initial distribution on what we, in capitalistic countries, call "ownership" terms.) The question is, how do we decide what proportion of his output is due to his own abilities, and what is due to the fortunate disposition of his resources? There's the rub. Any dolt willing to move his limbs will succeed hugely in the Garden of Eden; even the ablest will be hard pressed just to survive in the Sahara. To suppose that we can see, by some occult process of divination, how much is really the fruit of "his labor," and how much is due to luck, is to resort to mysticism.

The slogan, "From each according to his abilities, to each according to his needs," has two serious defects and one serious merit. It has merit insofar as it is, as we have maintained, the satisfaction of needs, among other things, of which utility consists. But the first defect is that 'needs' is too narrow a term. The satisfaction of any want or desire or interest is *prima facie* desirable. The second, and chief shortcoming is the suggestion that we would be right in requisitioning the output of an individual whose abilities were great but whose needs were small for the benefit of everyone else, without regard to that individual's wishes. Of course, we can (as the Chinese Communists do) indoctrinate him with the belief that he ought to devote his energies to society at no special reward to himself. But what if he isn't convinced? And what if the amount of effort expended in indoctrination is not compensated for by increased output anyhow? Besides, on our principles, "brainwashing" is *prima facie* immoral from the start, so the whole idea is pretty dubious.

What we need, then, is a principle for determining the share of an individual's output that should go to the rest of society at large, versus the share that should stay in the hands of the individual. Both of these quantities, obviously, should be as large as possible, *prima facie*. How to adjust it? The answer is implicit in the foregoing, I believe. What we must do is to think of the rest of society as a body, sitting across the bargaining table from each individual, so to speak. Society[21] regards the individual's share as an inducement to produce more. It wants to make the public's total as large as possible; this will not necessarily be done by making its share as large as possible. It depends on the effect of raising the public share on the individual's output.

Moreover, all bargaining is essentially competitive. If the public wants soap, there is nothing to do but offer the smallest price that will get it what it wants. (This might be accomplished by government ownership of industry, of course; the present construction is neutral on this question, the answer to which will surely vary with conditions.) What the price may be depends entirely on who happens to be interested in making soap at the time.

When society becomes thoroughly industrialized, the extent to which an individual's income is dependent on everyone else becomes so large as to make the maxim, "A man is entitled to the fruits of his own labor" virtually meaningless. What is one's "own" labor if your ability to use it requires (1) twenty years of education paid for almost entirely by other people, (2) the use of fabulously complex machinery which was designed and manufactured by others, (3) the existence of elaborate organizations for planning, marketing, communication, etc., (4) the cooperation of colleagues, (5) the cooperation of skilled and unskilled workers at the production end, and (6) as significant as any of the above, the existence of a market of consumers who at any time could, in principle, stage a boycott or shift to another product? In these circumstances, there is no reasonable way to determine "merit," except by bargaining in competition with others who are ready to perform the same line of work.

---

[21] Note that 'Society' here does not refer to government. It simply refers to the people other than the individual concerned. Naturally, government will be the bargaining agent in some transactions, and the model here described is intended to be applicable to the range of problems involving government.

(Again, it should be born in mind that these conditions are substantially the same in socialist societies.) The notion that goods have some kind of "general intrinsic value" apart from what people are willing to pay is as mythical as the notion of "general human merit" denounced above. Price ought to be measured by utility, but utility has to be measured by willingness to exchange, i.e., to pay.

In sum: the principal ends to bear in mind are the extension of opportunity as widely as possible, and the attainment of the best conditions of purchase possible by society at large with respect to any individual's output. A simple mechanism for achieving substantially this end might, for example, be to employ a (basically) free market with a graduated income tax, an exemption from the tax which increases with the increase of prosperity generally, subsidies in the form of education, health insurance, and provision of minimum living standards for those whose present abilities do not enable them to get "up to the line" under their own power, and sets of controls over any power centers capable of exerting monopolistic influence on the whole system. The graduation of the tax should be as steep as possible, regulated by observing the effects on personal income in the lower echelons. If reducing the steepness of the curve (which makes the rich richer) increases the incomes of the rest of the economy, then it should be reduced; but if increasing it increases the lower incomes, then it should be raised. This system keeps an eye on all of the relevant utilities, the ultimate goal being the raising of everyone's income as much as possible.

The general conclusion from this section, then, is that it is a mistake to oppose equitable distribution, where it is a relevant goal, to "maximum happiness." Once one rids oneself of the misguided analogy of "quantities of happiness" to quantities of liquids, gases, and other bulk substances, and instead considers the way in which such "quantities" are actually measured, it becomes evident that considerations of equal distribution are central to the whole conception of utilitarianism. In turn, an analysis of the various proposals about how we ought to distribute goods reveals that utilitarianism can account for what is plausible in each. On the basis of these considerations, I have

229

suggested a general theory of economic distribution which attempts to take into account all of the relevant factors, and a simple system which (if it works) might plausibly be thought to maximize all of them at roughly our present state of economic development.

The chief moral is that maximizing the general happiness is not a simple matter. It is not directly analogous either to maximizing the Gross Natitonal Product, or to maximizing the average net income, though both of these are obviously plausible goals; nor does it directly imply either of these as taking precedence over the others.

This is partly because happiness is not due solely to size of monetary income; and mainly because there is no simple set of monetary measures that necessarily apportions what there is to the different claimants. Utilitarianism acknowledges, *prima facie*, the claims of everyone generally (and argues for an equal distribution of income to the needy or disabled who could be assisted by an unequal share, and of those whose output is greater insofar as this is due to superior productiveness. Adjustment of these different claims is no easy matter, and there is no reason to believe that any given system, even if clearly the best at the time, will continue to be for long. Philosophers have apparently supposed that the goal of "maximizing utility," since it sounds simple, must imply some simplistic theory of distribution. But reflection shows that this is a mistake. Simplicity of basic theory, when conjoined with the complexity of the human situation, leads to complicated results.

CHAPTER VIII

Rounding Out the System

Duties of Society: Relief of Suffering and Equalization of Opportunity

Thus far in our discussions, we have been considering what ethical theorists have called "perfect" obligations, that is, principles demarcating acts which it is one's duty to do or to avoid on specific occasions, or whenever the possibility arises. A promise obliges one to perform a particular act or series of acts, and is only discharged when these have been performed or their nonperformance excused or justified; harms need to be justified always, not just sometimes. The general Principle of Duty, as I have called it, is peculiarly aimed at this category, for I have tried to show that all such duties can be thought of as instances of the duty not to harm people. It is ordinarily thought that we have other duties which cannot obviously be brought under this principle, duties such as the relief of suffering and contributions to charity. This category of duties has been entitled "imperfect" obligation, the idea being that we are not obliged to perform them on each and every occasion when it is possible to do so, since there is no end to opportunities of this type. One could work twenty-four hours per day at the relief of suffering, and could impoverish oneself contributing to charity, but it is felt that to require one to do this would be going rather too far.

It is commonly alleged that utilitarianism has just this consequence, and this is regarded as one of the objections to it as a theory. This is the opposite of the difficulty I have sketched above. If, as my general Principle of Duty asserts, our only fundamental duty is to avoid harm to others, then it is not a fundamental duty to relieve the sufferings of others. Thus, we seem to have a Scylla and Charybdis to steer between. According to the objection, we have too many duties, and according to my reply (which, after all, was made with reference to similar difficulties about overabundance of duties), we have too few. The matter evidently needs closer investigation.

Thus far, the account offered has yielded two categories of duties: those which are always with us, and those which we incur by acts of our own. The "fundamental" one, that of avoiding harm to others, might very well be called a "Natural" Duty, in the sense that corresponding to it we can think that there is a "Natural Right" not to be harmed. The point of calling it "natural" is simply that the primary types of harms are definable in a "state of nature": no organizations, institutions, or practices need exist in order to make bodily injuries possible.

It has been argued by Hobbes[1] that the whole notion of justice (and thus of the violation of a right) is inapplicable in a "state of nature." Hobbes, in effect, makes the contractual type of duty the fundamental one, and claims that we have no duty to avoid harming others when we have no guarantee, supplied by covenant, that they will not harm us. But Hobbes' argument shows that he doesn't literally mean it when he says that in a state of nature "everyone has a right to everything."[2] To say that one has a right to do something is surely to say that others may properly be prevented from, or punished for interfering with, one's performance of that act,[3] and obviously Hobbes does not mean this.[4] His whole argument implies that we are justified in taking measures, including the use of force, to prevent harm

[1] Thomas Hobbes, *Leviathan*, in *English Philosophers from Bacon to Mill* ed. E. A. Burtt (New York: Modern Library Giant, 1939), p. 162: "The notions of right and wrong, justice and injustice, have there no place."

[2] *Ibid.*, p. 163: "It followeth, that in such a condition, every man has a right to everything; even to one another's body."

[3] This, I take it, is by now commonplace. Cf. Hart's "Are There Any Natural Rights?" in *Philosophical Review* (1955), among others.

[4] The trouble is that in the context quoted, Hobbes identifies rights with "liberties," in a sense in which a liberty is simply an ability; later, (p. 164, for instance) he talks of "transferring" rights, which is clearly nonsense, if a right is a liberty, where a liberty is merely the "absence of external impediments" (see definition on p. 163).

to ourselves, and this is not due to any contracts whatever. It is, in fact, precisely what I have claimed is meant by calling the avoidance of harms to others a duty.

Now it seems to me that the relief of suffering is not, in this same way, a duty. It is always a kindness, of course, always morally valuable, but as we have emphasized all along, this of itself is not sufficient to consider it a duty. Under what circumstances do we owe it to a person to relieve him from want or suffering? Under what circumstances, in other words, is it reasonable to blame or punish a person for failing to relieve suffering?

To begin with, we need to draw a strong contrast between the relief of suffering (which is what most charity and much philanthropy consists of), and something else which for want of a better term I shall call "sheer benevolence." The distinction I have in mind here requires the concept of a sort of standard or "par" state of satisfaction. When a person is suffering, in need[5] as we say (in the narrowest sense of 'need'), let us say that he is "below par." It isn't just that his satisfactions are few, it's that he's positively in a state of dissatisfaction, involving pain, grief, anxiety, and the like. The object of charity is to raise him from this level to "par." But if a person is in perfect health, both physically and psychologically, enjoys a good income, and is doing pretty well on the whole, then the rest of us aren't really in a position to give him "charity." If such a person has a rich uncle who unexpectedly leaves him enough to double his income, that is a stroke of good fortune, and certainly an act of benevolence on the part of Uncle, but hardly the sort of thing to be considered Uncle's duty on general moral grounds. The distinction, then, is between restoring someone who is below "par" to a "par" state, and raising the level of satisfactions of a person who is already at or above "par." Clearly, we must consider only the former a matter of general moral duty, and not the latter. Only by special arrangements, such as contracts, or

---

[5] This word, 'need,' unfortunately has wider and narrower uses. Sparshott, in *An Enquiry into Goodness*, pp. 136–38, interestingly attempts to get at the wider sense, but I find this rather dark. Anyhow, my use does see some circulation, I think. The idea is that a 'need' (as distinct from a 'want') is such that something terrible will happen if it is not satisfied.

because of special status, such as liability for reparations, could the latter fall under the heading of duty.

Mill has suggested that the distinction between "perfect" and "imperfect" obligation is that "perfect" ones are:

those duties in virtue of which a correlative *right* resides in some person or persons . . . It seems to me that this feature in the case—a right in some person, correlative to the moral obligation—constitutes the specific difference between justice, and generosity or beneficence. Justice implies something which it is not only right to do, and wrong not to do, but which some individual person can claim from us as his moral right. No one has a moral right to our generosity or benevolence, because we are not morally bound to practise those virtues towards any given individual.[6]

This feature was adopted as the definition of 'right' in the preceding chapter: To have a right to do x simply is for it to be the case that others have a duty to avoid interfering with one's performance of x.

Now, Mill's analysis is born out to the following extent. In the case of the General Duty discussed in Chapter VI, there is indeed a corresponding right, namely the right to personal safety. The specific, or "incurred," duties in turn are of the kind which create a right in certain specific individuals, namely the promises of the contracting parties. (Sometimes third parties get the right, as when I promise you to give Hattie a ride to town. Here I acquire an obligation "to" Hattie, as well as "to" you. This ambiguity of 'to' in 'A has an obligation to B' is nothing to worry about, it seems to me, once we recognize that it exists.)[7] But what about the relief of suffering?

If we say that there is a duty to relieve suffering, we ought to be able to say whose duty it is. It is clear enough whose right is involved: the sufferer's. In saying that somebody or other has a duty to relieve suffering, we are saying that people have a right not to suffer, and this is a natural extension of the concept

---

[6] Mill, *Utilitarianism*, p. 46.

[7] There has been much confusion about this, especially as it relates to the "correlativity of rights and duties." Baier helps out considerably when he distinguishes the 'partner,' the 'ground,' and the 'content' of an obligation. *Moral Point of View*, p. 216.

of a right to safety. I suggest as a general answer to the question, whose duty is it to relieve suffering?, that it is the duty of "society."[8] By the expression 'duty of society,' I mean that every member of society has the duty to play some part in seeing to it that somebody performs the act in question. The steps taken might be of many different sorts, but in general, they will consist in creating and supporting a social institution. An example of a rule of this kind is that ordinarily, if a person is in a position to relieve a particular case of suffering without great danger or trouble to himself, then he is to do so. Another example is the creation of a medical system, whereby some members of society volunteer to become doctors, which results in those individuals' having both the ability and the duty to relieve certain kinds of suffering. An example of a practice prevailing in certain parts of western society until recently is that the sufferer, when cured, pays the doctor for the relief.

There are good reasons to put the relief of suffering in the category of "duties of society," if we are to classify it as a duty at all. Some of these reasons are as follows: In the first place, if Jones just happens to be in the neighborhood where someone is suffering in a way relievable by Jones, this is just luck. Any of us might have been there instead; Jones didn't do anything to deserve the imposition of having to forego his present activities in order to relieve suffering. Therefore, it is unreasonable to make the relief Jones' duty, as distinct from any of the rest of us. If we were to consider this a strict duty, that would be unfair to individuals who happened to be in a position to relieve suffering quite often. Secondly, the relief of many kinds of suffering requires specialized knowledge and/or skills which most of us do not have. We obviously cannot require someone to do what he isn't able to do; but also, it would be silly to require everyone to acquire the knowledge in question, even if they were able to acquire it. But a duty has to be someone's duty. It can't just be no one's in particular. Consequently, the thing

---

[8] For the interest of readers with a taste for symmetry and architectonic, we might mention that my "duty of society" is construable as the mirror image of Mill's "imperfect duty": in the latter, the duty is *to* no one in particular; in the former, there is an "imperfect right"—a right *against* no one in particular.

to do is to make it everyone's duty to do something, even if the "something" is just a matter of seeing to it that someone else does it. Those who are put on the "business end," such as the police, the medical people, firemen, etc., should of course be compensated for going to the trouble of performing these activities. The simplest solution is simply to make these professions supportable by the public.

The question is, then, why should relief be treated as a duty at all, even if only a duty "of society" in the sense explained? It seems to me that this should only be treated as a duty in a "society," as one of the (perhaps the chief of the) obligations of membership. It is here that the "contract" theorists were, I think, on the right track. It is always reasonable, in any state of human existence, to prevent people from harming others. But it is not reasonable to require people to trouble themselves to relieve suffering unless they are compensated for it in some way, and in particular, unless they have reason to expect similar treatment. There is, after all, no such thing as an obligation to be a member of society.[9] If a person wishes to become a hermit, we ought to permit him to become one, and this will mean that we shan't expect anything of him in the way of assistance in time of need. But if he wishes to remain a member, then it is reasonable to impose as duties on him that minimum which he in turn expects of society. The relief of suffering, where possible, is certainly going to be the minimum such condition.

In short, the fundamental consideration, when it comes to obligations imposed by society, as distinct from obligations incurred by an individual himself and duties which are completely unconditional, is that each individual gains more from having the obligation (provided everyone else is seen to have it as well) than he loses.[10] Under these conditions, we can expect a net gain in utility, and this is therefore the ultimate justification for regarding the relief of suffering as having the status I have described. For our original definition of 'duty' is 'an act the nega-

[9] Curiously, Kant thought it was, in *Metaphysical Elements of Justice*. But in the end, this would have to be a "duty to the self," which category is renounced below.

[10] This is different from Rawls' idea (objected to in Ch. VII, see n. 19) for here the individual genuinely loses something.

tive reinforcement of which would be morally good,' good being measured by utility. Since we have shown that we can expect an increase in utility when reliefs are considered a duty of society, while we cannot if we regard them as individual duties (since in that case the individuals who happen to go out of their way to relieve suffering are uncompensated for their trouble and thus lose), nor if we do not regard them as duties at all (since in that case the relief of suffering would be highly undependable), we can conclude that this is the status which utilitarianism must assign to these acts. Surely this is also very much the same status which the "ordinary moral consciousness" would assign to them; indeed, the classification as "duties of imperfect obligation" suggests as much.

The notion of 'par' discussed above is obviously a variable one. What counts as deprivation in one state of society might well amount to immoderate wealth in another. This is not only unsurprising, but just what one would expect on our account; for the amount of trouble which an individual or society as a whole would have to go to restore a person to a state of non-deprivation will be immensely greater in a very poor state of society than in a very wealthy one. There is a further reason for this, at least in any kind of society which we can expect now or in the near future. This is that there is a very prominent role assigned to competition in the acquisition of wealth in such societies (Communist as well as Capitalist; only the types of position for which people compete differ a great deal between the two). In any such society, a person must be able to compete. Inability to do so, caused by lack of the minimum conditions for competition insofar as society is able to supply them, is equivalent to deprivation. In such societies, the conditions comprising 'par' will have to include a good deal of education, together with whatever features of home environment may be requisite to its pursuit. Consequently, it becomes proper to regard these things as basic rights in any such society. They are "basic" only in the relevant kinds of society, however, and not basic rights of mankind everywhere and in any condition.

How much counts as one "society" is also a notorious problem. Eventually, there is reason to hope, the totality of mankind on earth will constitute "society," and already some nations are acknowledging the obligation to improve the lot of the poorer nations. Is this a genuine duty on the part of rich nations, or should it be classed as pure benevolence? (The motives of the nations in question are not in point here!) This is difficult to say, and I do not see any obvious reasoning to support one or the other view at present. On the other hand, wherever there is a genuine society, extending governmental functions to all persons in a certain area, the above results will clearly apply.

Finally, it is worth observing that there is the strongest argument for putting all of the functions classifiable as "duties of society" in government hands, and supporting them by general taxation. Anyone who argues that any such functions ought to be matters of private charity (or in the extreme case, as some people evidently believe, of private enterprise) unless he has some extremely strong practical reasons for the view, can be accused of insincerity. If a duty is genuinely a duty of society, then it is contradictory to say that it should be left up to individual consciences to be done, unless there is good reason to think that public servants just can't do the job. But if anybody can do it, government can do it,[11] and those who say it cannot are usually people with a vested interest in seeing to it that it doesn't. If, of course, there happen to be a lot of people in society who just enjoy relieving suffering, they're welcome to do so. But this won't do as a general social answer to any such problems. People who relieve suffering hardly ever do it because they enjoy it; they do it because their conscience tells them that they should. But if their consciences are correct, then it is no more their duty than anyone else's, and it is the responsibility of society to see that it is done without sanctioning special impositions on people of exceptional good will. Duties of society are duties, not gratuities; and they are duties of society, not of whoever happens to feel especially called on to perform them. It follows that the agents of society (i.e., governments) ought to see to it that these functions are carried out in a reliable, regular way without any special self-congratulating of the kind that private participants in charity sometimes indulge in.[12]

[11] Logic does not *require* civil servants to be incompetent.

[12] This is not to say that charity is a bad thing; obviously, it is *prima facie* a good thing. But to rely on charity, which is spontaneous, for the carrying out of what are properly duties of society is a bad thing.

Generosity, Works of Supererogation, and Ideals

We have now considered all of the kinds of acts which can properly be classed as duties or obligations, and there remain to be considered only those activities which go beyond the category of duty altogether. There is a tendency to regard this category as empty. According to such views, morality is equivalent to obligation. There is some point in so regarding it, but I think there is better reason for thinking of morality as including more than this.

I suggest that all acts of raising people above "par," as I called it, provided they are not required by some special relation between the benefactor and the benefited, should be regarded as praiseworthy, morally good, but not such that their nonperformance is blameworthy or morally bad. The argument for so regarding them is a simple extension of the argument of Chapters V and VI, in reference to "fundamental" duties. To class something as a duty, as we have seen, is to put an onus on the person whose duty it is, to hold him responsible for nonperformance, eligible for blame or other "negatively reinforcing" activity. If Jones regards Smith as having the duty to increase Jones' happiness, and the rest of us support him in this, then we are effectively doing Smith harm. We are, then, lowering his utility-level, which is a disutility. But if our only reason for doing this is to raise Jones' utility-level, then Jones' desire for such a "raise" is illegitimate. He would be putting something over on Smith. Thus it would be contra-utilitarian to regard any such act as a duty.

Utilitarianism, as we have emphasized so often, requires us to regard everyone as equal in point of satisfiability. It follows that I am doing precisely as much good (in the "objective" sense discussed in Chapter V above) by satisfying my own desires as by satisfying someone else's, other things being equal. Why, then, should we reward people for satisfying other people when we do not reward them for satisfying themselves? In part, this has been answered in Chapter III. People do not need to be rewarded for satisfying themselves, because they will do so anyhow if given the chance. On the other hand, we do not have any

motive, as such, for satisfying other people. Of course, everyone
has friends and favorites, people whom he wants to do good to,
whom it gives him pleasure to do good to, and this is all to the
good. But these are selective motives and do not prompt people
to acts of perfectly general, nonselective benevolence.

Now, it isn't all that easy to perform acts of "perfectly general, nonselective benevolence." In many cultures, it is almost
impossible; in our own, for example, people would think it extremely bizarre if one were to send Christmas cards at random
or leave presents at strange doors. Nevertheless, it is possible to
make contributions of this kind, with a bit of ingenuity. For
example, one can underwrite orchestra concerts which the community might otherwise be unable to afford; indeed, one can do
a lot by simply being friendly, smiling at people, being willing
to give them directions, etc. There is a moral point to rewarding
this kind of thing, even though one cannot seriously regard it
as literally obligatory.

Still, such actions fall within the purview of morality, for the
reasons supporting the practice of rewarding them are of the
moral kind. These reasons are "supreme" and "absolute," in the
sense discussed in Chapter II. An example will clarify this. Suppose that you happen to be interested in model airplanes. In that
case, you will be disposed to praise the constructors of exceptionally interesting models, just because they are exceptionally
interesting. Here, then, is a special reason for bestowing praise:
a "model plane enthusiast's reason." But even if you are totally
uninterested in model planes yourself, you nevertheless have a
reason for helping to make it possible for those who do have
this interest to satisfy it: namely, you have the same reason that
anybody has, that this activity brings some joy into some people's lives, satisfies some interests. The argument for regarding
this as a good reason will be considered in Chapter IX, but here
it is sufficient to point out that it is different in kind from the
enthusiast's reason. It holds for everyone, independently of particular interests. Praise for such acts will accordingly be moral
praise. We increase the general happiness by singling out for
praise acts which increase the general happiness when there is
no other motive for performing them.

It is possible for a person to become a "general happiness

enthusiast." Imagine a person whose only interest was to promote the general happiness, and who had no other interests of his own. This is very difficult to do, of course, for it is hard to imagine a person who gets no pleasure from eating different kinds of food, or from various activities such as sports, who is uninterested in art or science, and who is even devoid of sexual desire. Clearly, it is no one's duty to try to become such a person, to suppress all of his natural interests in favor of his moral interest in happiness-promoting. This is what makes Kant's conception of a community of Holy Wills [13] who have nothing but moral motives so strange. In such a community, there would be nothing for anyone to do: if the only interest that anyone had was to satisfy other people's interests, the game couldn't get started. The "ideal" of utter self-abnegation is thus a logically poverty-stricken ideal.[14]

Nevertheless, we can conceive of people who come pretty close to having nothing but other-interests, and so long as there were at least some people who weren't like that, these people would have something to do. The question is, then, ought we to regard their lives as *especially* worthwhile, more so than (say) those of tennis players, pianists, or (for that matter) perfectly happy day-laborers? My answer to this question is that we should not. We have here a question about the relative worth of different ways of life, and this, as I have emphasized, is not a specifically moral kind of question. For moral purposes, any life is as good as any other life so long as it makes an equal contribution to the general happiness; this is sometimes done by contributing mainly to one's own. It is true that the "general happiness enthusiast" performs activities which everybody has a reason for praising, whereas people will differ in their estimate of the value of being a piano player, a day laborer, a tennis player, a politician, and so forth. But the fact that we would

---

[13] Kant, *Foundations of the Metaphysic of Morals*, especially part III. Kant thinks that the notion of an "intelligible world" implies such a community; if so, I would suggest that "unintelligible world" might be more apt.

[14] I do not mean to imply that Kant favored this ideal. But I think this is an inescapable implication of his idea. My "The Two Faces of Kant's Normative Ethics," paper read before the Canadian Philosophical Association, Sherbrooke, Québec, June 17, 1966, argued thus.

not bestow moral praise on these people for living the kinds of lives they lead, whereas we would bestow it on the saintly type, does not mean that the saint's life is (necessarily) more valuable than that of the others.[15] Reckoned among the benefits of sainthood, of course, would be included the appreciation of others. A real saint presumably would not put any special value on this, except insofar as it was a sign that his efforts at promoting the general happiness were successful. (This is a peculiarly unreliable benefit, as the occasional martyrdom of saints suggests. However, saints are rarely if ever martyred just for being good; ordinarily, theological motives lurk in the background.) But then, that just means that we have to reckon among the reasons for not trying to be a saint the fact that it has peculiar occupational hazards: as soon as the saint begins to enjoy something, he starts suspiciously examining himself to make sure that the enjoyment is absolutely selfless, and such habits inevitably lead to neuroticism.

All this amounts to, really, is a reiteration of my oft-stated insistence that, from the utilitarian point of view, the choice of a way of life is absolutely up to the individual who is doing the choosing, so long as the way of life he selects is not immoral. The fact that one would enjoy being a gangster or a Nazi does not mean that it is morally permissible to do so; but short of this, any kind of life is as permissible as any other.

A great many people have, and have had, "Ideals" which they regard as moral ideals, and which do include recipes for the conduct of individual lives. What can we say of these? To begin with, the utilitarian view implies that such people have a reason to try to persuade other people of the soundness of their views. If I think that way-of-life x would be of extremely high intrinsic value, I presumably will regard it as my duty to encourage other people to follow it. If I succeed in persuading somebody to adopt it, then, so long as I haven't tricked him into it, I have ipso facto raised the level of his utility; for if I have persuaded him, what I have done is to show him that the type of life he was living is not as good as the one I am trying to "sell." Thus, if he is persuaded, it follows that he regards himself as better

---

[15] There is an interesting discussion of these matters in J. O. Urmson's "Saints and Heroes," in *Essays in Moral Philosophy*, ed. A. I. Melden (Seattle, Wash.: University of Washington Press, 1958).

off than he was before, and this by definition (Chapter II, Section 12) is to increase his utility. Thus, utilitarianism puts a special value on this kind of evaluative argument.

On the other hand, utilitarianism cannot grant any special validity to any one such conception as opposed to any other. If I try to persuade somebody to engage in way-of-life x, and I fail, then I just have to lump it, morally speaking. I may regard it as highly regrettable that he doesn't take up the particular cross I have to offer, but I have no right to force my view on him; and it would be immoral for me to try to get the community to adopt laws which would restrict his activity for non-acceptance of my view. This is just as true if 99 per cent of the community are of my way of thinking as if only I myself am, as is shown by the argument of Chapter VI.

Is there, then, any "Ideal of Life" promoted by the utilitarian creed? Well, no, except in the rather vacuous sense that the utilitarian would like to see everybody perfectly happy. But this only means seeing each person living a life which is as good by his own standards as it is possible for it to be. And what kind of life is that? Obviously, it is no one particular kind of life, nor is it a variety of types of life, necessarily. We can see that virtually every human being is likely to be happier if he is adequately fed, clothed, sheltered, and has opportunities to be active. We know from general human experience that if people have nothing to do, they get bored, that if they are continually exposed to danger, they get traumatized, that they do not enjoy being pushed around and persecuted, and so on. And we are therefore safe in promoting these particular ends, for the time being. But there just isn't any one kind of life which we have reason to believe would maximally satisfy everybody, and if anyone thinks he does know of such a life, his work is cut out for him: let him go and persuade everyone else that he is right. If he succeeds, he will have promoted the general happiness, and if he fails, then we hope he enjoyed trying and that those with whom he argued the view derived some benefit from the argument.

There is, in short, no such thing as "the utilitarian way of life" any more than there is such a thing as the "democratic way of life." It seems to me that we should strenuously object to the

243

common practice of supposing that every social question is a
question about "ways of life"—that our disagreement with the
Russians, for instance, is a disagreement about "ways of life."
These problems and these disagreements are nothing of the sort,
and to put them in that category is to put unnecessary obstacles
in the way of solving them. Properly conceived, these problems
all are concerned with ways of satisfying the general interest, i.e.,
with ways of improving everyone's life to his own satisfaction.
Whether a particular policy, system, or practice achieves this
or not is, in principle, knowable by observation. To erect any
of these means into ends, especially ends supposedly sanctioned
by some misty metaphysics, is merely to put people off the track.
This, I take it, is a point which Dewey was concerned to advocate,[16] and we owe him a great debt for having labored so
mightily (and with considerable effect) on its behalf.

Finally, it is necessary to repeat, in the interests of clarity on
the point, that I am not advocating "subjectivism" regarding
these non-moral matters. Questions about the value of ways of
life, aesthetic questions, and any other evaluative questions of a
non-instrumental kind, are real and important, and to label them
"subjective" just because they aren't specifically moral, would
be unjustified, especially if the point is (as it often is) to belittle
them by calling them so. No doubt some lives are intrinsically
better than others. What I object to is the move from "this way
of life is intrinsically better than that" to "therefore, it is your
duty to abide by it." There is no reason why one perfectly
"objective" proposition cannot be perfectly irrelevant to another perfectly objective proposition, and the same goes in evaluative matters. Nor am I in any way denying that there is objective reasoning of a prudential kind as well as of a moral kind.[17]
Indeed, some of the latter is, in a sense, suggested by the terminology of utilitarianism. For example, we can argue that a person
is being "unfair to himself" if he neglects his future welfare in
favor of present pleasures, that it is imprudent to concentrate
on long-range plans to the neglect of present satisfactions, that

[16] This is a recurring theme in *The Public and its Problems, Human
Nature and Conduct, The Quest for Certainty,* and other works.
[17] Cf., the next section of this chapter.

it is wise to cultivate the virtues of industry, patience, economy, and so forth. I neglect these questions simply because they are irrelevant here, and not because they don't exist or don't matter.

Self and Others

There are two opposite problems concerning self and others with respect to utilitarianism. On the one hand, there is a feeling, which I share, that self-regarding acts have no specifically moral worth, and that notions of moral duty "to the self" are out of place. But on the other hand, it is felt that one ought to prefer one's own family, friends, community, and nation to perfect strangers; and moreover, there is something to be said for the view that, other things being equal, one should prefer oneself to others.

In Chapter III, I argued that according to utilitarianism the central aim of morality is to get people to respect the value of others. That people already do respect their own values was held to be, in a sense, a trivial truth. Moral praise, blame, and criticism are to be bestowed with a view to getting people to do what they would not naturally do of their own accord, and what they do not have motives to do already (which comes to much the same thing). If a person has an interest in doing something, then there is no point in blaming him if he doesn't do it, or praising him for doing it. No moral point, that is.[18] For the purpose of morality is to maximize the general happiness, which is to say, to be concerned for others as well as oneself. But "having concern for oneself" does not mean having any special set of concerns: it just means having whatever concerns one happens to have, no matter what they are. If, of course, one happens to be

---

[18] Kant has put the point very succinctly when he says that one's own happiness "can never, without contradiction be regarded as a duty. What everyone of himself already inevitably wants does not belong under the concept of duty, because a duty is a constraint to an end that is not gladly adopted" (*Metaphysical Principles of Virtue,* p. 43.) The reader with a careful familiarity with Kant's work will notice a considerable similarity between positions argued for here and Kant's. (Cf., especially Ch. IX.)

so constituted that one naturally wants to promote the happiness of other people, then there won't be any need for moral predicates to be applied to one's behavior; if everyone were like that, then there would be no need for an institution of morality at all, though there might be use for other kinds of evaluatory activities.

Now Falk, for example, in his interesting essay, "Morality, Self, and Others,"[19] has pointed out that concerns for our own interests are often just as serious, and a need for self-discipline just as important, as other-regarding considerations, and of course he is correct here. But as he himself recognizes, "to say, 'you ought to' to another is always a kind of interference; and the propriety of *saying so* varies with the case."[20] The question is, would it be proper, on the utilitarian account, to invoke this interference against a person on his own account? And how much would it be proper to invoke? It is well known that the answer to these questions in Mill's *Liberty* is that it is never proper to force a person to do anything on his own account, whereas it is quite proper to force a person to do certain things on account of others (which things, we shall see below). Now in this, as I have argued, Mill is basically in the right, though the matter is not quite properly put in this way. The reasoning is as follows. Suppose that I am an exceptionally imprudent person and, reflecting in a cool hour, I perceive that the only way for me to protect my interests is to force myself to do certain things that I know I won't like to do at the time for doing them. Seeing that I doubtless won't have the means to carry out this plan myself, I might invoke the aid of others. In that case, if they assist in forcing me to do what I believe to be in my best interests, they are helping me out, because it was my value-appraisal of my situation that they are acting on. If, for instance, part of my plan involves your emptying a bucket of cold water on my head if I don't get up by x o'clock, and you do so, I may dislike it intensely, but by my own showing I have no right to complain. You are doing precisely what you should do on the utilitarian view and your action, if done without pay (for example), is morally good, despite the fact that you're causing me

[19] Castañeda-Nakhnikian, *Morality and the Language of Conduct*, Essay 2.
[20] *Ibid.*, p. 56.

a lot of discomfort. But the discomfort is in what I conceive to be my own interest, and that is exactly what you are supposed to go on, on the utilitarian view.

The reason why it is improper to speak of its being a "duty" in the moral sense for me to ask you to douse me with cold water in the morning is that it's my business, and I can call it off whenever I want. The matter is entirely up to my own judgment. But with moral duties this is precisely not the case. When I have a moral duty to do something, this is a genuine constraint on my behavior. I can't simply release myself from it, call it off whenever I feel like it or am so inclined. This characteristic is, I have argued, part of the definition of moral predicates (in Chapter II). If it is, then it is obvious that moral praise and blame just don't come into the self-regarding sphere. This does not mean that we are demeaning the self-regarding sphere or claiming that it is unimportant. Quite the contrary: in a sense, it is the only important sphere, for it is everyone's interest that is the concern of morality, and this means the same as everyone's "self-interest." The point is, there is no need for the peculiarly moral kinds of praise and blame, which have an impersonal authority independent of self-interest, in matters *of* self-interest.

It also follows from this last consideration that it would be wrong to employ moral predicates in contexts of self-interest. For to do so is to erase the distinction of moral and nonmoral, to assimilate the one to the other, and thus to run the danger of encouraging immoral behavior. To see this, consider for example a man who, as in Kant's example, is "wearied with life because of a series of misfortunes that has reduced him to despair" and so contemplates suicide. Such a person is likely to take the view that nothing is worth doing, life is meaningless, and it doesn't matter what he does. (Strictly speaking, this isn't quite what he thinks, for this person would not have a reason to commit suicide; he just wouldn't have any reason to do anything at all. But the suicide takes the fact that life, if he continued to live it, would be empty and meaningless as a reason for ending it.) Now, this is a prudential estimate, and it does indeed give him a perfectly good reason for committing suicide, which is exactly what he should do, if it is certain that a psychiatrist or someone could not restimulate his interests in life. But if the distinction between moral and nonmoral value is not alive in him, he would see no difference between dynamiting an airliner with himself in it, and thus killing a great number of other people who want to live as well as himself, and doing it in the privacy of some dark forest. This is an extreme example, of course, but there are innumerable examples on a less exotic scale.

It is perhaps worth pointing out that so-called "ideal" utilitarianism leads to the same disastrous result. Only utilitarianism holds that what basically matters morally is what people like and dislike, i.e., what they think is good, rather than some supposed intrinsic value. The suicide mentioned above is precisely the person who sees no intrinsic values in life, and this is a question which we may not be able to argue about with him. We may not be able to convince him that anything is intrinsically valuable. But for moral purposes, we don't need to. Whether anything *is* intrinsically worth doing is irrelevant: other people think that something is worth doing, and unless he can convince them otherwise he has no right to immolate them along with himself.

Perhaps I have overstated this contrast: Its validity is limited, perhaps, by certain conditions which do not necessarily obtain. For example, it seems that it is logically possible that people should "naturally" be more concerned for others than for themselves; in that case, it might be urged, the "moral" predicates would be the ones to apply to what we now call "self-regarding" actions, and the non-moral ones to what we now consider "other-regarding" actions. Is this a possibility?

Something of the general sort is a possibility, but it seems to me that the exact description given above could not apply to it. From our present point of view, we have been defining "self-interest" as consisting of whatever interests one happens to have. This is, of course, partly a stipulative definition. In ordinary discourse, "self-interest" is defined in part in terms of a certain range of interests: e.g., that in filling one's own stomach, as opposed to someone else's. The assumption, clearly, is that these interests are, in the relevant sense, "natural" ones. It is very difficult to conceive of a state of the world in which a totally different set of interests are natural. I suspect that the term 'self' would not be usable in such a world, and that some rather different concept would have to be employed. Thus, it seems to me that speculations of this kind must be inconclusive at present.

More to the point, however, are the following considerations. We can point out that there is a general evaluative province, which some would consider part of morality, and which we can at least include under the more general heading of "ethics," in which the problem is to set forth the criteria for evaluation insofar as they concern oneself. This would be the area of prudence. Now it might be suggested that just as there is a problem involving the use of reason and calling for the employment of self-control, in going from prudence to morality (in the substantive sense of learning respect for others), so there is a formally similar problem involved in going from one's present state, one's immediate concerns, to one's future concerns. Indeed, it has been argued that what defines a "rational" directive in this area is the principle that those of one's wants which are remote in time from the present are to be counted equally with those now prominent.[21] This would be a prudential "principle of utility," the essence of which would be the allotment of parity to all wants, whenever occurring, just as the essence of the (moral) principle of utility is allotment of parity[22] to all wants, no matter whose.

Now, I have argued in Chapter II that we must not simply define the term 'moral' in such a way that prudential values are ipso facto not moral, even though it is common to contrast 'prudential' and 'moral.' The meanings of the words are certainly to be distinguished, but their extensions could nevertheless be the same: indeed, it is the main business of my final chapter to see whether we can construct an argument to prove that they are not, and of course argument would be unnecessary if we could settle this by definition. Why, then, should we not permit considerations of prudence proper, in the sense described, to count as moral?

The reason for this, I think, is as follows. I have suggested that

[21] Cf. J. D. Mabbott, "Reason and Desire," *Philosophy* (1953).

[22] This is not to deny the factor of probability, of course. Other things equal, a good nearer in time should perhaps be preferred to one more distant, simply because of the lesser certainty of more remote events. But it seems wrong to make "propinquity" *and* "certainty" measures of utility, as does Bentham.

the differentia of morality consists at least partly in the question of who is authorized to use (verbal or nonverbal) force or stimulation. If this is correct, then the reason for including prudence would be, in effect, that one's future "selves," or "states of oneself," being distinct from one's present self (or state of self), are therefore entitled to be thought of as members of the "moral community," just as much as other people are (or, not to beg a question, "other" people differentiated nontemporally).

The reply, which is perhaps a lame one, is that one's future states of self—that is, that set of momentary "selves" which are related to one's present state (or "self") in such a way that the whole series constitutes a single person in our present sense of that term—are somehow too intimately related to one's present state to be put in the same category with other persons. It is true that if I make a mistake, my future self (or one of them, or should I say, some proper subset of them?) will suffer, and this is a reason for criticism of a kind. But it seems also that it is a reason for criticism by me, rather than primarily by others.

I call this a "lame" reply, because perhaps it will turn out in the end that the feeling that one's future selves are more intimately related to one's present self than are other people is simply a metaphysical prejudice. Indeed, perhaps the day will come when, owing to developments in brain surgery or in psychiatry or in psychological drugs, the distinction in question will be much blurred. In any case, the distinction would seem to be a matter of degree, in some way.

For the time being then, it seems to me that we need a suitable compromise, and that this in fact is what we have. There is one's present state, or self, one's future states (or selves), and other people, with one's future states standing somewhere in between. We suppose, in general, that people are going to be a good deal more responsible in the second area than in the third. The community, we might say, is welcome by invitation only until such time as a person has clearly lost his senses.

Thus, there is good reason to distinguish between moral praise and blame and nonmoral valuation. If we do, then on the utilitarian view there is every reason why moral praise and blame should not be used in purely self-regarding contexts. We have other expressions for this, which carry just the right connotations of critical tone. A man who lets his talents go to rack and ruin in the pursuit of frivolities is a fool, but he's not immoral. He is not doing anything contrary to duty, but he is being irrational, foolish, silly, or perhaps weak. These are serious charges, but if the man recognizes that he has these talents, wants to develop them, realizes that it would be in his interest to do so, and still doesn't do so, then these criticisms are quite justified. They are justified by reference purely to the man's own value-scheme, and if he doesn't care about these talents, doesn't care about the money he could earn by developing them, etc., then we shall be obliged to let him go his own way. Of course, all sorts of moral factors do tend to arise in such cases. If he's married, he may owe it to his wife and family to earn more money by developing his talents; and society can point out to him that, at any rate, they would benefit from his exercise of them (if they are of certain kinds). But we aren't considering these at the moment. The utilitarian view is that, so long as it's only his own interest that's concerned, moral criticism (i.e., the kind of impersonal criticism which in serious cases also leads to reinforcement), is out of place.

On the other hand, since everybody's interests are to be regarded equally, neither more nor less, a person has a perfect right to urge his own interests against others. We might regard him as a fool if he doesn't; on the other hand, he doesn't have a duty to stand up for his rights; but he does have them. And this also follows from the utilitarian view. Obviously, if everyone's interests count equally, then I have a right to advance my own claims where they are in question. I presume that most people would agree with the result that we have a right, but not a duty, to pursue our own interests equally with everyone else.

The view that we have a duty to prefer ourselves to others is, accordingly, false. But the view that we nevertheless *should* prefer ourselves to others is another matter. According to Baier:

If we ask ourselves to which reasons, other things being equal, we attach the greater weight, to the self-regarding or the other-regarding, the answer is that, if the two reasons are of exactly the same sort and importance, then we always (other things being equal) attach greater weight to the self-regarding reason.[23]

---

[23] Baier, *Moral Point of View*, p. 121.

It is difficult to evaluate this view, owing to the problem of deciding just what the force of "other things being equal" is. However, I think that on the most natural interpretation, Baier is correct and that the view is just what we would expect on the utilitarian principle. What Baier is saying, I think, is that if another person would enjoy something that I can do for him just as much as I would enjoy it if I did it for myself, and I can't do it for both, and I have no particular affection for the other person, so that I would not get any additional pleasure out of doing it specifically for him, then I should do it for myself. The reason is simple: it's more trouble to do it for him. The other fellow is, after all, someone else, another person with his own plans, activities, friends, etc. In order to do it for him, I not only have to sacrifice my own enjoyment, I also have to go to the trouble of doing it for him. Suppose, for example, I have an opera ticket and I happen to know that Jones would enjoy going to the opera just as much as I, but that Jones is a perfect stranger. Aside from the obvious embarrassment (in our society anyway) and absurdity of doing such a thing for a perfect stranger, there is the fact that he might have other plans for the evening, he might suspect my motives and I would have to go to the trouble of explaining that I am just being benevolent (but would he believe it?). Even if Jones is somebody I know, still, how can I be quite sure that he really would enjoy it just as much as I would? All in all, unless one has good reason to believe that the other person would enjoy it much more than oneself, and unless it wouldn't be any special trouble and one really wouldn't mind (and after all, one usually does mind missing out on an enjoyable experience), it's better to go ahead and do it yourself. The other chap can take care of himself. This seems to me to be the obvious conclusion on utilitarian grounds, and is surely in accordance with common sense as well. The above remarks also apply to the preferring of one's family, relatives, etc., to people one doesn't know. Clearly, one reason for doing things for those we know rather than those we don't know, is precisely that we do know them, and thus can be reasonably confident that they really would enjoy certain things and not others, that they wouldn't be embarrassed, and so on. It is also true that, by and large, we enjoy doing things for people we know more than for people we don't know, and provided there is no other reason to discriminate among recipients of favors, this gives one a good reason for bestowing them on friends, acquaintances, and family in preference to strangers. Finally, associating with people inevitably tends to involve one in obligations of the types previously discussed in Chapter VI. The utilitarian must deny, of course, that being someone's brother creates obligations to him simply as such; but it is unlikely that most people would think, on reflection, that it does. Most people have a psychological preference for their siblings and parents instilled into them by society. Thus, if told that someone hitherto thought to be quite unrelated to one is in fact one's brother, say, this will stir a certain interest in most people. But suppose he turns out to be a crook, or a bore? Clearly, the sense of obligation in these relationships is due to affection and association, and when these disappear, the sense of obligation declines as well.

In short, we might question whether the types of attitudes toward relatives (and fellow countrymen, for that matter) sanctioned in a particular society are good ones or not, and whether they could be changed for the better (would it be an improvement to try to instill the view that all men are equally one's "brothers"?); but the argument that certain rights and duties are built into the nature of things, sanctioned by biology or some other "laws of nature," simply won't wash.

Summing Up: The Limits of Morality and Odds and Ends

With the preceding section, I have concluded my exposition of utilitarianism as it bears on the principal issues of morality. It remains but to make a few general observations, among them one or two devoted to explaining the absence of certain discussions which might have been expected.

Some of the precursers of Bentham's utilitarianism, such as Gay, Paley, and Malthus, were of the "theological" variety, and it is perhaps worth including a brief note on the bearing, if any, of religion on the present discussions, or perhaps vice versa. Most religions are thought by their adherents, and by the general public at large in Europe and North America, to have some serious connection with ethics, and on occasion this has been made the ground of some sort of objection to the utilitarian view. Utilitarianism is generally regarded as a "secular" doctrine, and there is a sense, as we shall shortly see, in which they are perfectly justified in this.

Those who believe that there is an important connection between religion and ethics may be divided into two classes of very unequal sizes. The preponderant class consists of those who believe that it is our moral duty to be religious, in any of various ways; the smaller believes that it is our religious duty to be ethical. Of the second view, we may observe that so long as the substance of morality is determined by utility, there is no objection whatever to reinforcing moral behavior by religious motives, so long as this is not made the ground (as it often is) of reverting to the first view.[24] It is the first that is important. Plato first showed that God cannot set or create the standards of morals;[25] any number of modern authors have clarified this to a point which leaves little room for improvement.[26] This demonstrated, it follows without difficulty that it cannot be a (moral) duty to be religious. The only question remaining is whether religion is consistent with ethics. This has been thought possible, among utilitarians, by assuming that God is a utilitarian.

Unfortunately, the supposition that there is a utilitarian God is incredible, if not meaningless. On the utilitarian view, the ground for regarding something as a duty must be that its non-performance would harm someone or other. In the case of omnipotent beings, who can supposedly do anything without any cost of effort to themselves, the argument for this restriction becomes inapplicable. Since it would cost God no effort what-

[24] I see little to be desired in the account of this in the doctrine of "sanctions" in Bentham and Mill. Cf., *Principles, of Morals and Legislation*, Ch. II (sec. xviii) and Ch. III; *Utilitarianism*, Ch. III.

[25] Plato, *Euthyphro*.

[26] E.g., Baier, pp. 173–80; Sparshott, pp. 39, 40; Moore, *Principia Ethica*, Ch. IV; Frankena, *Ethics*, p. 84; Brandt, *Ethical Theory*, Ch. 4; Kai Nielsen, "Morality and God," *Philosophical Quarterly* (1962); C. B. Martin, *Religious Belief* (Ithaca, N. Y.: Cornell University Press, 1959), among many others.

ever to make everyone perfectly happy, then we are fully justified in regarding it as a duty on the part of God to do so. But obviously God has done nothing of the sort; and since he is supposed to have been our creator as well, he is literally responsible for the conditions of our well-being, which are notoriously imperfect. It is impossible to reconcile the supposition of the existence of such a being with the state of the world as we know it. What is done is quite different. It is supposed that somehow God is justified in creating a world of people of the kind we know because such people either could not be any happier than they are, or if they were made so, it would have to be at the expense of the supposed faculty of "free will." The former is beneath discussion, and the latter involves a gigantic misunderstanding. For free will, in any sense in which we attribute free will to people, is of no intrinsic moral value whatever. If another person, of his own "free will," goes about causing pain and suffering, then we are not only justified but obligated to restrict his activity, which means, of course, diminishing his "freedom." It follows that the possession of free will is not a value that overrides any negative values, and it is difficult to see what could have made philosophers think so, other than a penchant for obscurantism. The advocates of the existence of God ought to reflect with sobriety, instead of with metaphysical enthusiasm, on this difficulty.[27]

If it is claimed that it would not have been possible for God to make men perfectly happy because otherwise they would not be men, or because (as some now hold)[28] the concept of perfect happiness is self-contradictory or otherwise logically inapplicable, then it merely follows that God ought not to have created people at all. Only conceit, I think, compounded by bad reasoning, could make this the ground of an objection. If, of course, we had not been born (or otherwise created), then the problem of evil, and indeed any other problems, would not have arisen; but in any case, God would not have done us a wrong in not creating us, since there would then have been no "us" to do

[27] As an example, cf., John Hick, *Philosophy of Religion* (Englewood Cliffs, N. J.: Prentice-Hall, Inc., 1963), pp. 42 ff.
[28] E.g., George Schlesinger, "The Problem of Evil and the Problem of Suffering," *American Philosophical Quarterly* (July, 1964).

wrongs to.[29] But on the theological scheme of creation, coupled with the doctrine that God is a morally responsible being, we can only conclude that he has been doing a bad job of it ever since he did commit the initial mistake of creating us.

I conclude that discussions of religion in any way, shape, or form, are wholly irrelevant to ethical contexts.[30] The fact is, there's a great deal less to ethics than has often been supposed, and it is conceivable, I think, that races of intelligent beings could exist without any such institution. It is this sense of the limitedness of morality with which I should like to conclude this Chapter. Morality can be summed up, if the interpretative devices introduced in the foregoing chapters should prove sound, as that institution whose concern is the general happiness (conceived in the manner of Chapter III). The general happiness is merely everybody living the sort of life he would find best, according to whatever conception of the good life he happens to have. For most of us, this conception does not include any substantial specific concern for the general happiness, and does include a wonderful variety of other concerns. For any given one of us, then, these other concerns are our major business in life. Moral concerns crop up every now and then, to be sure, but by their very nature are secondary. Without other interests, there can be no moral interests. Thus, it is in the nature of the institution that they cannot be predominant, and indeed that action from specifically moral motives ought not to be predominant. We might say that in a morally ideal world, morality would be unnecessary.[31] For there is no moral value in the existence of moral problems. The world is perhaps more interesting because interests conflict and moral dilemmas arise, but this is no moral reason for supposing that there ought to be moral problems. Morality is not a matter of taste, even if the taste is in universes.

[29] The case is then parallel to the "new generations" problem: does one have a duty to have children if they would be happy? There is, in fact, no moral value in it as such, at all, since if one doesn't bring them into existence, the question of doing them well or ill doesn't arise.

[30] Irrelevant, that is, in the sense that no general moral principles depend on religious ones for their validity; but no doubt religious people could have moral problems which non-religious ones don't have.

[31] Cf., John Ladd's remarks on this point in "The Desire To Do One's Duty For Its Own Sake," in Castañeda-Nakhnikian, *Morality and the Language of Conduct*, pp. 322, 323.

CHAPTER IX

Foundations

We come now to the sometime vexed question of whether morality, and the utilitarian theory in particular, can be supported by proof. The word "proof" must no doubt be used advisedly in this connection, but it may be that these scruples should trouble us less than they have. At any rate, I do propose to offer what seems to me a rational argument for adopting the principle of utility, and against adopting any other "conception" of ethics.

What Are We To Prove?

Some philosophers have held, on occasion, that morality not only needs but can have no "proof," no justification. They reason thus: To prove that I ought to do my duty is to endeavor to show that I ought to do what I ought to do. But this is nonsense. If I ought to do something, then there can be no additional proof, and certainly need be no additional proof, that I ought to do what is so characterized (namely, as what I ought to do). Either I can offer a worse reason, a lame one, such as that I might enjoy it—but then, what if, as is often the case, I would not?—or I can offer the same old "reason" over again, viz., that it is my duty. Nothing stronger is available.[1]

This argument is decisive against its particular target. To call an act right or a duty is to say that one ought to do it, and so, to ask for "proof" for such statements as "you ought to do what

[1] This, of course, is taken substantially from H. A. Prichard's "Does Moral Philosophy Rest on a Mistake?" in *Moral Obligation* (New York: Oxford University Press, Inc., 1949).

is your duty" is simply misguided. But this is not the problem. The man who is worried about morality will not, in all likelihood, have his worry removed by such an argument. Just as King George wanted to know whether Scott was the author of "Waverley," and not whether Scott was Scott, so our man wants to know, if we must put the above argument to him, not whether we ought to do our duty, but whether anything is our duty, and in particular how we can know this.

In order to be able to offer a general, single-barrelled "proof" of morality, one must have a general, single-barrelled characterization of it which is nevertheless nontrivial. If we conceive of morality as consisting of a number of unrelated principles, then if one is to supply proofs, one will have to supply a different proof for each principle. Fortunately, utilitarianism is *par excellence* a single-barrelled theory, in this sense. It proposes that all right acts are utility-promoting, all wrong ones utility-defeating—in other words, that utility is coextensive with moral value. This being a general, but substantive, thesis, it makes sense to try to prove it. This ease of formulation is probably why the question of proof arises so naturally in the context of utilitarianism. It would tend to come up in any "monistic" theory of ethics clear enough to be discussable. (Many are not: that one's fundamental duty is to "realize the self" or to harmonize with the Absolute, for example, are contentions which inhibit sensible discussion.)

What Constitutes Proof?

When do we have a proof and when do we not? It is hard to give an informative answer to this. Doubtless, a good argument is one that is "capable of moving the mind" in the general direction of the conclusion: but what does this come to?

At least we can say what it is not. The skeptic, about whom more will be said below, very often seems to be demanding that we literally talk people into being good. This can sometimes be done, and is certainly a worthy aim; but to set it up as a general standard for validity would be quite unreasonable. For one thing, even people who believe that x is what they ought to do sometimes do not do it. It is even open to question whether a person who believes he ought to do x necessarily wants to do x. One cannot deny that there is some connection between the acceptance of moral principles and acting as they prescribe, but this seems too much. At very most, we must aim at convincing people that they ought to act in conformance with the principle of utility. But this isn't quite right either, for if our arguments in Chapter I are sound, then most of our readers already do believe this, since they believe that they ought to keep their promises, relieve suffering, avoid harming people, and so forth. What we apparently need to do is to produce a feeling of "rational conviction" in them. What is this?

To begin with, it is unfair to call rational conviction a "feeling," just like that. To have such a "feeling" is to think (that is, to be rather confident) that one *knows* whatever the conviction is about. Under what circumstances is one entitled to do this—particularly in the case of ethical matters? I do not think that we need a special characterization of this for ethical questions as distinct from others: to know is to have good reason for believing. And to have good reason for believing is to see that certain promises are true, and that they imply the conclusion in question.

It might be held that knowing is not always reasoned in the suggested sense. When I spot the bluebird in my back yard, I know that there is a bluebird in my back yard. Where is the "argument" here? Where the premises and the conclusion? But this overlooks the distinction between knowledge and those perceptual states that (in the relevant cases) are its prerequisites. Seeing is perceiving, but it is not believing: it is merely the prerequisite to believing, when what you believe is about what can be seen. And knowing is being able to produce a satisfactory defense of what you believe. "There was a bluebird in the back-yard this morning." "How do you know?" "I saw it." (If this continues, "How do you know that you saw it?," the answer might be, "Well, it was a perfectly clear morning and the branch is just six feet from our kitchen window," or any number of other things. But satisfaction is obtained when the knower shows that his utterance has been properly cued by his experience, and this can always involve an argument.)

Similarly, knowing that such-and-such is a duty is being able to defend satisfactorily the proposition that it is a duty. Such a defense consists in supplying premises which all parties to the argument accept, and then showing that the conclusion ("It was my duty," or whatever) follows. Of course, the relevant premises might themselves be called into question by some philosophical questioner, and then a new argument may be needed. When does this process end? It ends when we show the questioner that the denial of what we are out to prove would involve an absurdity or contradiction.

Some claim that not all absurdities involve contradiction. This may be so, but they are all near to it in one respect: namely, that we convict a man of absurdity when we find him maintaining (verbally) a view which contradicts either some of his other statements, or some statements which his behavior shows that he accepts. And when does one's behavior "show" that one accepts a statement, especially when one purports to be denying it verbally? When the behavior is of the kind which it is the purpose of the sentences in question to signify. If a man hits his finger with a hammer, he says "Ouch!"; and thus we know it hurt. If he claims that it didn't, and the exclamation was loud enough and clear enough, we conclude that he's kidding, or acting, or insincere, or that he hasn't mastered the meaning of the word 'hurt.'

It is in this way that we want to know what is right and wrong, and proof consists in getting us into this state.

Is Proof of Ethical Statements Needed?

In the Introduction, I gave reasons for thinking that proof in ethical matters was not impossible. The question might remain whether it is necessary, which has often been denied. Those who deny it, however, tend to maintain that "proof is as needless as it is impossible"; if they thought they could supply it, they would not deny that it was necessary.

The words 'know' and 'prove' are intimately related. The man who knows, as I suggested above, is the man who can give a good argument. And arguments are needed when what we believe is called into question. Whether proof of ethical statements is needed, then, depends on whether they are called into question. But of course, they often are, both in particular and in general. I contend, moreover, that there is no difference in principle between the type of argument called for in the case of the "general" question, and that called for in the "particular" one, though of course there will be differences in generality. The philosopher's business is to show with precision ("as much as the subject permits," no doubt; but this may be quite a bit) what the rock-bottom steps in such arguments should or could be.

Moreover, as Baier points out,[2] morality is an institution peculiarly requiring rational support. For it frequently requires us to do what we wouldn't otherwise have wanted to do; it calls for sacrifice of one degree or another, and sometimes these are serious. Such sacrifices need justifying, and it is the rational person in particular to whom the need for such justification will occur. Others may be "conned," duped, brainwashed, or otherwise habituated to unquestioning obedience, but the reflective will raise doubts. If these cannot be laid to rest, then suspicion arises that the whole institution may be a fraud. In any case, it could lose the support of these individuals, and this may well lead to a chain-reaction, as others come to ask why they too should not participate in the "luxury" of immorality.

Method

How do we, then, construct an argument both powerful enough and general enough to "support" so weighty an institution as morality? If my account of knowing is close enough to do, the general outline becomes clear enough. We need to search about for premises which anyone, or at least anyone capable both of participating in and raising questions about morality, will accept. But what sort of premises might these be?

[2] *Moral Point of View*, Introduction.

Clearly, the best kind of premises would be those we can with a clear conscience think of as "necessary" or *a priori*. More precisely, we want to search for premises which it would make no sense for a person who qualified as a member of our audience (which presumably is everyone, but possible exceptions will be noted eventually) to deny. Among these, certainly, will be principles of formal logic, but of course these will not be sufficient. We shall also need, most especially, analyses of the relevant portions of evaluative language. If we can show that the "very meaning" of expressions which our audience must employ is such that to deny the principle of utility would land one in absurdity, then the proof will be complete.[3] This calls, then, for an excursion into meta-ethics, which we have been to some extent eschewing in former chapters but clearly can no longer ignore.

False Starts

There are a number of pitfalls to be avoided, which happily the labors of recent theorists have pointed out for all to see. For example, there are the various forms of the definist fallacy, and the "naturalistic" fallacy in some understandings thereof. In Chapter II we have hopefully warded off such spectres; that was the point of denying that the principle of utility is "analytic." But the fallaciousness of such fallacies is exposed by the conditions of proof lately laid down. To adopt a definition that doesn't define the expressions in which the *other* chap's questions are couched is to lose your hold on him for argumentative purposes. If Jones doesn't mean by 'good' what my proposed definition says 'good' means, then the fact that utility-production is "good" in that sense is simply uninteresting. This, I take it, is a fundamental impetus behind "ordinary language" philosophy.

The same general consideration defeats many other possible efforts. Any sort of intuitionism, for example, fails as soon as

---

[3] Why this does not (hopefully) jeopardize the views in Ch. II about the "synthetic" status of utilitarianism will come out in the sections below. Cf., especially "Proof of Utilitarianism," and "Mill's Proof."

the audience fails to share our supposed "intuitions."[4] Appeal to theological premises is of no use, both because numerous members of our audience will not share them, *and* for various logical reasons well understood by philosophers.[5] Appeal to "human nature" in any very substantial sense is dangerous because implausible.[6] There is little point in saying that all men have the natural desire to help others, because the facts show that either they don't, or it's too weak to be of service in numerous cases.

The line that everyone would like to be able to take, and which some have attempted to take, is that of showing that in some way or other, morality is in one's interest. But the cruder forms of this pretty obviously won't work. One might be interested in making a lot of money, owning a yacht, keeping a mistress, and so on; and it is all too easy to conceive of situations in which cheating, breaking promises, or killing a few enemies will in fact help one to achieve these goals. The wily prudentialist will retort that these interests are of a kind the satisfaction of which won't really make their possessor happy. And he might even be right. Unfortunately, there is a good deal of evidence to show that he's wrong, if 'happiness' is not stretched in some way; but if it is stretched, then we have the same problem as the various fallacious starts mentioned above come up against. Our audience may not be interested in being "happy" in the newly defined sense.

It may be that in some extremely subtle sense, morality is in one's interest. But we must be careful of various obscure logical traps. For example, it is indeed true that if everyone were to promote [note: not 'try to promote,' but 'to promote'] everyone's happiness in the sense defined in Chapter II above, this would be in everyone's interest. Such is the premise of Baier's attractive and ingenious argument.[7] If everyone follows the rules of morality (rules which occasionally run counter to self-interest

---

[4] Powerful arguments against intuitionism are numerous. Nowell-Smith, *Ethics*, Ch. 3; Baier, *Moral Point of View*, pp. 22–24; Strawson, "Ethical Intuitionism," in Sellars and Hospers, *Readings in Ethical Theory*, pp. 250–63, are recommended, among others.

[5] See n. 26, Ch. VIII.

[6] Cf., for example, Sparshott, *An Enquiry into Goodness*, pp. 82–88; Moore, *Principia Ethica*, Ch. II; and Hospers, *Human Conduct*, pp. 92–101.

[7] Baier, *Moral Point of View*, Ch. 12.

for everyone), then everyone would be better off. Therefore, I should follow the rules. . . . *if.* . . . For as Baier recognizes, if I can depend on no one else to follow them, it is contrary to my interest to follow them, and so only if I have reason to suppose others will follow them, have I reason to follow them, and so should follow them. So everyone has reason to be moral so long as he is reasonably sure that others will be, too.

This argument requires close consideration; it is surely somewhere near the truth. But there are certain difficulties which may be decisive, and at least give us reason to hope we can do better. In the first place, we must be careful how we are to take the argument. One possible interpretation would be that "the best average life is a sufficient recommendation of the moral point of view, that the benefit of the group justifies acceptance by each individual,"[8] as David B. Gauthier puts it. The trouble here is that the argument seems unintuitive. We seem to be able to ask, "But *why* does the benefit of the group justify acceptance by me, if I can gain from a more selfish policy?" There is no use in saying that it *just does*, if our hope is to convince all rational beings; for it is precisely some rational beings (such as myself and, as it turns out, Baier) who question it. The other interpretation is that the argument shows that an individual can expect more satisfaction from adopting morality than from not doing so. The trouble is that even though this is perfectly true at the outset, yet there will come a time when it no longer is, namely when, as Baier admits and insists will happen from time to time,[9] morality requires a genuine sacrifice of me. At this point, it ceases to be true that the policy offers expectation of maximum benefit, even though at the outset I had reason to suppose it would. So I no longer have a self-interested reason to continue to follow the moral "policy." If self-interest really is the foundation of the policy, then it breaks down here. Self-interest, then, cannot sanction the general adoption of anything but a policy of (genuinely enlightened, to be sure) self-interest.

Finally, Baier's argument seems to work only among people whose power over others is limited. An extremely powerful individual who could control others as he wished, would appar-

---

[8] D. B. Gauthier, *Practical Reasoning*, p. 107.
[9] Baier, *Moral Point of View*, p. 314: "But while enlightened self-interest does not require any genuine sacrifice from anyone, morality does."

ently not have a reason to be moral by this argument (taking it, of course, in the second sense).[10] This seems unsatisfactory, for surely powerful people ought to help people, or at least not to harm them, just as persons of ordinary power ought to. It is absurd to make duties dependent on power in this particular way, Nietszche[11] to the contrary notwithstanding.

What we need, in short, is an argument, universally acceptable, which makes morality "coordinate with prudence," as Gauthier puts it. The fact that others will suffer must be shown to be just as good a reason for avoiding it as the fact that I will suffer. No argument which is based essentially on considerations of self-interest, it appears, can do this. What does this leave?

Self-interest

The form of our question has gradually evolved into one of self-interest versus the general interest. The reader will, I think, have considered this a natural evolution. It is unsurprising to be told that being moral is being unselfish. What makes it unsurprising is that nobody doubts that the fact that x would be in my interest is a good reason for doing x. The work of recent ethical theorists,[12] as well as many past ones,[13] suggests that

[10] Gauthier, p. 109, accuses Baier of this result. It is difficult to interpret the sense of the argument in *Moral Point of View* on this question, but in a symposium at the University of Waterloo (April 23, 1965), Baier agreed in a question period that so far as he could see, it would not be possible to have moral relations with a supremely powerful person (God, for example).

[11] According to whom: "One has duties only to one's equals." (*Beyond Good and Evil*, Ch. IX.) This selection is found in *Philosophic Problems*, ed. Mandelbaum, Gramlich, and Anderson (New York: Macmillan Co., 1957), p. 370.

[12] E.g., Gauthier, Sparshott, Baier, Nowell-Smith, and Castañeda in "Imperatives, Decisions, and 'Oughts'" (*Morality and the Language of Conduct*, pp. 219–92), and probably Toulmin, Hare, and Stevenson, among others. All of them say or imply that if one wants something, getting it will not interfere with the satisfactions of others, and it isn't contrary to any other important wants of one's own, then it would make no real sense to deny that I am justified in trying to get it.

[13] Plato, Aristotle, all of the Stoics and Epicureans in one way or another, and probably most of the medievals, would accept this; all, however, have special views as to what really is in one's interest, which makes it a bit more doubtful. Kant, incidentally, implies this in his famous view that hypothetical imperatives are "analytic."

there is something a priori about this, if I may put it so. It is felt that there is a logical connection between wanting something and its being good, or at least between wanting it and *calling* it good. (Hobbes: "whatsoever is the object of any man's appetite or desire, that he for his part calleth good.")[14] The logical niceties of this connection will not be explored very thoroughly here,[15] though part of the reason of it will be suggested below. But at any rate, we may sum this up by saying that each person assumes that the fact that something is in his interest makes it good, *prima facie*. 'Prima facie' needs to be added for two reasons. First, interests or wants sometimes conflict, and then one will have to adjudge one less good than the other, to the point where sometimes one will adjudge a want downright bad, as interfering with one's better wishes. And second, it is not self-contradictory to perform an action which is seen to be contrary to one's interest as a whole (unless we trivialize it by calling one's moral principles one's "interests").

Again it is necessary to warn against misinterpretations of this. Nothing about "human nature" is being assumed here, and nothing about the internal character of one's interests. These may be to any degree ascetic, inspiring, or what-have-you; they may also to any degree be essentially directed at the welfare of others, though as a matter of common observation they often are not. In order to understand the status of this principle, and especially its bearing on the construction of our argument, we must next consider the logic of evaluative expressions.

The Logic of Evaluation

What (if anything) are we saying about something when we call it good? By this time, philosophical analysis has reduced the area of reasonable disagreement to a rather narrow circle. It is agreed on all hands that to say that something is good is not,

[14] Hobbes, *Leviathan*, in *English Philosophers*, ed. Burtt, p. 149.
[15] The accounts in Nowell-Smith, Sparshott, Baier, and Gauthier all deserve careful study; I would not presume to improve on them in this matter, nor to be able to do so here.

in the most obvious sense of the word "quality," to attribute a quality to it.[16] It is, at least and in some way or other, to come out in favor of it, to recommend it. On the other hand, though goodness is not a quality, the man who calls something good is necessarily attributing some or other qualities (in the ordinary sense of "quality") to it. In calling something good, one is saying that there are reasons for preferring it, for being in favor of it, for using it, or whatever the appropriate attitude or activity may be. To say that there is a reason for preferring this particular thing is to say that it is of such a kind as to be preferred: to say, in short, that it is to be preferred because it is the sort of thing it is, or has the qualities it does.

Saying that something is good is not just expressing approval, then; it is purporting to have reasons for approval. It may or may not be that we could say, instead of "this is good," "this has qualities A, B, C, . . . so, take this!," or again, "this has qualities A, B, C, hooray!"[17] Quite likely each is correct in some contexts, incorrect in others. But the essential point is that in evaluating, we are supporting choices, preferences, lines of action which are alternative to other possible ones. We are, one can equally well say, defending them. No wonder, then, that we think of our wants as *prima facie* conferring value on their objects. For if I am willing to pursue a want, I have a reason for defending it. The man who condemns a certain line of activity in himself, while doing it, condemns himself, in a sense; and if he applies the language appropriate to condemnation but seems totally cheerful about it, we may assume that he is insincere. Applying evaluative language puts logical pressure behind some choice or activity.

In short, evaluating is reasoning: supplying reasons in support of choices and the like. From this, it follows logically that the application of evaluative predicates is intrinsically "generalizing."

---

[16] Sparshott, *An Enquiry into Goodness,* Ch. 6, finds reason to call goodness a "quality," but also reason not to. His subtle discussion of this is worth close attention. But it is, I think, compatible with the account attributed to "philosophical analysis" here.

[17] This, of course, is from Stevenson's "second pattern of analysis." Cf., *Ethics and Language* (New Haven, Conn.: Yale University Press, 1944), Ch. IX. See also the useful criticism of George Kerner's *The Revolution in Ethics* (New York: Oxford University Press, 1966).

To say of a thing that it is good is to voice a preference or to suggest or advocate preferring it, because it is A, B, C . . . . . But to say this is to say that if another item is also A, B, C, then it too is to be preferred. I can't say both that x is good because it is A and that y is bad (or indifferent) because *it* is A, unless I have further explanations.[18]

These two features of evaluative language are, I think it fair to say, pretty universally regarded as essential to it; the same goes for the "language of obligation," "ought," "wrong," and so on. The difference, as we have suggested in Chapter III, is mainly that "obligational" language is stronger in its committing functions. These features are the ones concentrated upon by Hare,[19] whose argument is substantially similar to the one I shall develop.

Refutation of Egoism.

G. E. Moore was the first to produce a refutation, on purely logical grounds, of egoism, the ethical view that everyone ought to act only on reasons of self-interest.[20] He has since been followed by others whose treatments differ in detail from Moore's.[21] I shall follow a similar line of reasoning.

Egoism is a theory, not an attitude. Let us, for the sake of simplicity, call the latter 'egotism,' denoting by this the tendency to act in the way recommended by egoists. The egoist, then, is the philosopher who recommends to all men that they pursue only their own interests, taking no essential account of anyone else's. Note that he is a theorist: he is arguing that this policy has the support of reason. This is equivalent, I think, to saying that the egoist says that we ought to follow self-interest only, that this is the best thing for everyone to do. To regard egoism as an ethical theory is to regard it as applying the moral vocabulary systematically on the basis of self-interest.

[18] See Kerner, pp. 21–24, especially 32 ff.
[19] See Hare, *Freedom and Reason*, Part I.
[20] Moore, *Principia Ethica*, Sections 58–62, pp. 96–105.
[21] E.g., Baier, *Moral Point of View* p. 188–190, and Brian Medlin, "Ultimate Principles and Ethical Egoism," *Australasian Journal of Philosophy* (1957).

Consider, then, the situation in which two people, A and B, have incompatible interests, in the sense that A's is satisfied if and only if B's is dissatisfied. Clearly there are frequent occasions on which this happens. Since the egoist holds that the satisfaction of A's interest is right, he is obliged by logic to hold that the dissatisfaction of B's is right; but since he is also committed to holding that the satisfaction of B's interest is right (hence that the satisfaction of A's is wrong), we have a contradiction. The satisfaction of either interest is both right and wrong. The egoist is rooting for both teams; which would be rather odd, but not self-contradictory, were it not that he claims to be rooting with the support of reason. It is this claim that proves fatal to his theory.

We must be careful to ward off a misconception about this argument. Some would reply that after all, the egoist is merely saying that if doing x would satisfy A at the expense of B, A would be justified in doing x "from his point of view," and that if doing y would satisfy B at the expense of A, B would be justified in doing y from *his* point of view. But this is an evasion, as G. E. Moore correctly saw in discussing the expression "my good":

In what sense can a thing be good *for me?* It is obvious, if we reflect, that the only thing which can belong to me, which can be *mine,* is something which is good, and not the fact that it is good. When, therefore, I talk of anything I get as 'my own good,' I must mean either that the thing I get is good, or that my possessing it is good. In both cases it is only the thing or the possession of it which is *mine,* and not *the goodness* of that thing or that possession. There is no longer any meaning in attaching the 'my' to our predicate and saying: The possession of this *by me* is *my* good. Even if we interpret this by 'My possession of this is what *I* think good' the same still holds: for *what* I think is that my possession of it is good *simply;* and, if I think rightly, then the truth is that my possession of it *is* good simply—not in any sense, *my* good; and if I think wrongly, it is not good at all . . .[22]

Some have missed the point Moore is making here, by supposing that it depends, for its acceptability, on his theory that 'good'

[22] Moore, *Principia Ethica,* pp. 98–99.

connotes a special property. This is not so. The word 'good,' and other evaluative words, are logically incapable of denoting any sort of "private" objects (a fact, incidentally, which may itself be employed to refute the theory that goodness is a simple intuitable property). As Moore saw, to say that so-and-so is my good is either to say that I think it good, or that its being mine is good. To say that I think it is my good could mean that I think that its being mine is good; but in this last sentence, it is nonsensical to qualify 'good' by 'my' or by 'according to me.' In saying that I think it is good, all the qualifying that needs to be done is done. "I think that I think it's good" adds nothing to, and perhaps subtracts something (viz., intelligibility) from 'I think that it's good.' And if one supposes that 'according to me,' or 'I think. . . .' must always be added to any occurrence of 'good,' infinite regress looms large before us: for even in 'I think that I think it's good,' we have an occurrence of 'good,' so that the whole would again have to be expanded into 'I think that I think that I think . . . ,' which is as ridiculous as it is boring.

If the egoist were saying nothing more than that when something is in a person's interest, he, for his part, will call it good, then this is not only perfectly acceptable but has already been insisted upon above. Only it isn't ethical theory. An ethical theory (as distinct from a meta-ethical theory) must use evaluative expressions, not mention them. Theories about what people think is right or wrong are not theories about what is right or wrong. In order to become such, a theory must side with some or other of the parties in question, or declare both mistaken. The trouble with egoism is simply that it attempts to side with all parties at once, which is contradictory when some of them disagree with others.

Another misinterpretation of the foregoing refutation of egoism goes as follows: What the egoist is saying is not that A ought to do x and B ought to do y, but rather that A ought to *try* to do x and B ought to *try* to do y. What about this? It is, in fact, either another evasion, or else a shift in the theory. For suppose we were to ask, of the conflict which would result if A tries to do x and B to do y where x and y cannot both be done, Which party *ought to win?* The egoist must either answer or refuse to answer this question. If he answers that one or the other ought to, then he is immediately contradicted by his principle that anybody's interests justify him in doing what would satisfy them, and the refutation is the same as before. He might refuse to answer, or he might answer, "may the best man win!" These, however, come to the same thing. If the egoist claims that his theory only issues in sanctions for trying, and not for succeeding, at any given aim, then he is tacitly underwriting the stronger side. "May the best man win!" would contradict egoism if the application of 'best' were determined on any other basis than that of satisfaction of the interest of the party concerned. But the trouble is that on that basis, we get contradictions, since the interests are incompatible. And our question, remember, was "who ought to win in this contest (quarrel, fight)?" As a reply to this question, the answer "I refuse to answer," or the answer "the stronger" are both equivalent to, "Well, whoever wins ought to win." This is a new theory altogether: the theory, namely, that whoever does win in contests due to conflicting interests ought to win. But this is incompatible with egoism. For consider little guys who can't win, or just anybody who doesn't like to fight. The theory that those who would win at fights ought to win conflicts with their interests, and hence with a theory that says that whatever your interests are, they ought to be achieved. The doctrine that might makes right is a different doctrine from egoism. Pure egoism, then, is inextricably ensnarled in contradiction.

Proof of Utilitarianism

Let us consider what really results when we take seriously the evaluative principle assumed by each person, namely that "the satisfaction of my interests *prima facie* is *good* (hence, *prima facie* justifies me in doing whatever will attain it)." We have seen that if we generalize this theory leaving off the '*prima facie*,' we get contradictions. But why, it might be asked, do we need to generalize at all? Let us, by way of reply, consider a "non-generalized egoism" and see what happens.

Suppose, then, that someone promulgates the theory that the

271

criterion of right and wrong is satisfaction, or dissatisfaction, of Jones' interests, where Jones is some particular person. We do not, at the moment, much care who he is, and it is not even necessary that the advocate be Jones himself: Jones might be a supposed Messiah, and the advocate one of his prophets. (In fact, certain religions approximate rather closely to just this model: the ultimate criterion of right and wrong is satisfaction of God's interests, and this view is advocated by priests, prophets, and miscellaneous clerics.) What is important is merely that we remember that it is satisfaction of his *interests* that is made the *ultimate* criterion, to which no further appeal is supposed to be possible.

Now let us ask the question, why ought we to accept this "principle" that satisfaction of Jones' interests is the ultimate criterion of right and wrong? It might be replied that since it is being put forward as an ultimate criterion, no answer to this question could possibly be legitimate. (If I read him rightly, this is precisely the view of Kierkegaard,[23] and probably most "existentialist" theologians, about God). This reply is a misunderstanding. The fact that something is an ultimate criterion can always be explained, though of course the criterion itself cannot be deduced from a further criterion. But the latter is not what we are asking; only the former.

This question, Why should be accept Jones' interests as the ultimate criterion of right and wrong?, is equivalent to asking why we should accept *Jones'* interests, not why we should accept Jones' *interests* for this criterion. For we would all like our own interests to be such a criterion, and therefore can understand perfectly well what the word 'interests' is doing there. What we want to know is, why Jones'?

There can be only two answers to this question. The first possibility is "Because Jones' interests are of type ϕ"; the second is, "Because Jones is Jones, and that's the end of it." Let us examine each by turn.

---

[23] One gets this impression from *Fear and Trembling* (New York: Anchor Books, Doubleday and Co., Inc., 1954); but Professor Alistaire MacKinnon assures me that it does not apply to the later Kierkegaard. On the general issue, cf., my "Existence and Particularity," *Southern Journal of Philosophy* (Spring, 1965), and further discussion below.

The first reply will not do at all, for it contradicts the supposition that Jones' interests are the ultimate criterion. Perhaps all of Jones' interests have some property ϕ, but to make this the real answer to our question is to affirm that ϕ-ness, not the satisfaction of Jones' interests, is the ultimate criterion. Suppose that Jones' interests were to change. Then what? If they were no longer ϕ, should we hunt with Jones or run with the ϕ's? We would be unable to do both, and this first reply to our question bids us leave Jones for the ϕ's sake.

My discussion of this first answer has perhaps been overly abstract, and some examples should be mentioned in order to bring home the point, as well as to enable our forthcoming discussion of Reply No. 2 to carry its due weight. Suppose, then, that our prophet's reply of Type 1 about Jones is that we should satisfy Jones' interests because Jones is stronger than anyone else. This again is a "might makes right" theory, of sorts, and implies that if, perhaps *per impossibile*, Jones should grow weak, we ought to stop taking his interests as critical for value. (The theologian might reply that Jones (i.e., God) *cannot* become weak, being infinitely strong. This is irrelevant. If strength is a defining property of Jones, then 'Jones' is no longer a proper name, and the theory is not of the type we are discussing.) Again, it might be said that we should regard Jones' interests as criterial because Jones can do Z better than we can. This makes Z-performing the ultimate criterion, and if Jones did not have this ability, his interests would cease to be criterial. And so forth. Any such answer will relegate the satisfaction of *Jones'* interests to a logical second place, behind whatever we pick for ϕ.

So let us turn to Reply No. 2, which is that we ought to regard Jones' interests as ultimately criterial just because they are Jones'. Now, this might be taken to be equivalent to saying that we ought to do so for no reason at all. But this would reduce the position to nonsense, in view of our analysis of evaluative language. Saying that we ought to do it, that it would be right or good to do so-and-so, is saying that there is a reason, and not that there isn't a reason, for doing it. Sometimes, indeed, the reason for doing something is "Just for the heck of it," which in a sense is doing it for "no reason at all." But this doesn't help. In the first place, "just for the heck of it" is automatically not a compelling reason. It would be absurd to say that you ought morally to do something "just for the heck of it," for this "reason" implies that if you don't want to, you don't have to. Moreover, "just for the heck of it" does not mean "despite the fact that it will kill us," or in general, despite the fact that it will dissatisfy our interests, but rather, that it might be fun, and at least will satisfy an interest in variety for its own sake. In neither case is this relevant to our present question, in which we are considering the proposition that the satisfaction of Jones' interests is the ultimate criterion of right and wrong, bearing in mind that 'right' and 'wrong' are *moral* words, whose meanings have been partially analyzed in Chapters II and V.

Thus the "reason" offered amounts to, "because Jones is Jones, and nobody else." But can the "fact" that you are you, that I am I, or that Jones is Jones, be the sort of thing which can logically be advanced as supplying a characteristic (reason) in virtue of which anything might be thought to be better or worse than something else? Let's take an example. Suppose that we have two identical Ferraris before us, which we shall call 'A' and 'B.' (Note that we could just as well have called them 'B' and 'A' respectively.) Suppose that each will travel equally fast, wear out at the same rate, be equally comfortable, impress people equally, and so forth. There just isn't any discernible difference between them. Under these circumstances, would it make any sense to say that A was a superior car to B? Of course not. Saying that A is superior to B is saying that there is *something about* A in virtue of which it is preferable to B, and 'being identical with A' does not indicate a difference between them, other than the fact that there are two of them. 'Being identical with A' can't operate as a reason supporting a differential evaluation, because it isn't a "characteristic" at all: we could equally have called A 'B,' in which case 'being identical with B' would have been the same "characteristic" as 'being identical with A' is now. This means that the "fact" in question simply amounts to the "fact" that it is identical with itself. And this is true of *everything*. So if this is what is meant, then if 'being identical with Jones' gives any reason for anyone's doing anything, then 'being identical with Smith' or 'being identical with Narveson' would work equally well. Since everything is identical with itself, 'being identical with itself' logically cannot act as a reason for supporting differential evaluations. Insofar as it acted as a "reason" at all, it could only support identical evaluations. Yet a differential evaluation is what would be *needed* to support Jones' claim to have his interests preferred to everyone else's.

What follows from all this is, of course, that if my (or anyone's) interests are going to be advanced as ultimately supporting evaluations, then everyone's interests do the same. But this is all that we need, for it is precisely what utilitarianism asserts: that satisfaction of everyone's interests (that is, "everyone's interests equally," as shown in Chapter VII) must be the ultimate criterion, and hence the criterion of moral value (Chapter II). Given that interests are what support evaluations, the fact that they are mine rather than someone else's is logically irrelevant.

Is It a Verbal Trick?

This proof, which derives from Hare,[24] in some respects and Gauthier[25] in others (and indeed, goes back to Kant and to Mill as well), may have the appearance of sleight-of-hand. For example, critics may suppose that I have, after all, attempted to fish a value out of a fact. The argument, it may be thought, starts with the premise that everyone in fact regards his own satisfactions as good, and then attempts to derive the conclusions that the satisfaction of everyone is good. This is one of

[24] *Freedom and Reason*, especially Part II.

[25] *Practical Reasoning*, pp. 87–89, surely makes much the same point that I am advancing here, although it is not emphasized so heavily. That it is not, is due (I think) to differing attitudes between Professor Gauthier and myself. He apparently does not regard this as an argument supplying a "justification" of morality. Differences between us on this matter could probably be split fairly satisfactorily. I find the same principle stated with the author's usual pungent conciseness in Sparshott's *Enquiry into Goodness*, pp. 168, 169: "By arguing in terms of goodness one claims, however wrongly, that one is not simply seeking one's own way . . . the fact that I am I or you are you can never by itself constitute a ground of relevance." See also David Hume, *Enquiry Concerning the Principles of Morals*, Conclusion (New York: Liberal Arts Press, Bobbs-Merrill Co., Inc., 1957), p. 93.

the errors imputed to Mill, who argued in something rather like that fashion (of Mill's proof, cf. below). But this is not the argument, although the assumption in question does play a part. The argument is that anyone who proposed to regard his interests, as such, as providing reasons in support of evaluations, is logically forced to admit the similar relevance of anyone else's interests. Thus the premise which any particular person uses, concerns *his own* interests, and asserts of them that they are to be regarded as criteria of evaluation, which is an evaluative, not a factual, premise. The statement that everyone does so regard his own interests, is relevant only because it reminds us that everybody is a party to the argument, and hence that it appeals to everyone.

What I have purported to prove is, in effect, that it is irrational to deny the principle of utility, if one regards one's own interests as supporting evaluations. The point of supposing that this argument is somehow a verbal trick or sleight-of-hand must be to call into question something about it. What? Not, I trust, its logic. Indeed, it would not be attacked as sleight-of-hand if the logic were unsound, for in that case, one could merely call it unsound and be done with it. What people really have in mind when they use this particular mode of criticism must be something else. And we may well suspect what it is: they doubt that this argument really will move people to be virtuous. This is doubtless true (though it might move some, and especially, might keep some from abandoning virtue). However, I have not claimed that the argument will do this. I have claimed only that it will move rational people to virtue, in so far as they are rational; which is just another way of saying that it is valid. People do not necessarily act rationally. But that an action is irrational is itself a criticism of it, and that actions contrary to the principle of utility are thus to be criticized is simply another statement of what I have set out to prove.

A more serious criticism, it might be thought, is that the truth of the conclusion depends upon that of the premise, and that people might wish not to accept the premise. This was, it will be recalled, that my interests (each person taking 'my' to refer to himself) are to be regarded as supporting evaluations, or in other words, that my interests ought (*prima facie*) to be satisfied.

Let us consider what denying this might consist in. It means, for one thing, that if you beat me up, I have no right to complain, in any sense of 'complain' worth noticing. For obviously, only justified complaints are worth noticing. If I scream or say 'Ouch! Quit it!,' but deny that you ought to quit it because what you're doing is wrong, then nobody need listen. Only justified complaints deserve our attention.

The truth is that it makes no sense to refuse to apply evaluative expressions on behalf of one's own interests. This is merely a dodge. When a man says, "well, I for my part refuse to regard the satisfaction of my interests as good," he's being insincere, and the reason is very simple: he wouldn't say this unless he regarded his refusal as *justified*. He is trying to use his refusal as a way of impugning the validity of an argument, and this is to supply a counter-argument of one's own. But arguments about what to do cannot be carried on without the use of evaluative terminology.[26] This is why the skeptic's position is incoherent at bottom, and why our hypothetical critic's position is in the same boat. The skeptic, when he says, "Nothing is really good or bad" (offering perhaps as his reason that evaluative terms are "meaningless" or "merely subjective") is attempting to offer us reasons for avoiding the use of evaluative terminology. If he is not, his argument is pointless, and he may just as well clam up. As Aristotle rightly says, the man who denies the law of contradiction is no better off than a vegetable. But to claim to be justified in refusing to use evaluative terminology is to apply evaluative terminology to one's refusal, and this is self-defeating.

In short, what the skeptic and our critic are really trying to say is this: one ought not to employ evaluative terminology. The absurdity of this remark needs only to be pointed out. There just isn't any way for anyone who is capable of talking about values to make out a coherent argument against the practice of employing evaluative language on behalf of his interests; and thus, there is no way for him to make out a coherent argu-

---

[26] If 'argument' is taken in the epistemic sense, then perhaps this is true of all arguments, and not merely of arguments about what to do. Whether such terms as 'know' are at least partly evaluative is a vexed question. Cf., R. Chisholm, *Theory of Knowledge* (Englewood Cliffs, N. J.: Prentice-Hall, Inc., 1966), pp. 11–14, for example.

ment against the principle of utility. This result is as much as it is possible for the theoretician to achieve: but it is also as much as he needs to achieve. For the reasonable person is precisely the person who acts on the basis of reasons, and those who do not can only be influenced by non-rational means, such as force. But they are also precisely the ones who cannot complain at its use, as we have seen.

Other Dodges: Hare's Fanatics

In *Freedom and Reason*, R. M. Hare outlines a procedure for moral argument not unlike the foregoing, in point of the purely logical apparatus employed. Hare calls attention to the two essential features of evaluative discourse, that it commits people to action, and that it purports to supply reasons, which (therefore) must be of a general kind. But Hare's account differs importantly in one respect. Instead of employing merely the general principle (if that's the right word for it) that my interests support evaluations, he proposes that we apply a universalization method to each particular one of our proposals for action. His procedure is thus reminiscent of Kant's, in which we are supposed to universalize the maxim of our acts. If its universalization is consistent, then action on it is morally permissible; otherwise not.[27] The defects of this procedure are the same for

[27] I have not emphasized the differences between Kant, Hare, and myself on this matter of "universalizability" in the text, but it should be pointed out that none of us is to be identified with any of the others. I have distinguished Singer's procedure, singled out for criticism in Ch. V, which consists in asking whether it would be disastrous or undesirable if everyone were to perform the sort of thing in question. Hare, on the other hand, usually asks the question, How would I like it if I were in the other man's shoes? He is, in other words, mainly concerned with "reversibility," as Baier calls it (*Moral Point of View*, pp. 202–03). This has been criticized interestingly by Alf Ross in *Danish Yearbook of Philosophy* (Copenhagen: Munksgaard, 1964), in his article, "On Moral Reasoning." Kant's view, according to which a necessary (and sufficient, I think) criterion for the permissibility of a principle of action is that it be "capable of being made a universal law" has been interpreted along Singer's and Hare's lines, by various people, but doesn't seem to me to be quite identical to either, though more similar to Hare's than Singer's, certainly. My view seems to

both Kant and Hare, and are worth going into here; they apply also, with some reservations, to Singer's method. First, if my interest is in, say cultivating roses to the exclusion of all else, we shall get results which all of these authors would concede were irrelevant; namely, that for extraneous reasons having to do with the nature of things and the constitution of the human frame, we cannot all cultivate roses to the exclusion of all else. Singer, as we have noted, patches this up by talking of "invertibility" and "reiterability"; Kant, I believe, does not even recognize the difficulty, and his interpreters have had to patch him up as best they can.[28] Hare's moves are somewhat similar to Singer's. All of this complicated logical maneuvering is unnecessary, of course, on the utilitarian theory. If I plant roses, there is no reason to think it will harm anybody, and so there's no problem. It's as simple as that. Second, and related to it: some people might like doing things which other people dislike. Now Hare's formula goes:

If, when we consider some proposed action, we find that, when universalized, it yields prescriptions which we cannot accept, we reject this action as a solution to our moral problem—if we cannot universalize the prescription, it cannot become an 'ought.'[29]

Of course, the consequences which I can accept might be quite different from what others can accept. Thus, if I happened to like being in prison, the fact that upon universalization of a certain line of action ("let all debtors be put in prison") I would find myself in prison (being a debtor), might not bother me at all. Hare recognizes this, and to a certain extent sees the consequences. In his chapter on "Utilitarianism," he takes up Braith-

---

me to be most similar to Kant's, of the three, but is not quite the same as any of them. Kant and I agree in that we do not ask anything of the form, "What would happen if," or "What would I think if" everyone were to act on the proposed rule, but rather "Is the proposed rule consistent?" But Kant is obscure in interpreting 'consistency' (to put it mildly). My procedure seems to me the most abstract of the four, in the sense that it appeals only to the "logical generality," or "supervenience" (as Moore called it) of ethical terms. In a sense, this procedure implies the usable parts of the procedures of each of the other three.

[28] See Paton's article referred to in Ch. IV, n. 11.

[29] *Freedom and Reason*, p. 90.

waite's example of the chap who likes classical music and lives in a thin-walled apartment, next door to a man who plays jazz on his trumpet.

Now it is obviously of no use for B to ask himself whether he is prepared to prescribe universally that people should play trumpets when they live next door to other people who are listening to classical records. For if B himself were listening to classical records (which bore him beyond endurance) he would be only too pleased if somebody next door started up on the trumpet.[30]

The solution is, of course, that

B has got, not to imagine himself in A's situation with his own (B's) likes and dislikes, but to imagine himself in A's situation with A's likes and dislikes. . . . The natural way for the argument then to run is for B to admit that he is not prepared to prescribe universally that people's likes and dislikes should be disregarded by other people, because this would entail prescribing that other people should disregard his own likes and dislikes . . . It does not follow from this that he will conclude that he ought never to play the trumpet when A is at home, only that he will not think that he ought to have no regard at all for A's interests.[31]

Now this comes very close to my argument above, except that the conclusion is properly to be stated that he ought to have equal regard for A's interests, it remaining true that this does not make the precise solution in any given case self-evident. What I want to point out is that this general result is really implied from the beginning, and renders unnecessary the employment of the "universalization" procedure on each particular problem. The same, precisely, applies to Kant. If what sets the whole stage for moral questions is the universalizability *of my inclinations* (desires, "willings," wants), then the result we inevitably are going to arrive at, if we commit no logical blunders and introduce no irrelevant metaphysical considerations about the "purposes of nature" (as Kant does), is utilitarianism, i.e., the position that the essence of morality consists in regarding any desire, no matter whose, as *prima facie* worthy

[30] *Ibid.*, pp. 112–113.
[31] *Ibid.*

of satisfaction. We can then simply apply the principle of utility to particular cases. This is a much better method because it does not get stuck in particular cases by concentrating on just the one desire or set of desires that happen to get it going, but also all incidental desires bearing on it at the time; and it immediately bids us see that the fact that one person's desires are different in structure from another's is only to be expected, and not a special source of theoretical difficulty calling for hedging devices.[32]

Why isn't Hare satisfied to rest with his method as a proof of utilitarianism, then? Because of the possibility of people he calls "fanatics." The fanatic is the person who is willing to take *any* consequences of the universalization of his desire. Thus if he is a fanatical anti-Semite, who holds that all Jews ought to be put in gas chambers, he might, upon seeing that this implies that if he were a Jew he too ought to be gassed, accept this consequence. "Logic," as Hare says, "does not prevent me wanting to be put in a gas chamber if a Jew."[33] The fact that this would be contrary to my interest, were I a Jew, he regards as indecisive, for:

A person who was moved by considerations of self-interest and was prepared to universalize the judgments based on it, but had no ideals of this fanatical kind, could not think this; and it might plausibly be said that a man who professes to think this is usually either insincere or lacking in imagination—for on the whole such fanaticism is rare. But it exists . . . His [the fanatic's] ideals have, on the face of it, nothing to do with self-interest or with a morality which can be generated by universalizing self-interest; they seem much more akin to the aesthetic evaluations discussed in the last chapter. The enormity of Nazism is that it extends an aesthetic style of evaluation into a field where the bulk of mankind think that such evaluations should be subordinated to the interests of other people.[34]

[32] The devices in Singer, discussed in Ch. 5, may be so classified. It is well-known that Kant ties himself into knots on the failure to make any allowances for conflicts of principles conforming to the Categorical Imperative (see his "On a Supposed Right to Tell Lies from Benevolent Motives," in the Appendix to Abbot's edition of Kant's *Ethical Writings* [New York: Longmans, Green, and Co., 1873, 1954]). He would get into similar difficulties here.

[33] Hare, *Freedom and Reason*, p. 110.

[34] *Ibid.*, p. 161.

This is a powerful-looking objection, for if Hare is right, then contra-utilitarian theories could be logically coherent after all. But I believe that Hare is mistaken about the role of the expression 'self-interest.' In believing that it is possible for a person not to be "moved by self-interest," he mistakes the "principle" as I called it above, for a genuine substantive hypothesis. My contention urged in Chapter III and elsewhere, is that this supposition that people are self-interested is wholly vacuous; and part and parcel of this is the corresponding view that the "assumption" discussed in the section above, that people employ evaluative expressions in support of their interests, likewise is vacuous. It is not just "plausible" that a man who professes what Hare's Nazi professes (professes to profess?) is insincere: it is certain. Or in other words, the Nazi is confused, if he is "sincere."

Why? Let us recall that I too have contrasted aesthetic with moral evaluations (Chapter II) and have admitted, or even insisted, that there are questions of "intrinsic value" of which aesthetic questions are either the best examples or, perhaps, the only basic examples; and that these questions are perfectly genuine. But none of this matters. It is either true or false, perhaps, that the world would be intrinsically best if it were ϕ; and let 'ϕ' be such that the gassing of Jews is an integral part of any world characterized by it. But my reason for acting on this cannot, logically cannot, be that such a world would be intrinsically best. My reason for acting on this, or rather, what makes it my reason, is that I *think* it would be best. What I think when I think it would be best is, of course, that it would be best; but it is logically impossible for it to be the case that its simply being best is what (rationally) moves me to act. Only the belief that it is best can do this. Of course, I might get so involved with this belief that I might allow the interest in making the world conform to it to dominate all of my other interests, including those which keep me alive. That is what fanaticism is: it is having some interest so intense that no other interests count; one is willing to die for it and will not hear contrary reasons. But this does not necessarily mean that all fanatics are irrational. Doubtless they are, in fact, but we can conceive of a rational fanatic, or perhaps, someone just like a "fanatic" except rational. Such a person would be willing to die for the realization of his dominant interest and would do absolutely anything to see it realized, *except* something immoral. For he would realize that his reason for acting to satisfy his interest is that it is in his interest, and if he wants to defend his activity on that ground, then he has to give equal weight to other people's interests as well. It is true that people generally abandon their ability to reason morally as well as prudentially when they become fanatics. This might, as I say, be part of what is meant in calling them 'fanatics.' But this verbal issue is unimportant here, for Hare is not trying to defend irrationality, but to claim that fanatics might be consistent in their fanaticism because they might be willing to abandon self-interest. If my argument is correct, the expression 'abandoning self-interest' is logically inapplicable, except in the secondary sense that one might throw prudence to the four winds, i.e., might subordinate all of one's other interests to one or a few which then dissatisfy the others (e.g., lead to death or permanent disability). But here Hare's stricture is appropriate: we call such people imprudent, but a person might regard one of his interests as superior to all others, and there's nothing for us to do about it except try to talk him out of it (or advise him to see a psychiatrist).

I conclude that fanaticism is a dodge, just as the effort to refuse the use of evaluative expressions on one's own behalf is a dodge. Every effort to escape morality is a dodge, in fact, just as, and for the same reason as the effort to escape "rationality" is. We hear of people who profess to be against rationality, in some sense or other. The futility of this is transparent: all of these people employ words like 'therefore,' 'not,' and the rest of the vocabulary of reason, and could not state their "views" without them. But all that this shows is that the only way to do without rationality is to join the vegetables, which must perforce remain silent.

Mill's Proof

The fourth chapter of Mill's *Utilitarianism* has become a classic example, though usually regarded as a classic bad example rather than a classic good one, for beginning students of philosophy. In a way, I suppose, this is unfortunate, for it is not very easy to assess the effort as a whole, and not at all obvious that the famous blunders of which he is accused have actually been committed. It is perhaps the duty of an advocate of utilitarianism to add his bit to the understanding of the argument Mill supplies, and I shall try to do so here very briefly and without much detailed attention to the opinions of other critics.[35]

As we all know, there are thought to be two crucial turns in the argument. The first of these is the famous parallel between 'desirable' and 'audible':

The only proof capable of being given that an object is visible, is that people actually see it. The only proof that a sound is audible, is that people hear it: and so of the other sources of our experience. In like manner, I apprehend, the sole evidence it is possible to produce that anything is desirable, is that people do actually desire it.[36]

Mill goes on to assert that people do actually desire happiness, and indeed nothing but happiness, the critics nipping at his heels all the way through. What are we to say?

The odd thing here is that what Mill actually asserts is unquestionably true: the only proof you can give that something is desirable is that it is desired (or anyway, would satisfy a desire). Any serious amount of attention paid to the way in which arguments about the desirable go will verify this point, and unsurprisingly so.[37] The only question is whether what we are trying to prove when we try to prove that something is desirable is the same sort of thing as what we are trying to prove when we try to prove that something is audible, allowing for the differences between desiring something and hearing it. (At

[35] These are numerous. For some samples, see those of Everett Hall, "The Proof of Utility in Bentham and Mill," *Ethics* (1949); Carl Wellman, "A Reinterpretation of Mill's Proof," *Ethics* (1958-59); Norman Kretzman, "Desire as a Proof of Desirability," *Philosophical Quarterly* (1958); and Evelyn A. Masi, *Mill's Methods of Moral Inquiry* (unpublished Ph.D. dissertation, Department of Philosophy, Radcliffe College, 1956).

[36] Mill, *Utilitarianism*, p. 32.

[37] This is well put in Arthur Murphy's book, *The Theory of Practical Reason*, p. 44, wherein he says, "The question is . . . "what *is* it reasonable for me to do?" It is this latter question that cannot be sensibly asked or answered without a reference to the "thing wanted . . . without an intrinsic reference to our wants there could be no practical reasons."

least one important author, Sparshott, claims that it is, and his argument is worth serious consideration.)[38] Moreover, the common contention that 'desirable' means 'worthy of being desired' rather than 'capable of being desired' does not cut as much ice as needs cutting here.[39] For one thing, 'capable' is a little thin in the nonevaluative contexts. 'Audible' surely means 'apt to be heard (under normal conditions)' and not just 'capable' of being heard (by whom? Gustave Mahler, or the rest of us?). And desirable things *are* apt to be desired by those who take the trouble to acquaint or interest themselves in the kind of thing in question, and could not intelligibly be held to be desirable if they weren't. We do not, as Sparshott justly points out, pay any attention to the desires of parties who just aren't interested, when it comes to talk of 'good' ('desirable').[40]

The other major move is from "each person's happiness is a good to that person" to "the general happiness is a good to the aggregate of persons." People have accused Mill of a fallacy of composition in this passage, but this is an implausible accusation. In fact, the main thing puzzling about this move is in the 'to' phrases. In "each person's happiness is a good to that person," 'to' is clear enough: it just means that he thinks it a good. This I have endeavored to support on logical grounds above. But in "the general happiness is a good to the aggregate of persons," 'to' is puzzling, since the aggregate is not capable of having an opinion on this unless it is meant that *each* person thinks the general happiness is desirable, and of course that may or may not be true but doesn't follow from the premise, and is not part of his argument anyway. Nor is it what Mill needs, which is why the "fallacy of composition" interpretation is unsatisfactory. For surely what Mill meant to try to prove is that the general happiness is a good, period. Moreover, he says so in one of his letters, where he declares that he meant merely that if A's happiness is good, B's good, and C's good, then the happiness of all of them (or the "sum" of them, i.e., the "general" happi-

---

[38] *Inquiry into Goodness*, Ch. 5 and Ch. 6, especially.

[39] The common contention in question is advanced in *Principia Ethica*, No. 40, and (in ref. to Dewey rather than Mill), by Morton White in his "Value and Obligation in Dewey and Lewis," in Sellars and Hospers, pp. 332 ff.; and in other places too numerous to mention.

[40] *Inquiry*, pp. 143 ff.

ness) must be a good.[41] Only this confuses the issue because in this explanation, he has the premise different from what it is in the passage from *Utilitarianism*, which has it not that A's happiness is a good, but that it is good to A, i.e., A *thinks* it good. Thus we must admit that Mill was apparently muddled about this. But the argument isn't. As we have seen, the premise from which the proof of utilitarianism proceeds is precisely that each person thinks his happiness a good, and the conclusion is precisely that the general happiness is a good, and the conclusion does follow, in the required sense and as a matter of strict logic rather than as a matter of psychology. As to its being the only good, on the ground that happiness is the only good, we have seen what to say about all of this.

There are a number of peculiarities, certainly, elsewhere in the chapter. The most peculiar thing of all is the statement that people desire happiness, understood as being parallel to the statement that they desire money or virtue. Some of the peculiarity is dispelled by Mill's qualifications and explanations, though not all of it. Critics have trodden very heavily on Mill's discussions about virtue becoming "part of the end," though not originally so, and here again I think that Mill may be interpreted as making perfectly sound points, though in a rather confusing way. He says, e.g., that

Virtue, according to the utilitarian doctrine, is not naturally and originally part of the end, but it is capable of becoming so; and in those who love it disinterestedly it has become so, and is desired and cherished, not as a means to happiness, but as a part of their happiness.[42]

All of this is acceptable, if we sort things out a bit. To begin with, when he says that virtue is not originally part of "the" end, we have to take him to mean that people do not originally in fact aim at it, not that it isn't something they *should* aim at, since obviously every moralist wants to defend the latter. Understanding him in this way, what he says is quite true: you in

[41] H. S. R. Elliot, *Letters of John Stuart Mill* (London, 1910), Vol. II, p. 116. Cited by Hall in *Ethics*, 1949 (cf., note 29).
[42] *Utilitarianism*, p. 34.

general have to *train* people to be virtuous, and there are probably no exceptions at all to this, though there is much variation in the degree and kind of training needed.[43] Secondly, there are two kinds of good people. those who enjoy making other people happy (and thus include the activity of making them so as "part of their happiness"—part of the life they see as a good kind of life to live), and those who perform their duties grudgingly, in order to ward off attacks of conscience, or with a view to public acclaim and reward. Both of these latter types regard virtue as a means to their own happiness, not in the sense that they enjoy it, but in the sense that they get something out of it which they do enjoy (or at least relief from the pangs of conscience for bad performance). The analogy with money is to a degree apt here, but I think Mill doesn't quite appreciate its aptness, for in fact to say that virtue is desirable is just as misleading as to say that money is desirable. Both of these are inherently worthless, in one sense: virtue just consists in doing good, and it is what is done that is good, morally speaking, not the activities apart from their consequences; similarly for money, as Mill says. But on the other hand, to say that they are "inherently worthless" is a bit misleading too, for virtue is inherently a matter of trying to achieve certain consequences, and money is inherently a means of exchange: in neither case are the things just accidentally related to their effects, but rather, are so named because of their intended effects. The difference is that it is silly to get a fixation on money apart from what it will buy, whereas there is something to be said for people who pursue virtue "apart from its consequences" (since it cannot be pursued apart from its consequences, whereas money can: you can accumulate heaps of buying power without spending it, but you can't do heaps of virtuous acts without making people happy, or at least by preventing unhappiness).

But Mill does not clearly realize that the principle that people "desire happiness" is merely verbal, and this is why his efforts to prove this are strained and sometimes inappropriate. I attribute this failure to the general intellectual atmosphere of the time. Only recently have we begun to see through some of the psy-

[43] This point, familiar since Aristotle, is well reinforced by Nowell-Smith, pp. 255–59; in a somewhat different way by Baier, Ch. 7.

chologisms of the last century, as in reality "logicisms." The proof is not very much the worse for wear for that, for the idea behind it all is sound.

The truth is, that the best way in which the proof could have been stated is scarcely bothered with. I refer to the passage in which Mill says, "Happiness has made out its title as one of the ends of conduct, and consequently, one of the criteria of morality."[44] Very little attention is given to this 'consequently.' In the first chapter, he does say that "All action is for the sake of some end, and rules of action, it seems natural to suppose, must take their whole character and colour from the end to which they are subservient."[45] In Chapter II, he says in reference to an immediately preceding discussion of happiness, "This being, according to the utilitarian opinion, the end of human action, is necessarily also the standard of morality."[46] The idea being expressed in these few meager places is certainly the central idea of the whole utilitarian viewpoint: that the purpose of morality is to forward the ends which people severally have, whatever they may be. If Mill had concentrated on this way of putting it, instead of the rather obscure and "psychologistitc" way he does, he probably would not have been the subject of nearly as much fuss as he has been. But what we have is a great deal better than nothing, and indeed not really wrong at all, though inadequately explained and clarified. Thus, at any rate, he may be interpreted.

On the Nature of Practical Reasoning

My arguments have purported to show that it is irrational to deny the principle of utility; and I have also claimed that it makes no sense to suppose that there is an open question whether one ought to be reasonable. The net effect of these arguments, then, would seem to be that rationality is somehow logically linked to sociality. The dice of reason are loaded in favor of the

[44] Mill, *Utilitarianism*, p. 33.
[45] *Ibid.*, p. 2.
[46] *Ibid.*, p. 11. E. A. Masi, in the Radcliffe College Ph.D. dissertation mentioned in n. 35 of this chapter, concentrates interestingly on this set of passages.

general interest. This seems to require an explanation of some sort, one which would clarify the connection between reasoning in practical matters and society's interests. Let us consider how such an explanation might proceed.[47]

Certainly the most popular philosophical theory about the nature of reason, until recent times, has been the one deriving from Plato, and occurring, in more detailed form, in Kant. According to this general type of explanation, Reason is a Faculty of the soul, one among others. In the case of Plato, there are two others, Appetite and Will, while in Kant only one is relevant, Inclination. The soul is pictured as being capable of internal conflict, Inclination issuing one set of orders and Reason issuing another, often contrary, set. Views of this type have a certain charm, no doubt, but they simply won't do. The overwhelming objection to them is that they don't explain what they set out to explain. If the commands (or advice?) of Reason are so characterized simply because they happen to come from Faculty X rather than Faculty Y, then the question why we ought to obey one rather than the other becomes open. There is then no answer possible to the question, Why does the Faculty of Reason issue the particular commands it does, rather than some other commands? For in saying that 'Reason' is simply the name of this faculty, all we can say is that Reason just does issue those commands and no others. Nor will it do to go on explaining, in a sort of proto-biological fashion, "why" Reason issues those commands ("Well, you see, Reason happens to be equipped with the Principle of Non-Contradiction, the Law of Causality . . .": compare with, "Well, there's this cog and it turns this wheel, which moves that lever, and thus . . ."). What we want to know is whether those commands are reasonable, regardless of who issued them. The explanation of rationality in terms of an appeal to a Faculty of Rationality, then, accomplishes noth-

[47] Baier discusses to good effect some suggestions about this, pp. 89–92, and is very good on the motive power of reason, pp. 147–48. But I do not think he quite answers to our satisfaction the question raised here of the relation between the "essence" of reasoning and the resulting bias toward the general interest. I think this is in part because that "bias" is not (as we saw in a previous section of this chapter) so thoroughgoing as I make it out; and partly because, in the end, there is no real difference between Baier's own view and the view of Hume as he presents it.

ing. We should just have to engage in discussion with the Faculty of Rationality to see whether its commands were justified, and this is what we wanted to know in the first place.[48]

For precisely the same reason, it will not do to fix on some plausible principle and proclaim that this "just is" one of the defining principles of Reason. This move also seems to make the whole thing arbitrary. If "reasonable" principles just happen to be this particular set of principles rather than that, then the question why we ought to follow them again seems to be open.

This is difficult territory, and I offer the following account in a spirit of exploration; perhaps, in the end, it will prove no more satisfactory than the others.

Reasoning, to begin with, is a verbal activity; it is also, by and large, a social one, and unsurprisingly so, since we need to be trained to talk by those who already know. Why engage in it? In particular, what are we doing (i.e., what are our purposes) when we reason about practice?

To reason is to criticize and rebut criticisms. When we raise the question, "Why?" in any context, whether theoretical or practical, we envisage the possibility that something may have gone wrong. The supposition is that whoever supports the stand, the assumption, or whatever it is which is being called into question, is attempting to do a certain thing and possibly failing. In the case of actions, to ask "Why?" is to call for a justification of the action in question. The possibility that rectification is needed is implicit in the asking: those who are supremely confident do not ask it, except perhaps in a purely rhetorical way.

But also, questions have an audience, sometimes (usually) social, but sometimes consisting only of ourselves. Still, it doesn't matter how large the audience is, for to level a question *at* a particular audience is automatically to make them parties to the questioning. It would be pointless for me to raise a question before an audience if I had no intention of listening to their reactions or taking account of them if they had them; and pointless

---

[48] There is a clear connection between this view of Reason, and views which put the ultimate authority of ethics in God, or in Conscience, or indeed anywhere; for in form, this is an authoritarian view. "Reason" is treated as a sort of abstract and ghostly authority.

to raise it at all, then, if no possible audience's reactions are envisaged as being worth taking into account.[49]

To engage in the defense of a line of action, now, is to imply that the members of one's audience have certain characteristics which make their opinions worth taking into account. It is, in particular, to assume that they can understand one's presentation, and are able to respond with intelligible criticism. But this in turn means that one concedes a potential (at very least) of practical reasoning on their parts. To see, in the light of this, why "the dice of reason are loaded in favor of the general interest," we can reflect that it would be absurd (i.e., pointless) to raise questions and make defenses of one's acts to other people, if one were not prepared to acknowledge similar weight to similar claims on their part. If I presume to defend what I am doing before an audience consisting of Jones by saying, "Well, I enjoy this sort of thing," but am not prepared to allow Jones to defend what he is doing with the same sort of argument, then I might as well not have bothered. It makes no *sense* to address people in the terms of reason if one isn't prepared to grant them any status as reasonable beings. This, I conceive, is the dialectical problem facing proponents of nondemocratic forms of government: arguments on their behalf can hardly be addressed to everyone in general, with a straight face. The same is true of moral arguments. There is no point in being prepared to argue if one doesn't envisage any possible terms of settlement; and one cannot hope for settlement if one's "arguments" are going to be arbitrarily loaded in favor of oneself.

Those who would retreat into their shells and argue only with their alter egos, however, gain no advantage from the tactic. They either must use, as their reason for refusing to face their fellow men in argument, the assumption that all other men are fools—an assumption which has to be put to the test before it can be accepted with any pretense of rationality—or must eschew the use of "reasons" altogether, in which case any monologues they may care to indulge in likewise abandon any pretense

---

[49] The paper by Haworth, mentioned in Ch. VII, n. 19, makes use of similar considerations. See also some of the thoughts of Bernard Mayo in his book, *Ethics and the Moral Life* (London: Macmillan Co., 1955), especially Ch. IV.

to rationality. Even in talking with oneself, one assumes that one is capable of understanding one's own arguments, assessing them, etc.: how, then, can one defend a refusal to listen to others who have the same capabilities, or worse, a refusal to find out whether they have them?

The answer, then, to our question why rationality in practical matters leads inexorably to acknowledgement of the general interest as the standard of judgment is that to raise a critical question about behavior, and especially to defend one's own behavior, is to start an argument; to start an argument is pointless if it cannot be settled; and it cannot be settled unless all parties to it have the same arguments available to them.

This leads us to formulate the argument for utilitarianism in an alternative way to the rather abstract-sounding one propounded in the foregoing pages. To argue for morality at all is to claim the assent of all rational beings. But the only principle mutually acceptable to all rational beings is one which regards all of their interests as equally worth satisfying (less, therefore, those which are incompatible with others). Everyone can agree to this because everyone's interests are respected. No other view of morality can claim universal acceptance unless by accident. If the alternative morality involves recognition of some particular type of activity as intrinsically superior, or of some particular person as intrinsically superior, then it automatically debars itself from the assent of anyone who doesn't agree with that evaluation. And on the other hand, the utilitarian principle implies the desirability of acts based on the recognition of those superiorities if everyone recognizes them, since in that case, it will ipso facto be in everyone's interest to perform those acts. Thus in the event that conditions for universal acceptance of some logically alternative position are met, the principle of utility will automatically sanction acts based on that position anyway.

In the light of the above, it becomes still clearer why the depiction of rationality as one agency of the soul among others, whose business is to deliver a particular set of (unpleasant) orders, is unsound. Anyone capable of handing down orders is, especially if he is worth listening to, going to have to be capable of giving reasons for them: thus anybody, or any agency for that matter, purporting to be Reason incarnate, automatically invites derision. If he (or it) purports to have reasons for his orders, then he (or it) has to concede the equal claims of the other parties to the discussion, while if he (or it) has no reasons and claims that his orders are to be obeyed without question, his pretension to being the incarnation of reason is exposed as a sham. Conscience stands unmasked as just another one of the boys. Perhaps, in the end, all that Kant meant with all of his talk of Faculties and Transcendental authorities is what we have said above: that there could be no point in reasoning unless one was prepared to concede equal weight to the interests of all the participants in the discussion, and consequently, if we conceive of everyone as being in on it, of everyone. In the end, then, there is no genuine difference between the position that morality is "founded on" pure reason, and the position that it is "founded on" a sentiment or feeling of sympathy, unity, or benevolence toward one's fellow men.

Index

43–44; prospective, 89; pleasure-seeking, 15. *See* Hedonism
Population, utilitarianism and size of, 44, 47–50
Precision, 38, 41
Presumptive reasons, 165
Price, Richard, 72
Prichard, H. A., 100, 257
Prima facie, 102
Principle of Utility: nontriviality of, 23–24; statement of, 92–93
Principles. *See* Moral principles
Pro-attitudes, and evaluations, 89
Promises, 14, 189–97
Property, rights to, 204, 224–29
Propositions, ethical. *See* Truth
Proof, and simplicity, 28–29; defined, 258–60; whether needed in ethics, 260–61. *See* Argument
"Protestant" view of moral judgments, 31, 32–37 *passim*
Prudence, 247–50
Psychological harms, 183
Psychological hedonism, 15, 51, 53, 57–67; role in proof of utilitarianism, 271 ff, 283 ff
Public *vs.* private happiness, 46
Punishment, of the innocent, 153–73 *passim*; 116; Hart's criticisms discussed, 170–72

Q

Quality, *vs.* quantity of pleasure, 79–82
Quantity, *vs.* quality of pleasure, 79–82; sense in which utility is one, 42, 212. *See* Measurement
Quine, W. V. O., 13*n*

R

Rashdall, Hastings, 16*n*, 67, 74
Rational conviction, and proof, 259

Rational ends, 74
Rationality: 289–93; and psychological hedonism, 60–61
Rawls, John: 236*n*; "Justice as Fairness" discussed, 219–23; moral persons, 87; marginal utility, 215*n*; "Two Concepts of Rules" discussed, 186–88, 194–95
Reiterability, 131–32
Relativism, 73
Relief of suffering, 226, 233–38
Religion and ethics, 39–40, 254
Reparations, 177–80
Rescher, Nicholas, 136
Retribution, 173–76
Rights, defined: 204–5; right to liberty, 221–22; Rawls' theory of, 219–24. *See also* Duty
Rigorism, 102, 103, 281
Robinson, Richard: 160; truth, 4; envy, 216
Ross, Alfred: on Hare, 278*n*
Ross, W. David: evaluation and obligation, 14, 145; Ideal utilitarianism, 70; intrinsic good, 75; *prima facie* duties, 102; promising, 189, 194–95
Rules, types distinguished, 186
Rule-utilitarianism, 16, 25; defined, 123; discussed, 123–29; Mill and, 123–24, 142; Brandt's type, 125–29; 144; Rawl's type, 186, *See also,* Searle
Russell, Bertrand, 72
Ryle, Gilbert: pleasure, 64

S

Saints and saintliness as a moral category, 242
Sartre, Jean-Paul, 106, 110
Satisfaction, 55–56, 75–76. *See* Pleasure, Psychological hedonism
Schlesinger, George, 255
Schneewind, J. B., 124*n*

INDEX

Universalizability, 275, 278–81. *See*
Generality; Generalization
Urmson, J. O.: Mill as a rule-
utilitarian, 16*n*, 25; Rule utilitarianism, 124; supererogation,
242
Utility: definition, Chapter III; of
advocating utilitarianism, 109*n*

V

Value. *See* Intrinsic
Values, of individuals and utility,
66 ff
Verbal activity, and rationality,
291

Verifiability, in ethics, 3–7
Verification. *See* Truth; Verifiability
Vote, question of obligation to,
132–33

W

Warnock, G. J., 29
Way of life, evaluations of, 83–84;
utilitarianism as a, 241–44
Wellman, Carl, 284*n*
West, Henry, 134*n*
White, Morton, 285*n*
Wieting, Hardy Lee, Jr., 218
Wolff, Robert P., 44*n*

designer:	Gerald A. Valerio
typesetter:	Maple Press
typefaces:	Jansen
printer:	Maple Press
paper:	Mohawk Tosca
binder:	Maple Press
cover material:	Columbia Fictionette